IMAGES
of America

ELIOT

On the cover: Campers are enjoying reading time in the living room above the barn at the Lanier Camps. Elizabeth Lanier is sitting in the rocking chair. (Courtesy of Dr. and Mrs. William Gilbert.)

IMAGES
of America

ELIOT

Margaret A. Elliott for the Eliot Historical Society

ARCADIA
PUBLISHING

ISBN 978-0-7385-3771-9

Published by Arcadia Publishing
Charleston, South Carolina

Printed in the United States of America

Library of Congress Catalog Card Number: 2004116674

For all general information, contact Arcadia Publishing:
Telephone 843-853-2070
Fax 843-853-0044
E-mail sales@arcadiapublishing.com
For customer service and orders:
Toll-free 1-888-313-2665

Visit us on the Internet at www.arcadiapublishing.com

Contents

ACKNOWLEDGMENTS

A deep debt of gratitude is owed to Mary Dennett and Joseph W. P. Frost, who spent countless hours on this project. Special thanks go to Wendy Gilbert, Julie Johnson, Rosanne Adams-Junkins, Mara Frost Marshall, Florence Moulton, Jeanette Paul, Lisa Raitt, Kenneth Tuttle, Edward H. Vetter, Donald Webber Jr., and the William Fogg Library.

This book is dedicated to Dr. John L.M. Willis (1856–1924), who believed that Eliot's citizens should honor their history. Founder and first president of the Eliot Historical Society, Dr. Willis also edited and published the magazine *Old Eliot*. Dr. Willis's commitment to the town and its history should be an inspiration to us all.

Introduction

The area now known as the town of Eliot was once part of the Piscataqua Plantation, which also included Kittery and the Berwicks. In the early part of the 17th century, people began settling along the water. Original immigrants included Shapleighs, Frosts, Leightons, Stapleses, and many others. Early occupations included fishing and lumbering. Tidal mills sprang up along rivers and creeks. The Piscataqua River was the primary means of transportation and the venue for goods bound for ships traveling to England and other ports.

In 1639, the land between the Piscataqua and Kennebec Rivers became the province of Maine by order of England's King Charles. In 1647, the Piscataqua Plantation became the town of Kittery, the first town to be incorporated in Maine. The province of Maine submitted to the government of Massachusetts in 1652. The signing of the submission took place at William Everett's tavern, on River Road in what is now Eliot. This move assured residents protection from American Indian raids in exchange for governing by Massachusetts. However, the area still endured many attacks by the natives. By 1675, there were at least 18 garrison houses within the settlement, attesting to the instability of the region. The massacre of several residents, including Maj. Charles Frost, occurred on July 4, 1697, at Ambush Rock, near Goodwin Road. Today a memorial marks the site.

Early inhabitants farmed for their own sustenance. Some larger farms shipped crops to other colonies and to England. Marshland in tidal areas and along the river and creeks produced salt hay, a commodity exported in the early days of the province of Maine.

By the early 19th century, the north parish, or the "garden of Kittery," as the Eliot area was known, moved toward separation from Kittery. Being a farming community, the north parish had different political and economic interests. On March 1, 1810, the "garden of Kittery" became the town of Eliot. Until 1820, when Maine became a state, the town was Eliot, Massachusetts.

A popular explanation for the town's appellation suggests Rev. John Eliot of Boston requested that the town be named for him. In return, he promised that he would provide a meetinghouse bell, a promise never kept because the church did not have a belfry at the time.

Along with maritime occupations, gristmills and sawmills were the earliest enterprises in the area. The first mill was built around 1625. Later, shipbuilding became the primary industry. William Hanscom's shipyard on the Piscataqua began doing work in 1828. The Hanscom Shipyard closed in 1855. Today a marker memorializing the yard stands in the vicinity of the Green Acre Baha'i School on Main Street.

Brickmaking began before the Civil War in the River Road and Sturgeon Creek areas. Close proximity of sand and clay led to the development of this industry. By 1870, there were five brickyards in Eliot. Bricks were shipped down the river on gundalows or small schooners. At one time, about 17 Eliot brickyards operated simultaneously.

Eliot's citizens have long been aware of the value of education. Some of the earliest schooling took place in Noah Emery's woodshed on Goodwin Road. Later, the area had one central school, but it was too far away for children in outlying locations. In 1803, what was still the town of Kittery divided into several school districts and soon built district schoolhouses.

Eliot had the first normal school in Maine. Not only a normal school, it also prepared students for college. Eliot Academy, built in 1839, operated from 1840 until 1875, when it burned.

The end of the 19th century and the beginning of the 20th century found Americans with more leisure time. Several camps, both for children and adults, sprang up in Eliot. The age of tourism had begun. What started as the Eliot Hotel in 1890 soon became the Green Acre Baha'i community through the vision of Sarah Jane Farmer. At Green Acre, Sarah raised the world's first peace flag in 1894. In 1905 Japanese envoys visited Green Acre after signing the Russo-Japanese Peace Treaty at the Portsmouth Naval Shipyard.

Ushering in the modern era were the railroad and electric streetcar. In 1842, the Boston and Maine Railroad laid tracks from Kittery to South Berwick on what is now Route 236. The first electric streetcar ran through Eliot on July 24, 1902. The cars traveled through Portsmouth, Kittery, Eliot, Dover, and York.

Many notable citizens have resided in Eliot, including Rev. John Rogers, the town's first and longtime minister, serving from 1714 to 1768; William Fogg, teacher, genealogist, and postmaster from 1817 to 1847; Dr. John L. M. Willis, physician, historian, and founder of the Eliot Historical Society; Gov. John Fremont Hill; and Prof. Moses Gerrish Farmer, electrical engineer, teacher, and prolific inventor.

With the demise of shipbuilding, brickmaking, and large-scale farming, many of Eliot's citizens sought employment out of town, at the Portsmouth Naval Shipyard or in nearby cities and towns.

Today the quiet community of Eliot has approximately 6,000 residents within its 20.3-square-mile boundary. Its unassuming temperament belies its vibrant and intriguing past. With this book of photographs we hope to bring that colorful past alive once more.

One

Eliot Landmarks

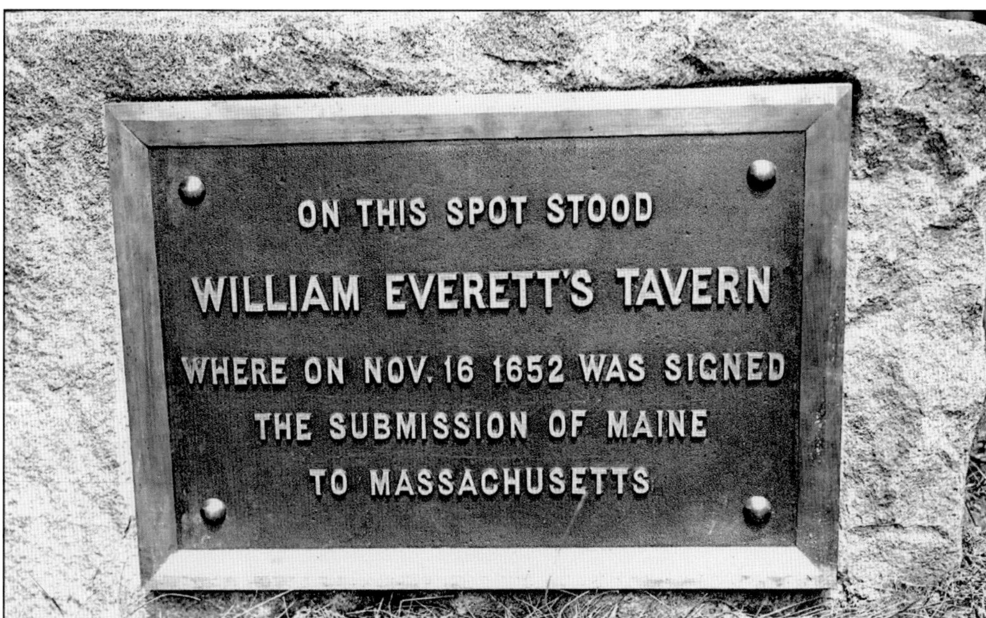

A plaque now marks the site where William Everett's tavern once stood on River Road. Captain Everett built the tavern before 1648. Many public meetings were held at this location. On November 16, 1652, the document proclaiming the province of Maine's submission to Massachusetts was signed at the tavern. (Courtesy of the William Fogg Library.)

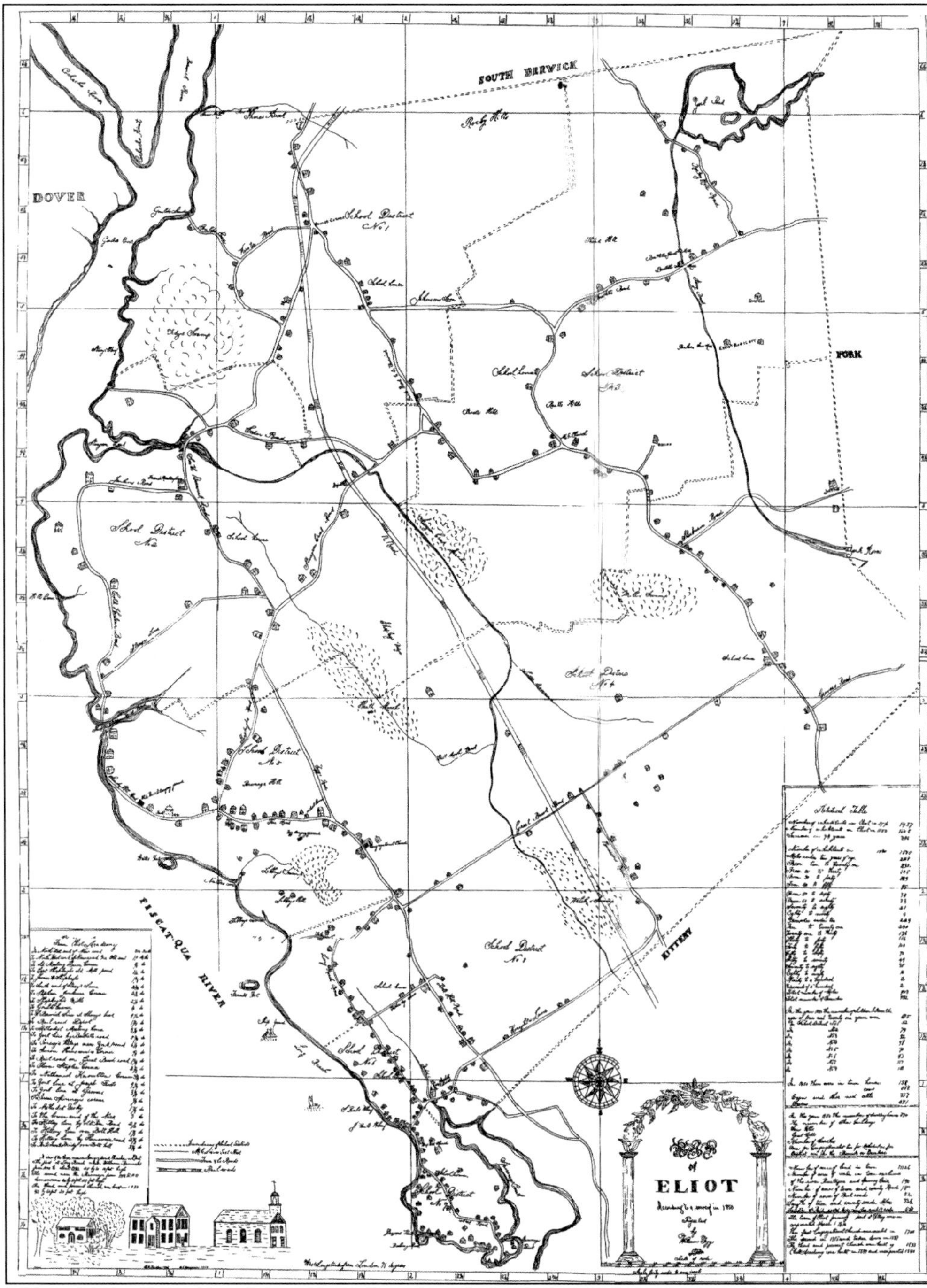

William Fogg, historian and genealogist, created this map of Eliot in 1850. At that time, the town of Eliot had about 1,800 residents. (Courtesy of the Eliot Historical Society.)

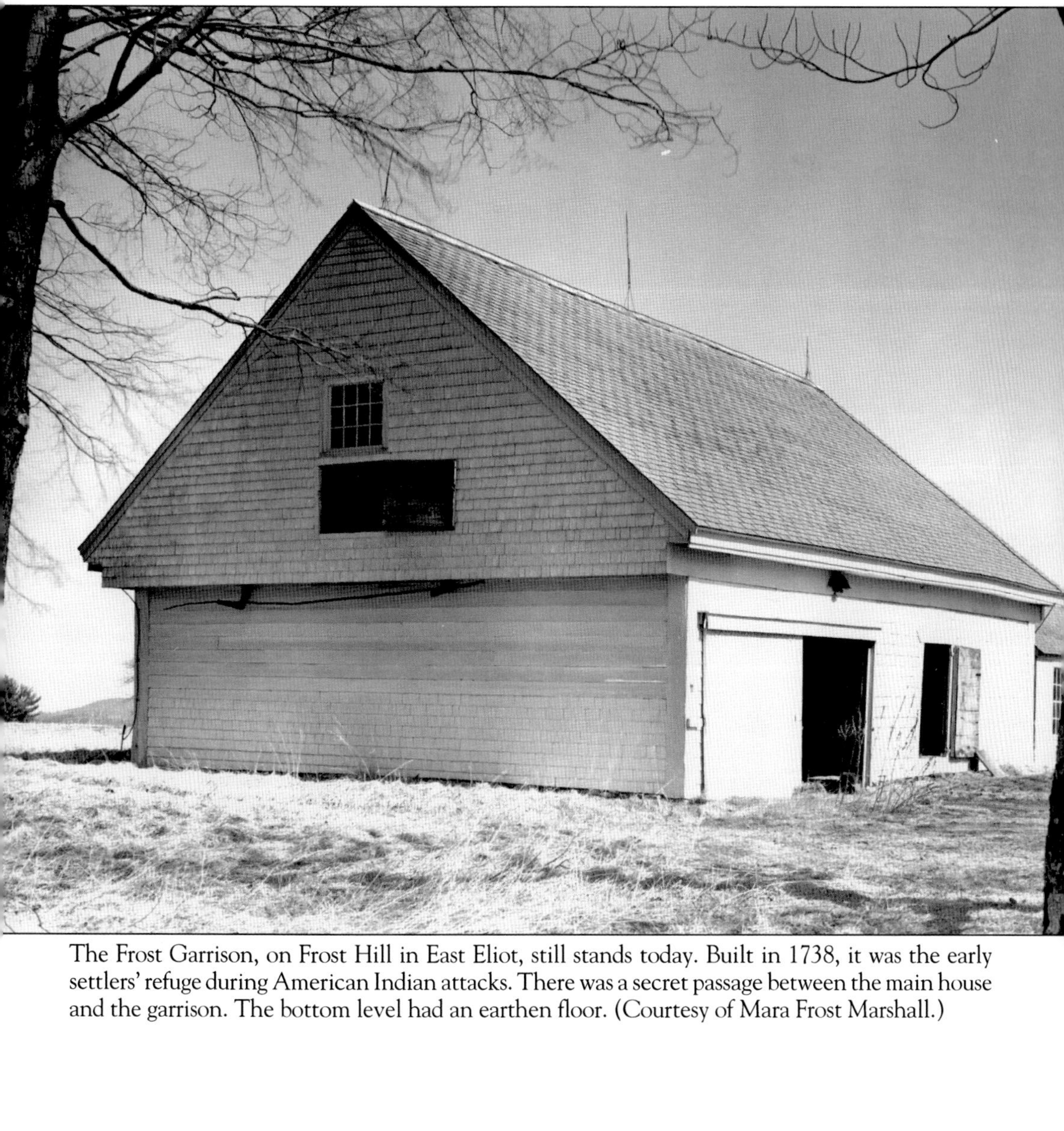

The Frost Garrison, on Frost Hill in East Eliot, still stands today. Built in 1738, it was the early settlers' refuge during American Indian attacks. There was a secret passage between the main house and the garrison. The bottom level had an earthen floor. (Courtesy of Mara Frost Marshall.)

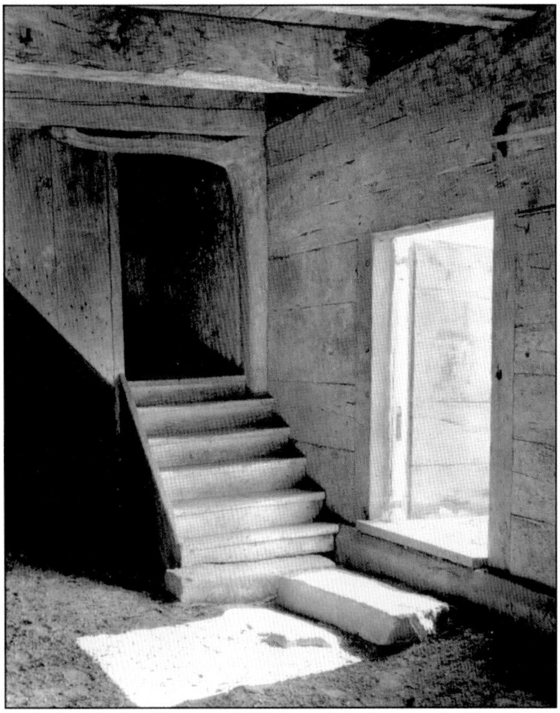

The lower level of the Frost Garrison housed animals during American Indian raids. The people fought off the attacks from the second floor. The walls of the garrison were seven inches thick. (Courtesy of Mara Frost Marshall.)

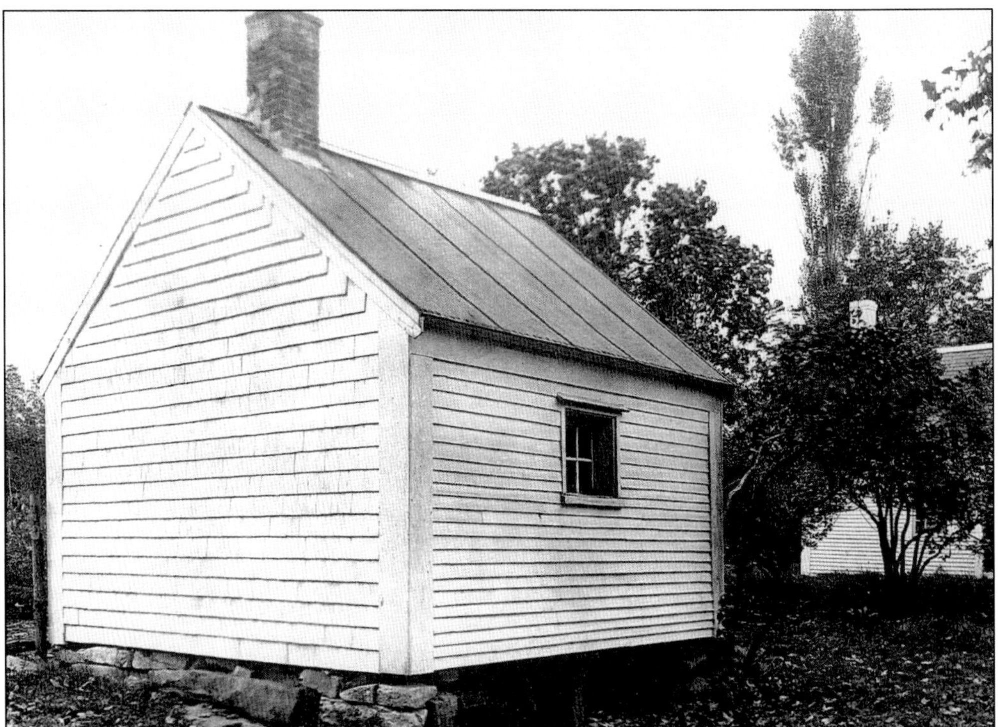

Built in 1734, the small garrison (or blockhouse) on the Frost property in East Eliot was used as a powder house. Originally, it had slots near the roof to let in light. Both the Frost Garrison and Frost Block House are on the National Register of Historic Places. (Courtesy of Mara Frost Marshall.)

On July 4, 1697, American Indians attacked a group of people who were returning from Sunday meeting at the Old Fields Meeting House in the Berwick district. Today a plaque marks the site on Goodwin Road. (Courtesy of the Estate of C. Edward Bartlett Jr.)

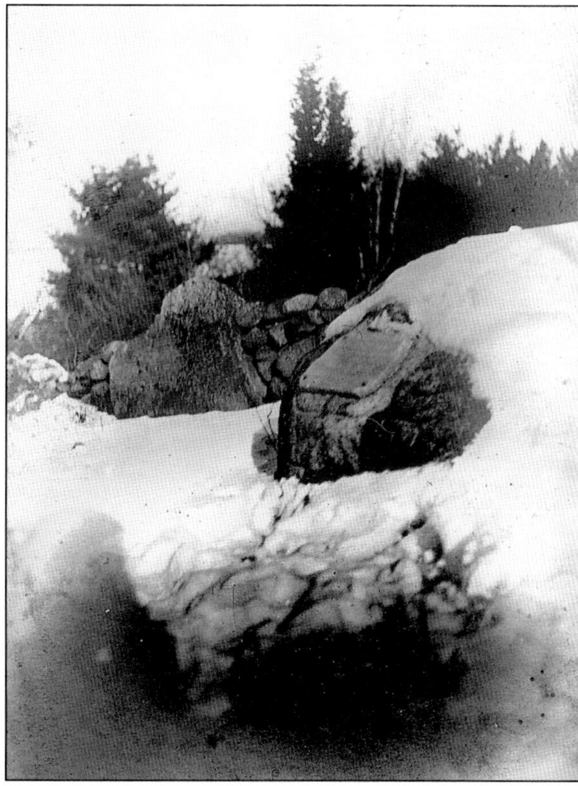

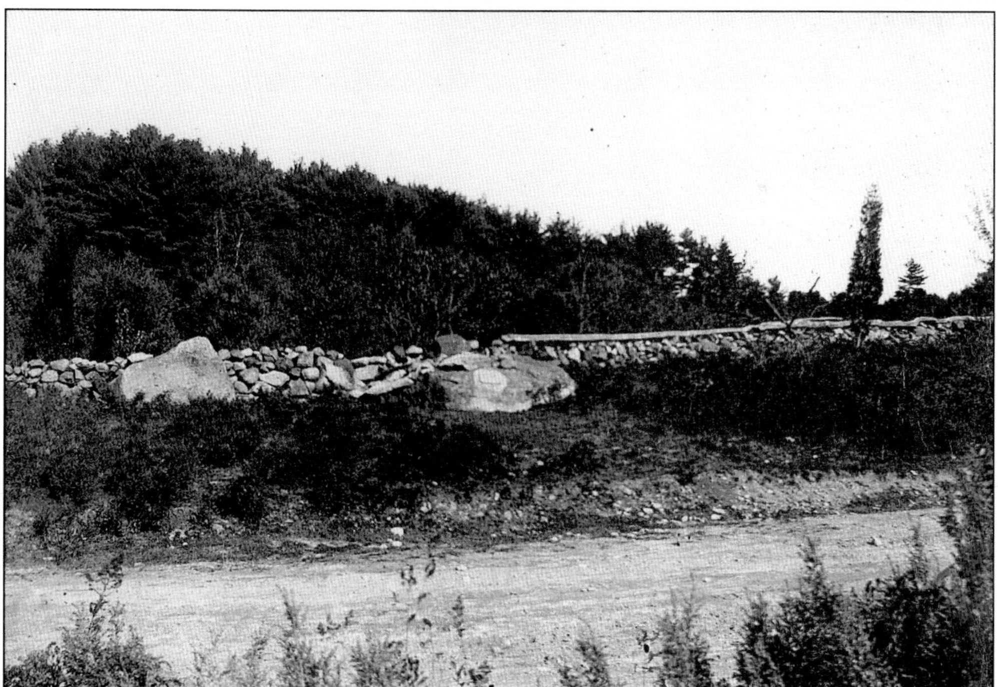

Maj. Charles Frost, Phebe Littlefield Heard, and Dennis Downing died at Ambush Rock. (Courtesy of the Paul Family Association.)

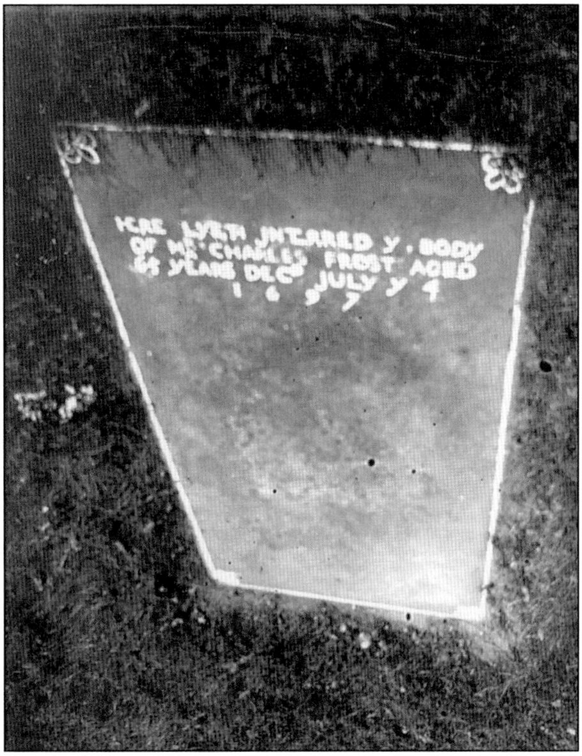

Maj. Charles Frost is buried on the land where he lived and where his descendants continue to live today, off Goodwin Road. Major Frost served his community well as a captain and commander in chief of the militia of Maine, a judge of common pleas court, and a sergeant major for Maine. (Courtesy of the Paul Family Association.)

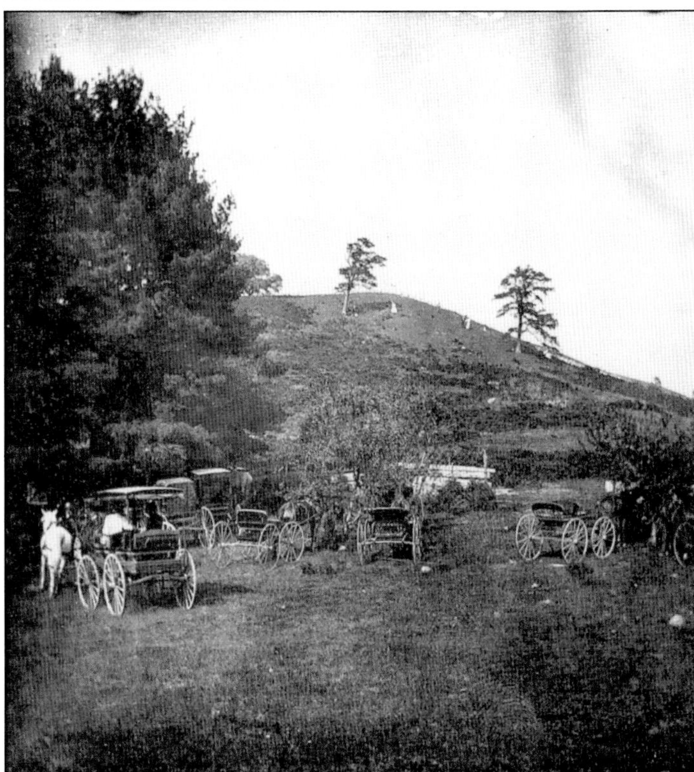

On July 5, 1897, the Eliot Historical Society held a commemoration ceremony marking the 200th anniversary of the death of Maj. Charles Frost. Society members left their carriages at the base of Great Hill and proceeded on foot to Ambush Rock. (Courtesy of the Paul Family Association.)

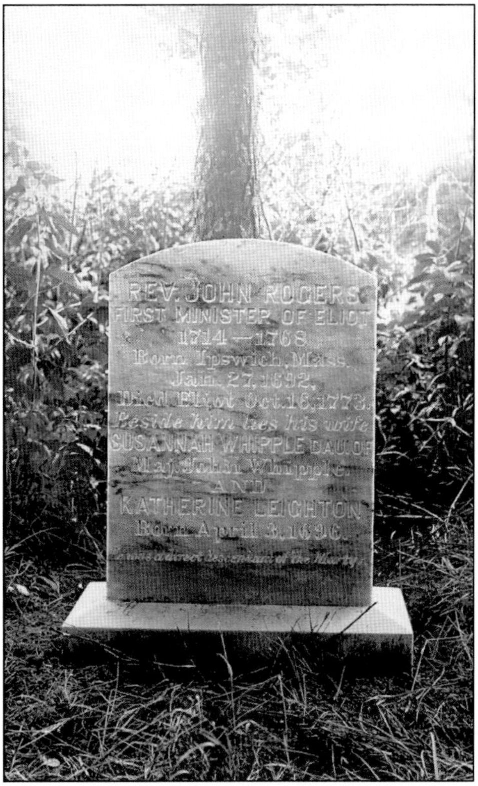

This gravestone, in the old parish burying ground on River Road, memorializes John Rogers, the first minister in Eliot, who served from 1714 to 1768. Born in Ipswich, Massachusetts, on January 27, 1692, he died in Eliot on October 16, 1773. The stone, a gift of former governor John F. Hill, was unveiled during the town's centennial celebration in 1910. (Courtesy of the William Fogg Library.)

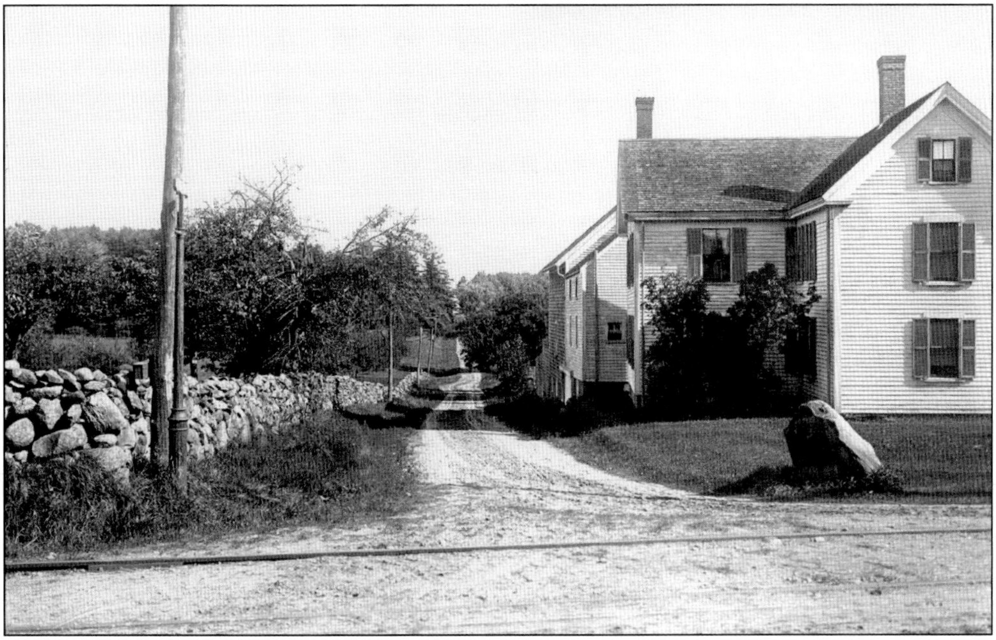

Eliot's first meetinghouse stood at the corner of Greenwood and Main Streets from 1699 until 1732. Later, the home in the photograph sat in the same location until it burned in 1923. Today a Cape-style home rests on the spot, and a marker memorializes the meetinghouse. (Courtesy of the Gov. John F. Hill Collection at the William Fogg Library.)

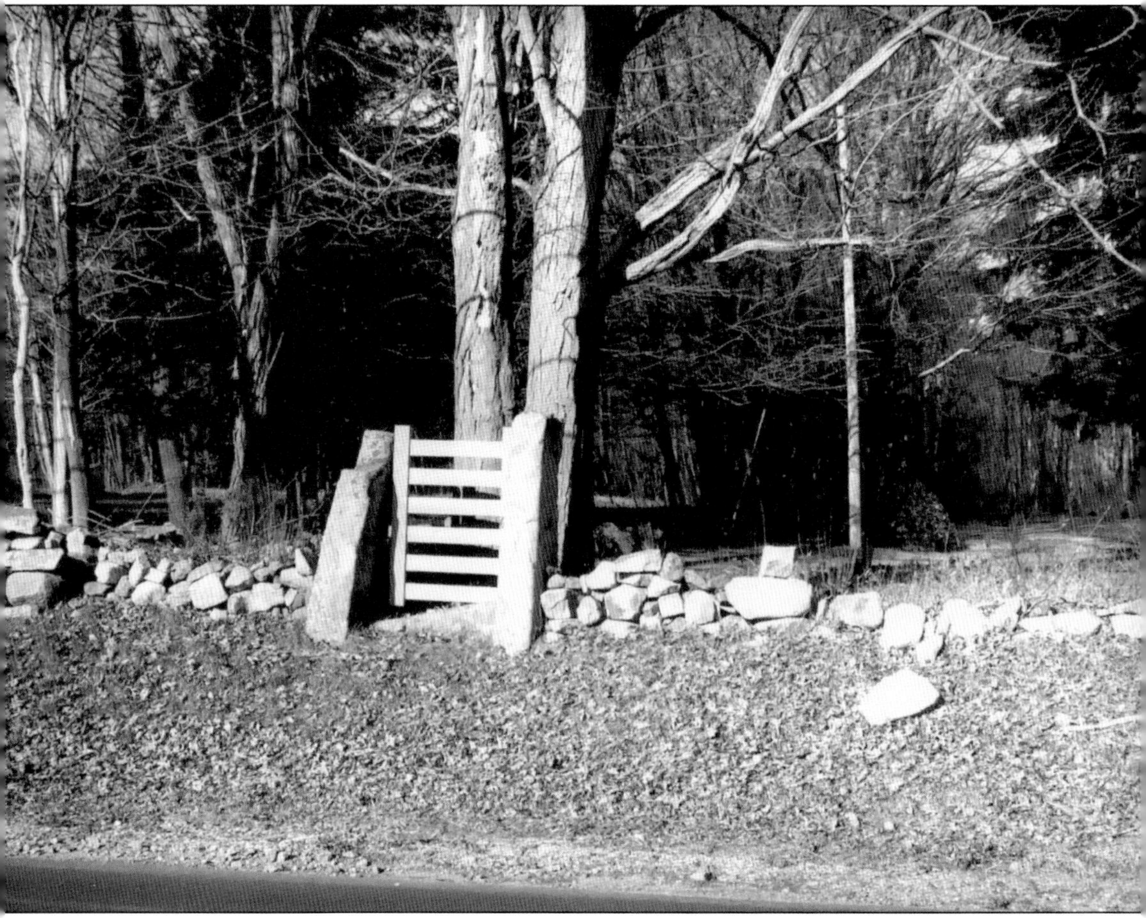

In the early 1800s, stray animals were placed in the town pound on Goodwin Road until their owners could claim them. The pound had fallen into disarray, but the family of J. Lyndon Leavitt is in the process of restoring it as a memorial to him. (Courtesy of Edward H. Vetter.)

Benjamin Kennard, a baker who later became a tavern keeper, had a swing sign advertising his business. His tavern was famous during the Revolutionary War period. In the 1830s and 1840s, many meetings took place there. (Courtesy of the Paul Family Association.)

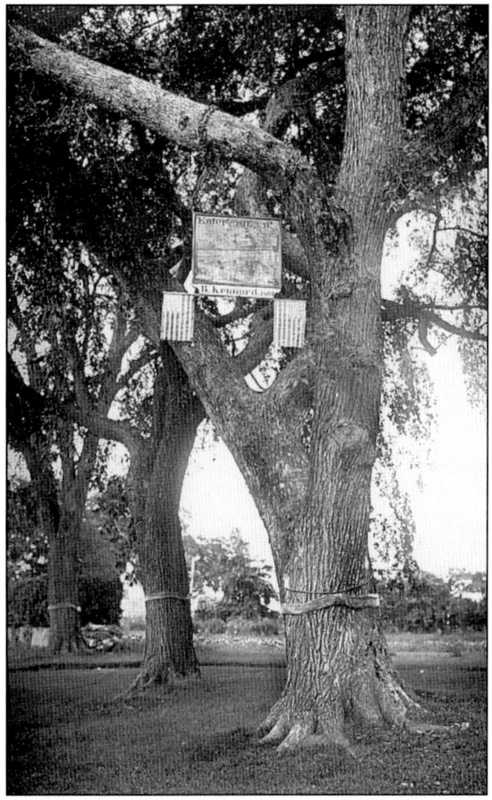

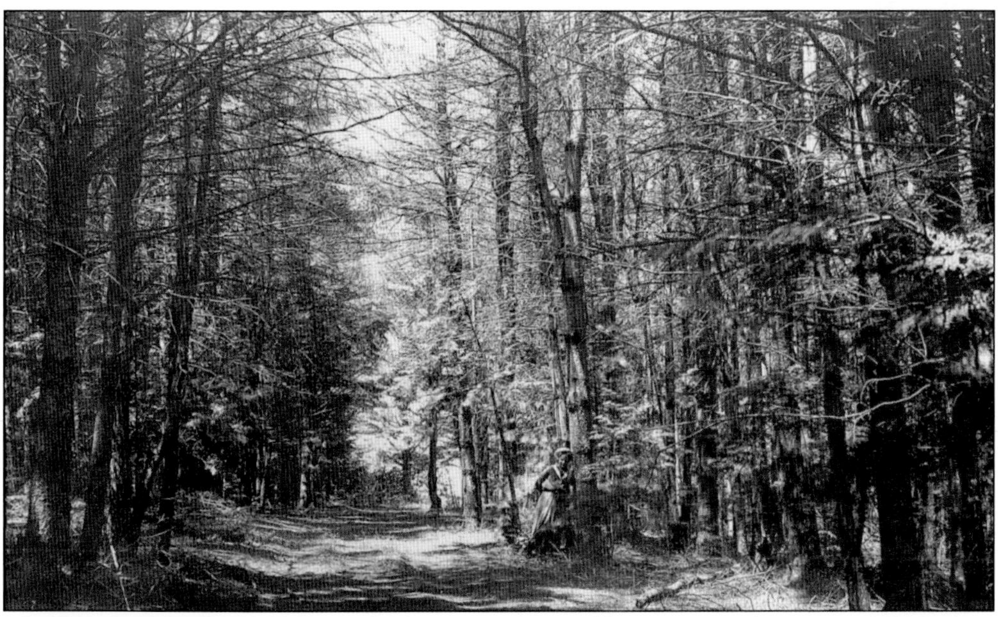

The Eliot Pines at Green Acre are also known as the Lysekloster Pines. The trees include Persian pine and Swami pine and were purchased by Mrs. Ole Bull for Sarah Jane Farmer, founder of the Green Acre School. (Courtesy of the Estate of C. Edward Bartlett Jr.)

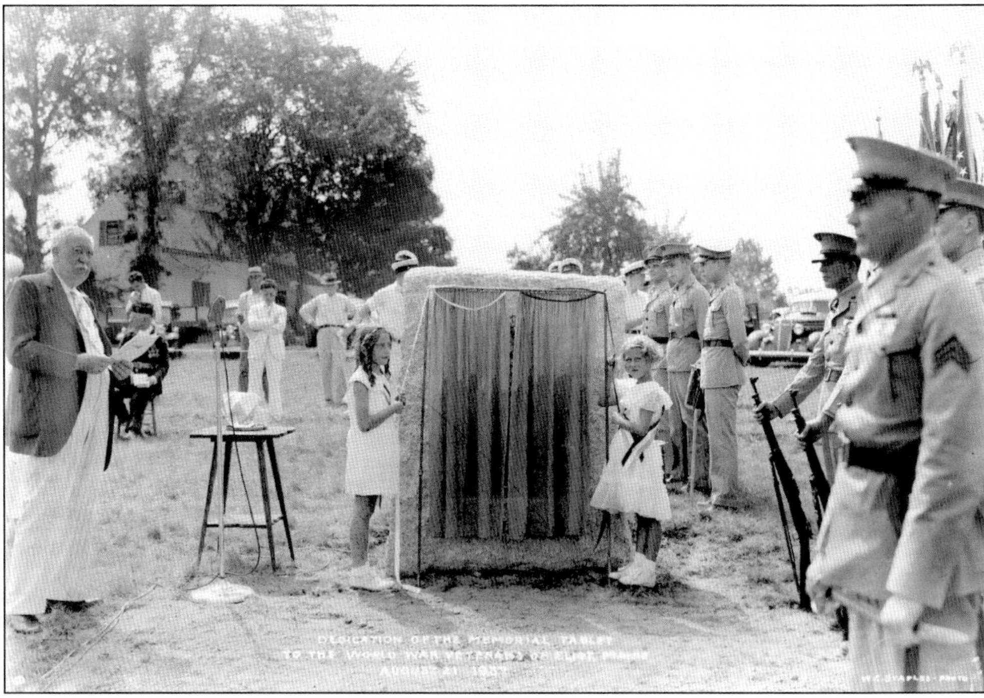

The memorial honoring Eliot's World War I veterans was dedicated on August 21, 1937, on the grounds of the William Fogg Library. The photograph above shows the unveiling of the memorial. The little girls in the photograph below are Ruth M. Drake (left) and Marjorie A. Hoyt. Dr. Henry I. Durgin, wearing the striped trousers, stands next to Hoyt. (Above, courtesy of the William Fogg Library; below, courtesy of the Paul Family Association.)

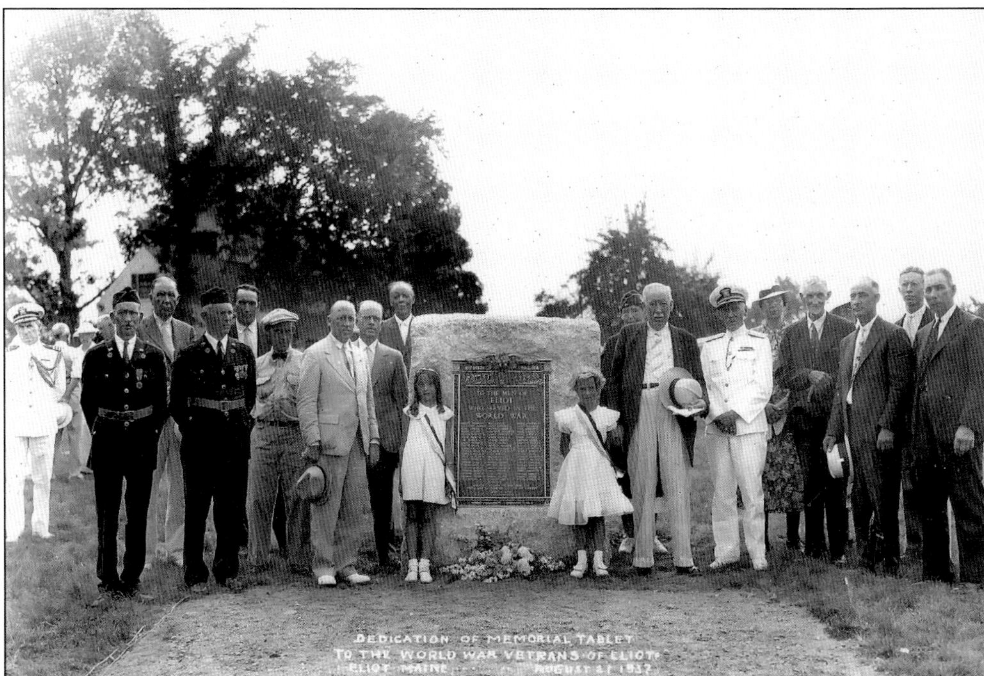

Two

Around Town

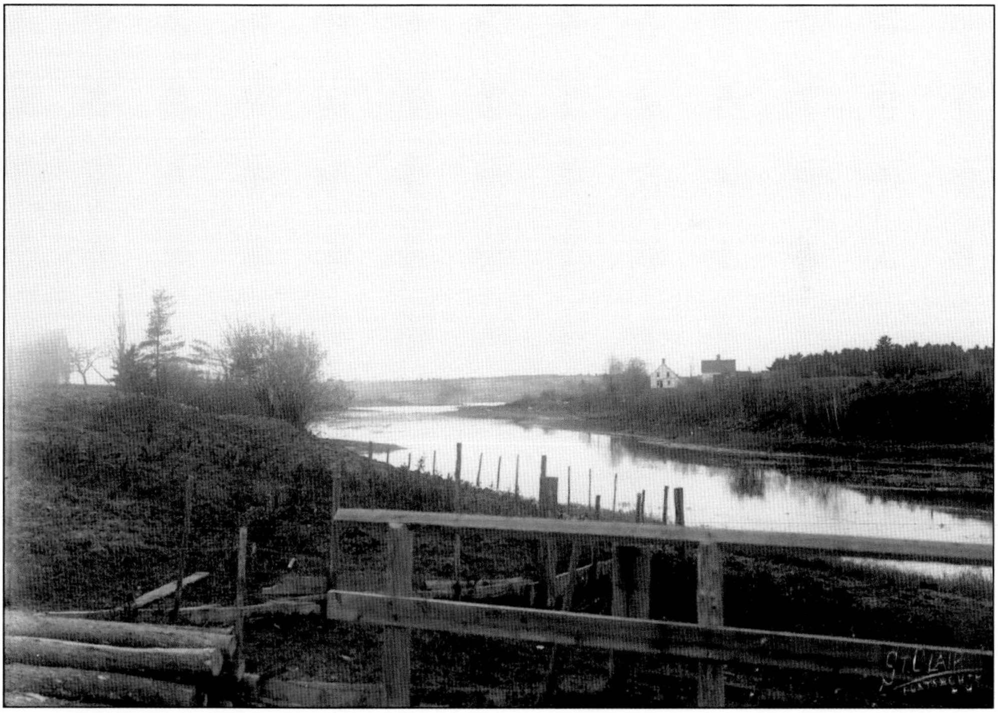

One of Eliot's first settlers, Nicholas Frost, sailed up Sturgeon Creek in 1639. This area was first the site of many mills and later brickyards. (Courtesy of the Gov. John F. Hill Collection at the William Fogg Library.)

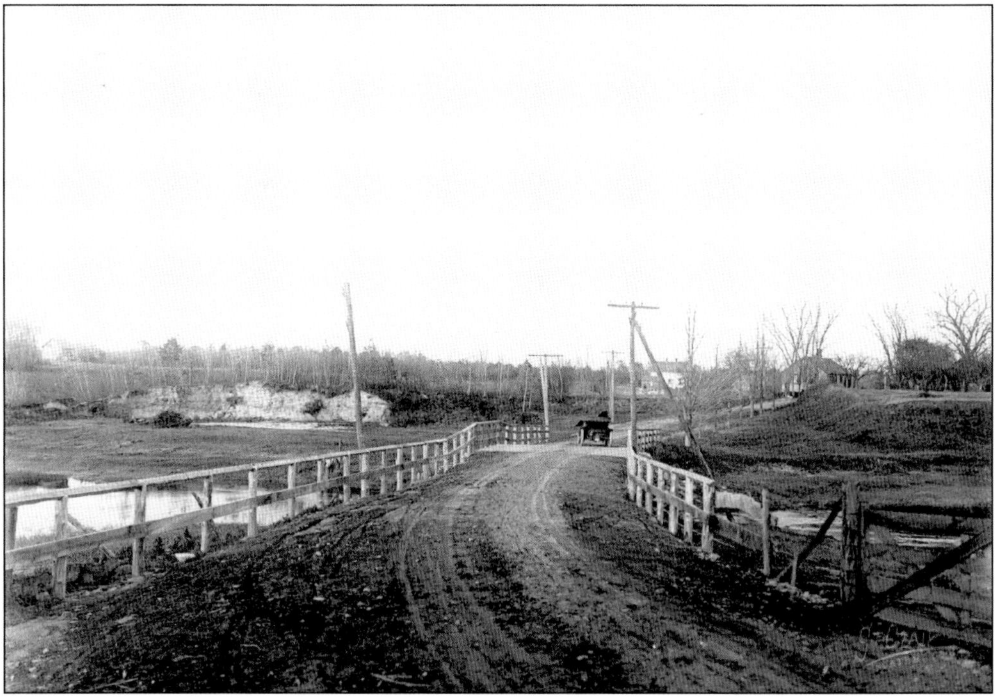

This view of Sturgeon Bridge on Tidy Road was taken in 1910. Eliot's earliest pioneers settled in this area. Sturgeon Creek provided a route out to the river for transportation of goods and lumber to Portsmouth and beyond. (Courtesy of the Gov. John F. Hill Collection at the William Fogg Library.)

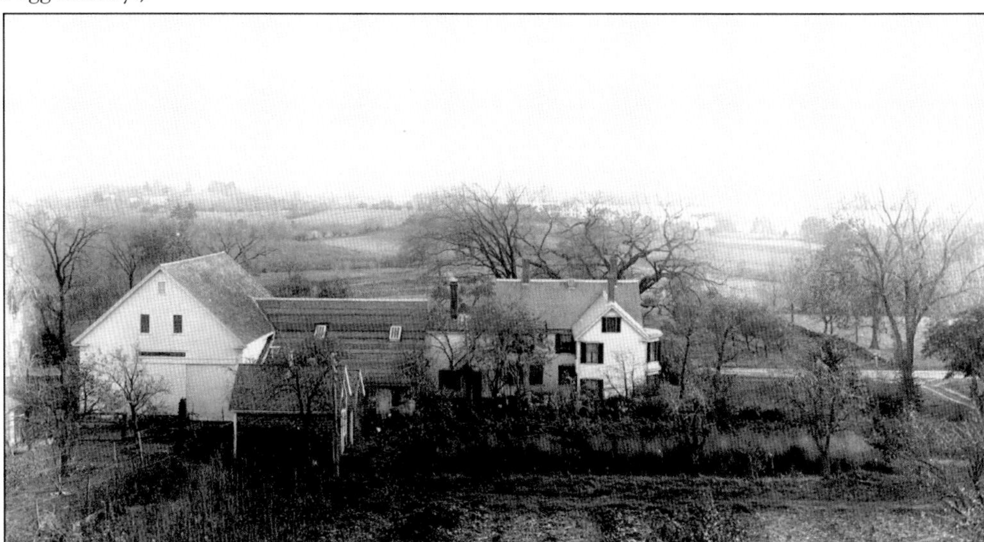

Looking south from Old Road, one can see Frankfort Island. Before 1631, the island was known as Frank's Fort, named for Francis Williams, overseer of a company doing experimental work in the salt industry. In 1775, during the Revolutionary War, New Hampshire men captured guns and powder from Fort William and Mary at New Castle and buried them on the island, later to be used at the Battle of Bunker Hill. (Courtesy of the Gov. John F. Hill Collection at the William Fogg Library.)

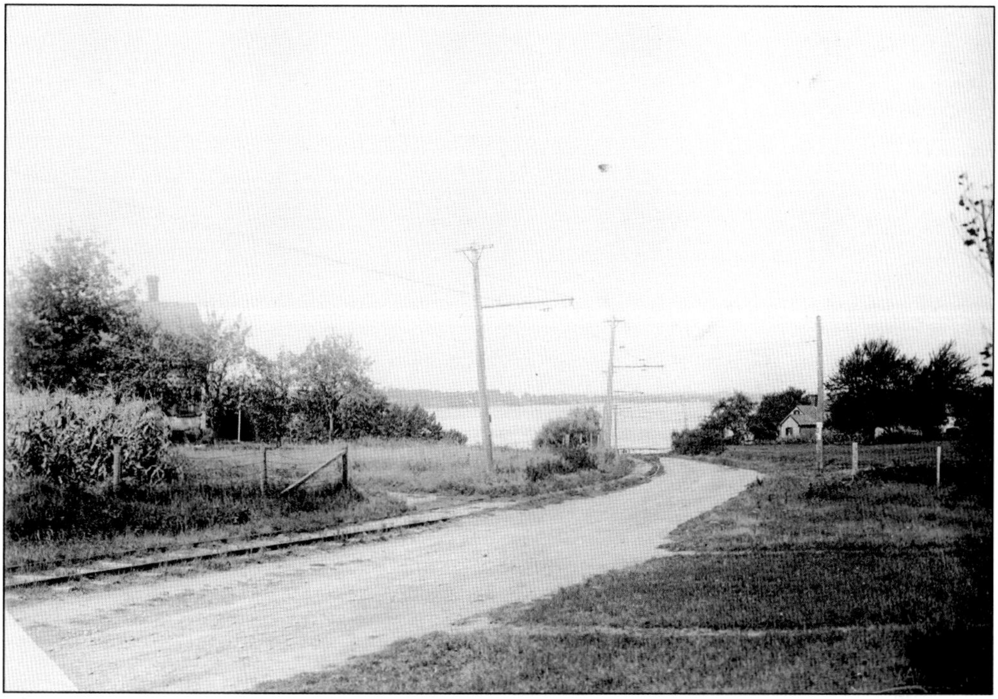

The Long Reach riverfront runs from what was once Watt's Ford (off Laurel Lane) to the Frank's Fort area. (Above and below, courtesy of the Gov. John F. Hill Collection at the William Fogg Library.)

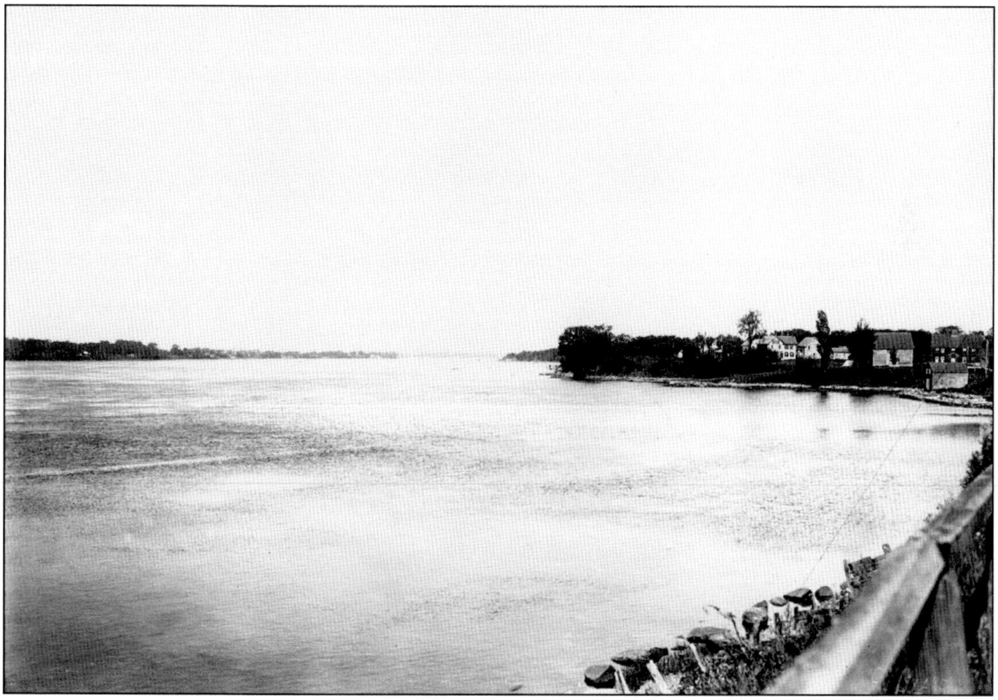

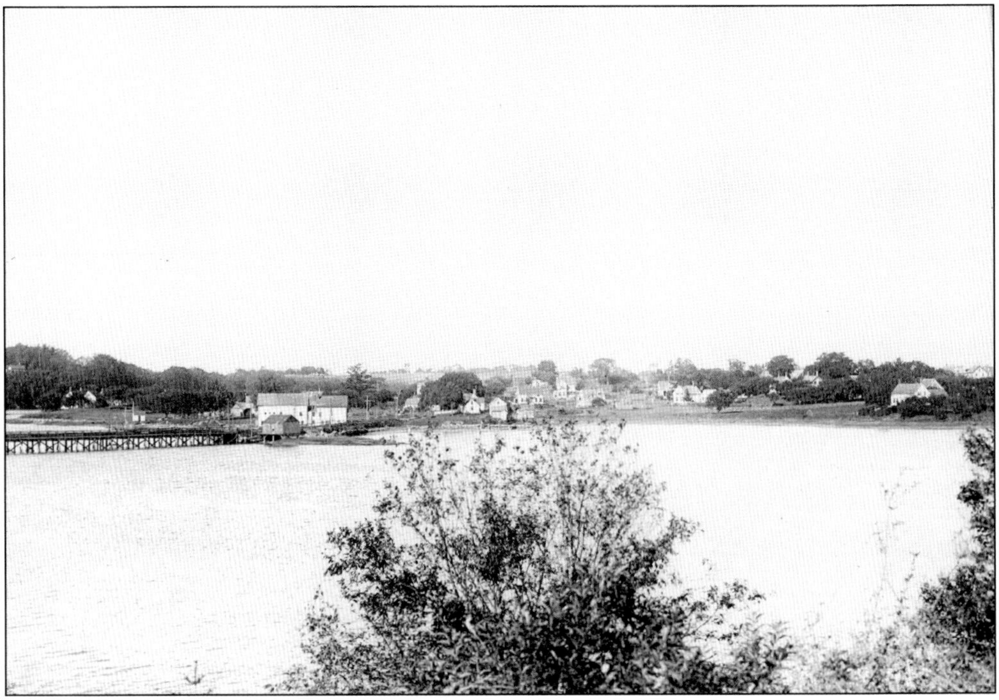

Spinney Creek in South Eliot marks the boundary between Kittery and Eliot. The creek flows into the Piscataqua River at Eliot Neck. (Courtesy of the Gov. John F. Hill Collection at the William Fogg Library.)

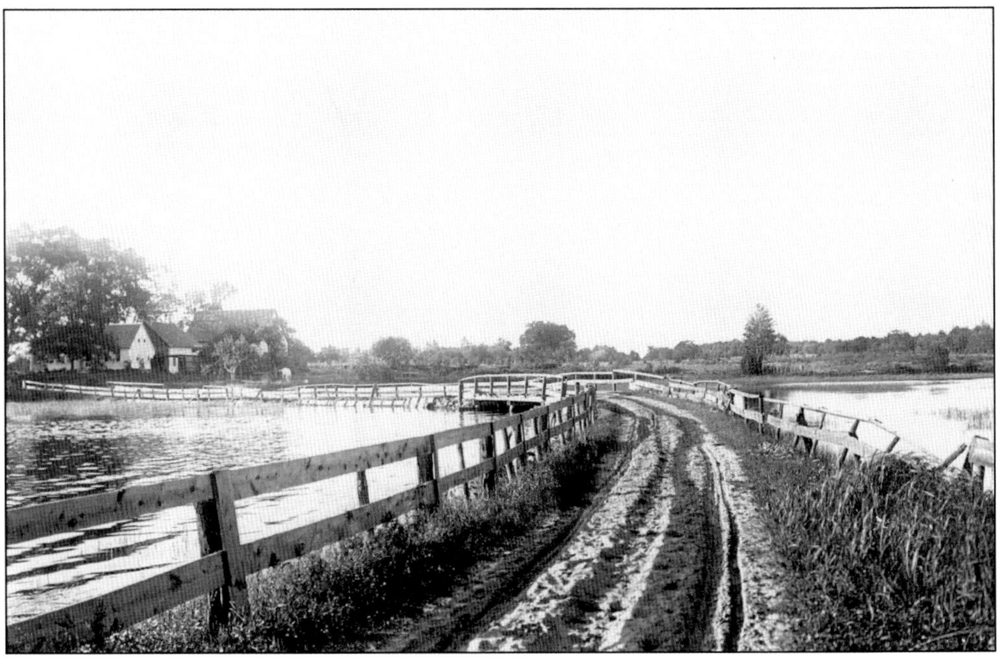

Cammock's Creek is also known as Stacy or Shapleigh Creek. Tidal-powered saw- and gristmills stood here in the 18th and 19th centuries. (Courtesy of the Gov. John F. Hill Collection at the William Fogg Library.)

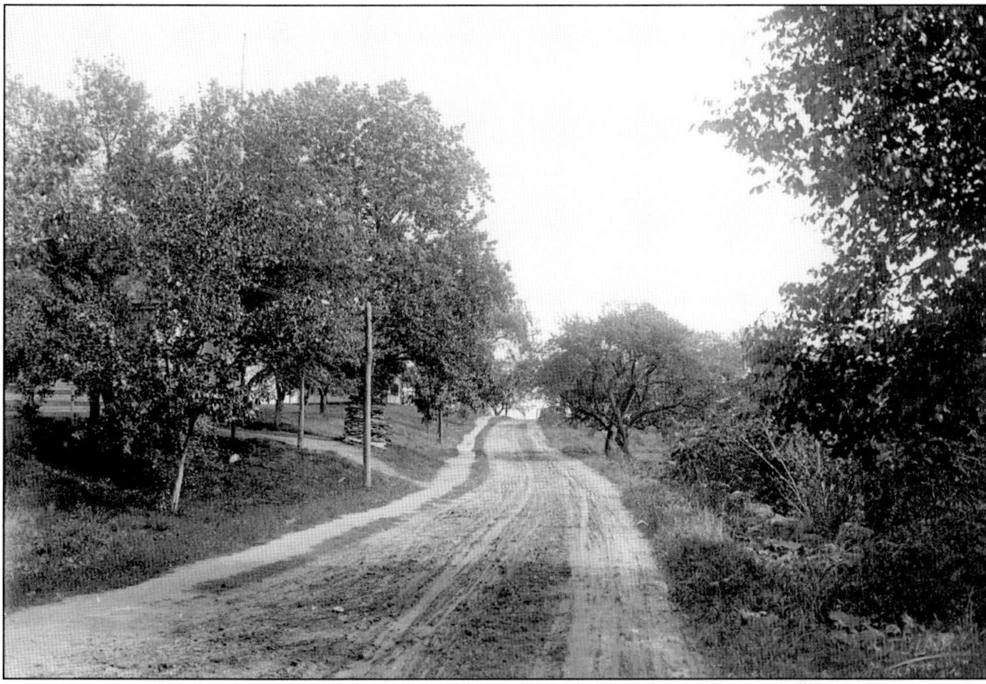

Historian William Fogg (1790–1859) described Old Road as the oldest continuously traveled road in Maine. It was originally an American Indian trail. (Courtesy of the Gov. John F. Hill Collection at the William Fogg Library.)

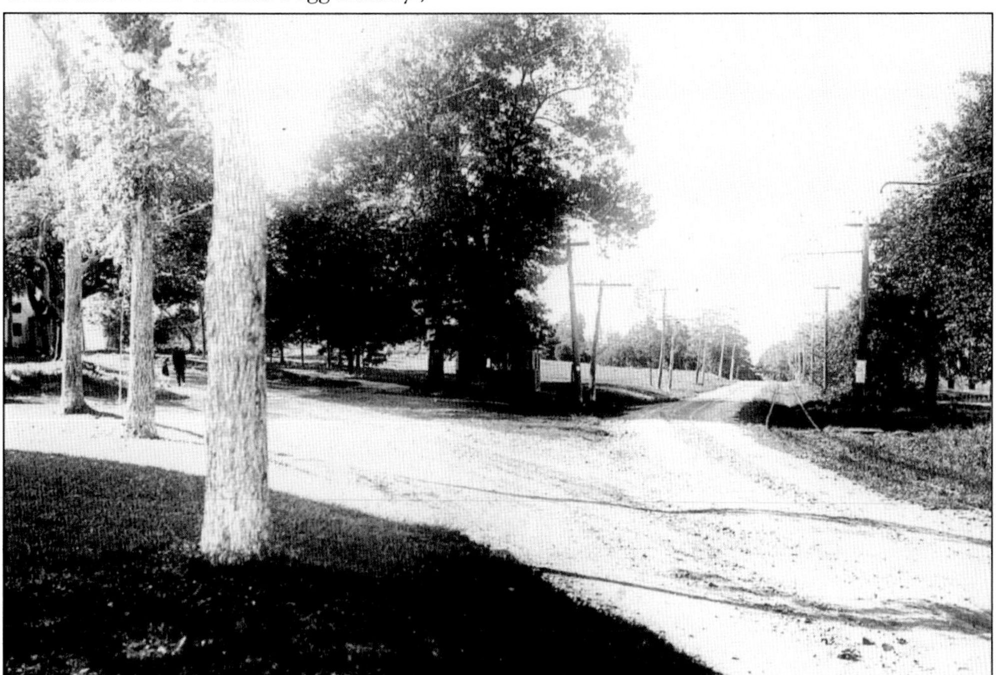

The area of Kennard's Corner was once the site of Kennard's Tavern, the Eliot Academy, and a schoolhouse. It is near the William Fogg Library. This photograph was taken in 1910. (Courtesy of Kenneth Tuttle.)

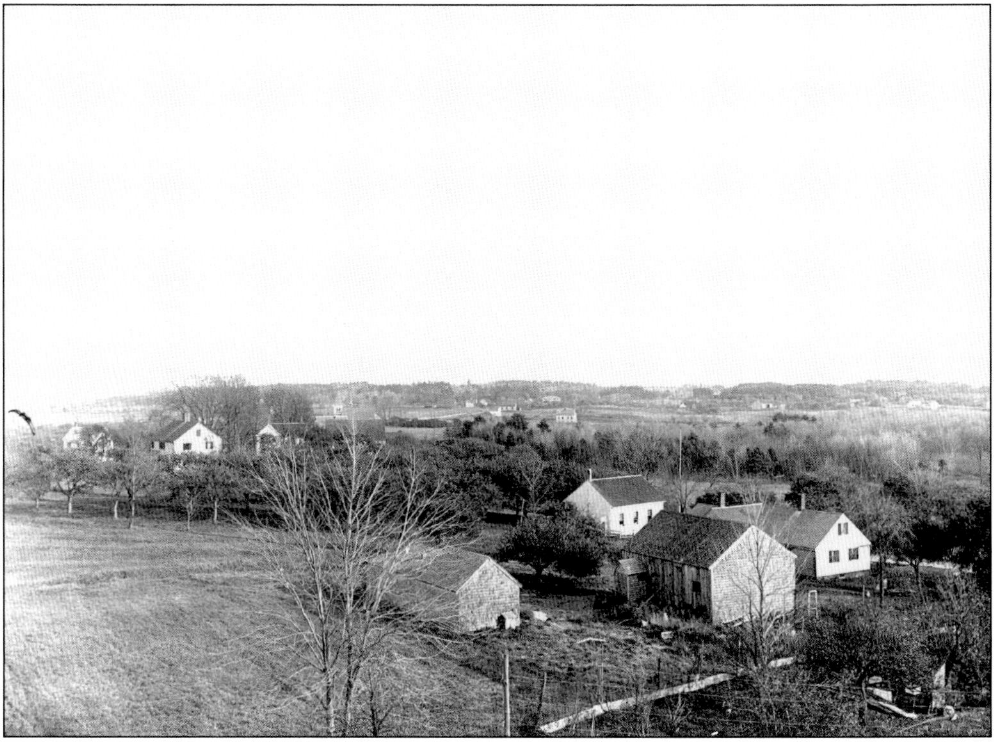

This bird's-eye view shows Kennard's Corner, where State and Old Roads intersect, as it appeared in 1910. (Courtesy of the Gov. John F. Hill Collection at the William Fogg Library.)

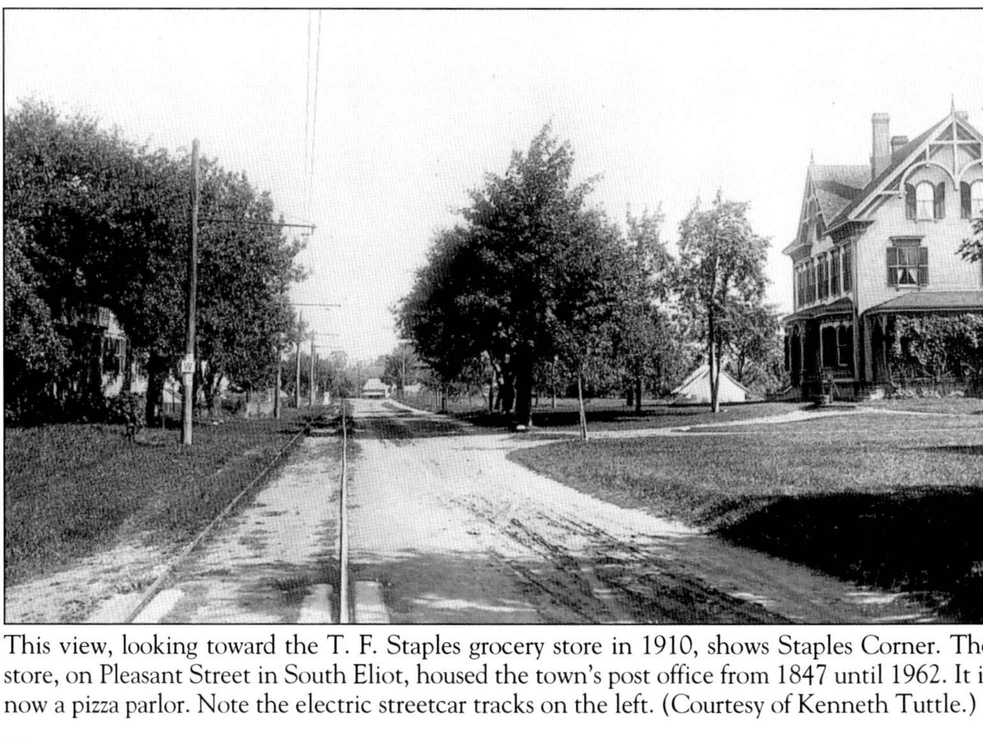

This view, looking toward the T. F. Staples grocery store in 1910, shows Staples Corner. The store, on Pleasant Street in South Eliot, housed the town's post office from 1847 until 1962. It is now a pizza parlor. Note the electric streetcar tracks on the left. (Courtesy of Kenneth Tuttle.)

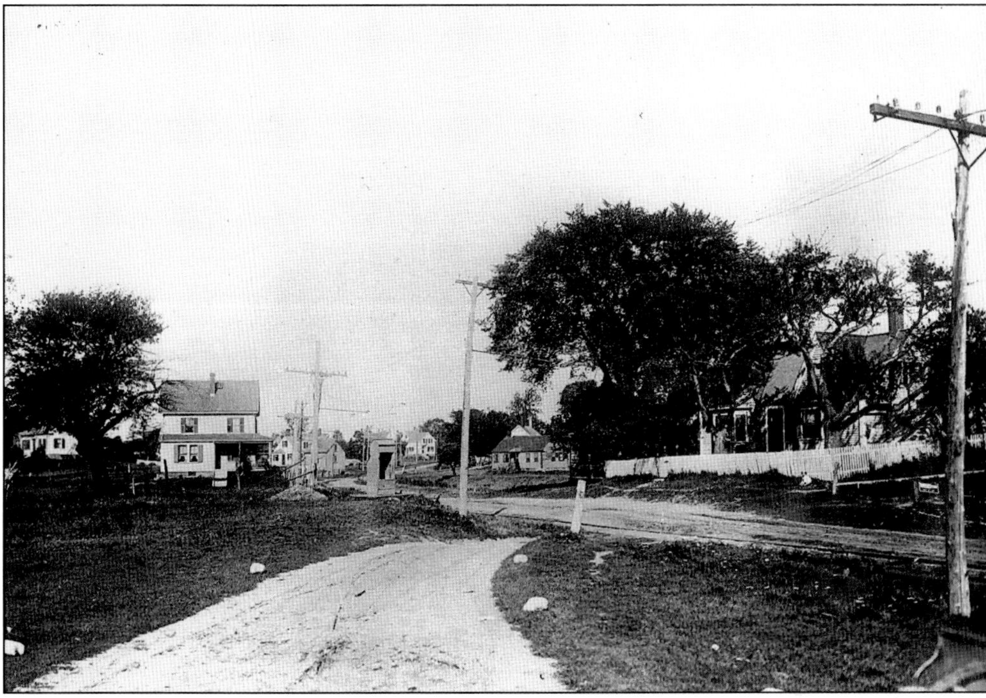

Taken in front of Harris Spinney's store at the tip of Eliot Neck, this 1910 view looks west to King's Highway in South Eliot. (Courtesy of Kenneth Tuttle.)

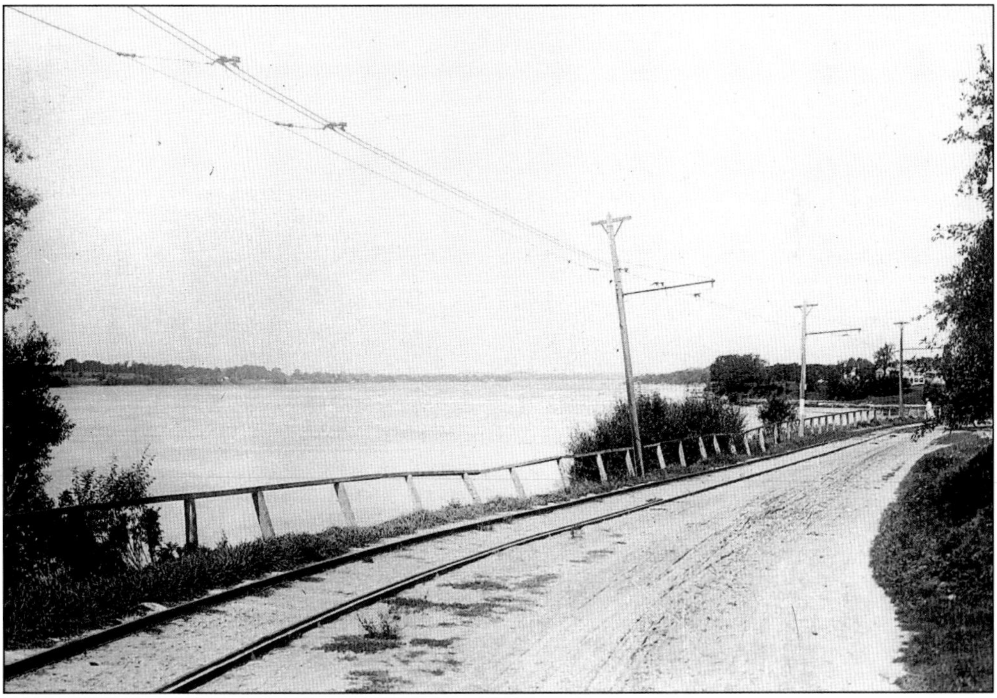

In 1910, when the landscape was still vacant of construction, one could look across the water on Pleasant Street to Newington, New Hampshire. (Courtesy of Kenneth Tuttle.)

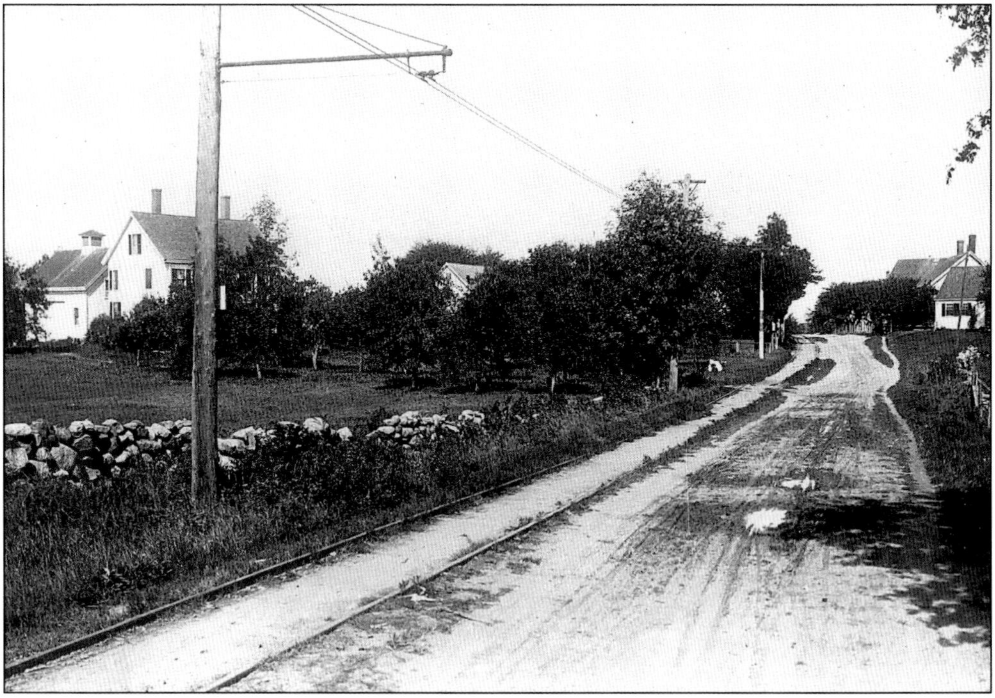

In another 1910 photograph of Pleasant Street, near Cross Street, one can see electric streetcar tracks. The Pleasant and Main Streets area was a heavily populated section of town, with smaller homes built more closely together. Many of the area's residents worked at Hanscom's Shipyard when it was in operation. (Courtesy of Kenneth Tuttle.)

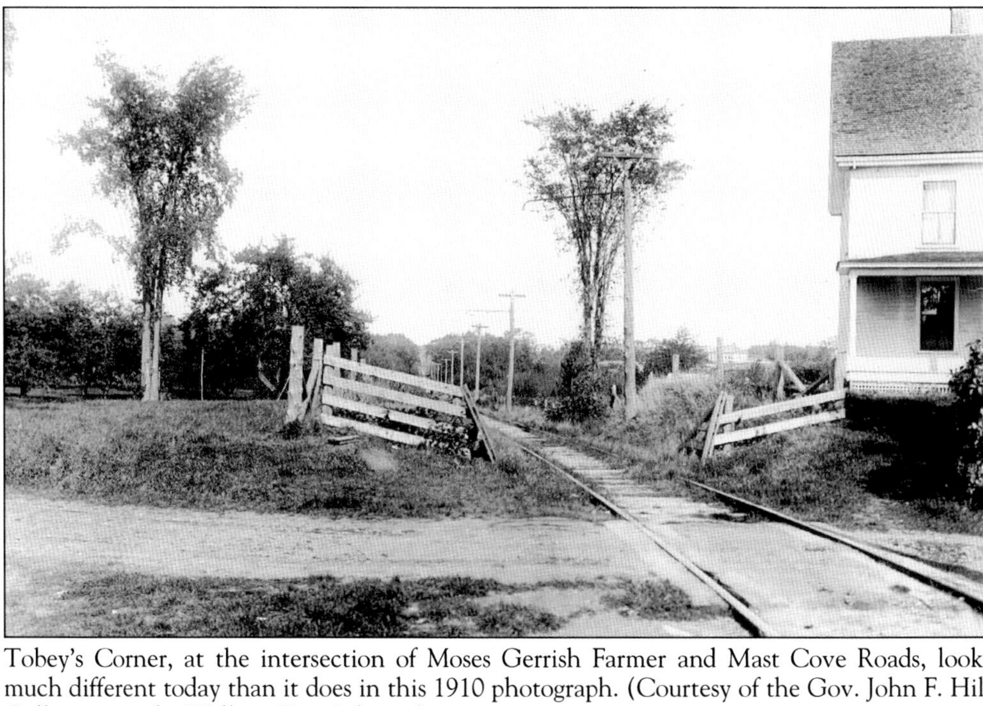

Tobey's Corner, at the intersection of Moses Gerrish Farmer and Mast Cove Roads, looks much different today than it does in this 1910 photograph. (Courtesy of the Gov. John F. Hill Collection at the William Fogg Library.)

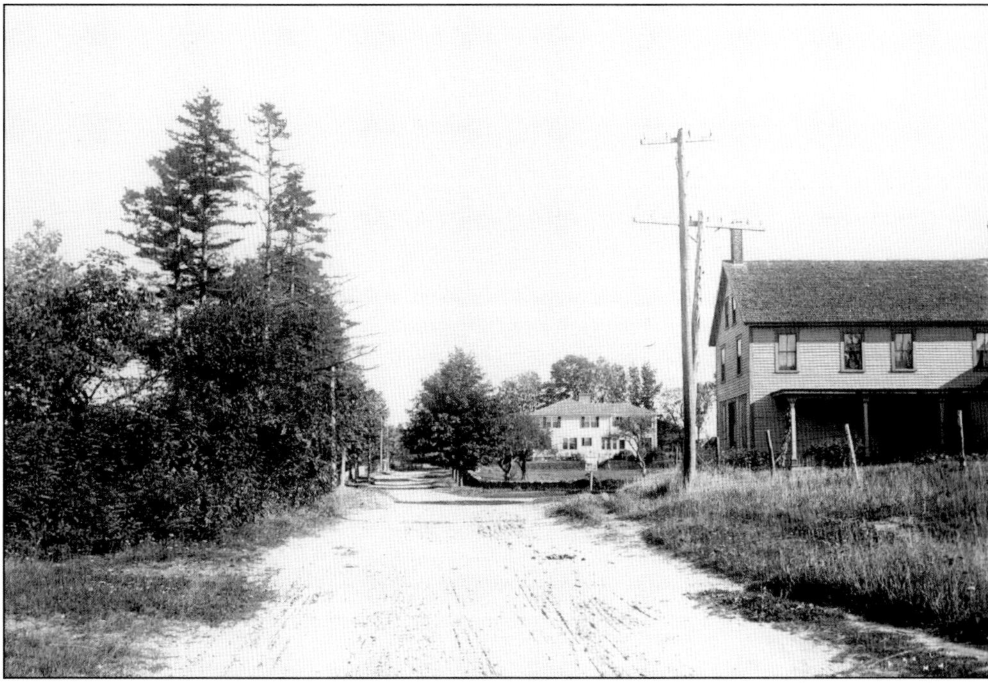

Liebman's Corner, at the intersection of State and Moses Gerrish Farmer Roads, looked like this in 1910. The building on the near right is now the location of the Eliot Meat Market. The house in the distance was Sarah Farmer's residence. (Courtesy of the Gov. John F. Hill Collection at the William Fogg Library.)

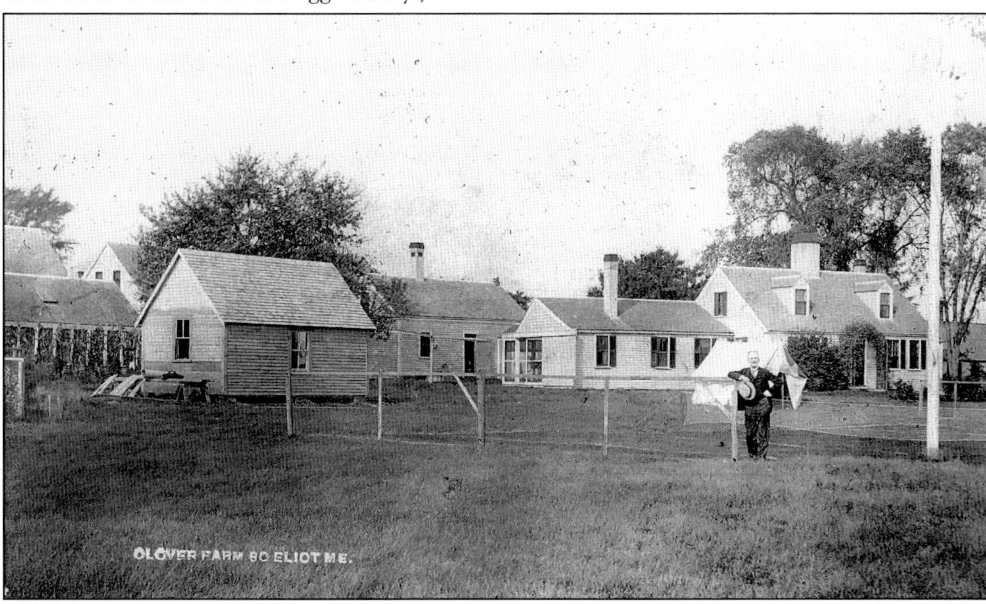

According to the present owner of Clover Farm in South Eliot, the property was at one time a chicken farm. The farm, built around 1750 and remodeled in 1950, first belonged to the Remicks and later to the Hanscom family. The house was put together with wooden pegs. Rumor has it that Teddy Roosevelt once slept here. Today there is an antiques shop on the property. (Courtesy of the Paul Family Association.)

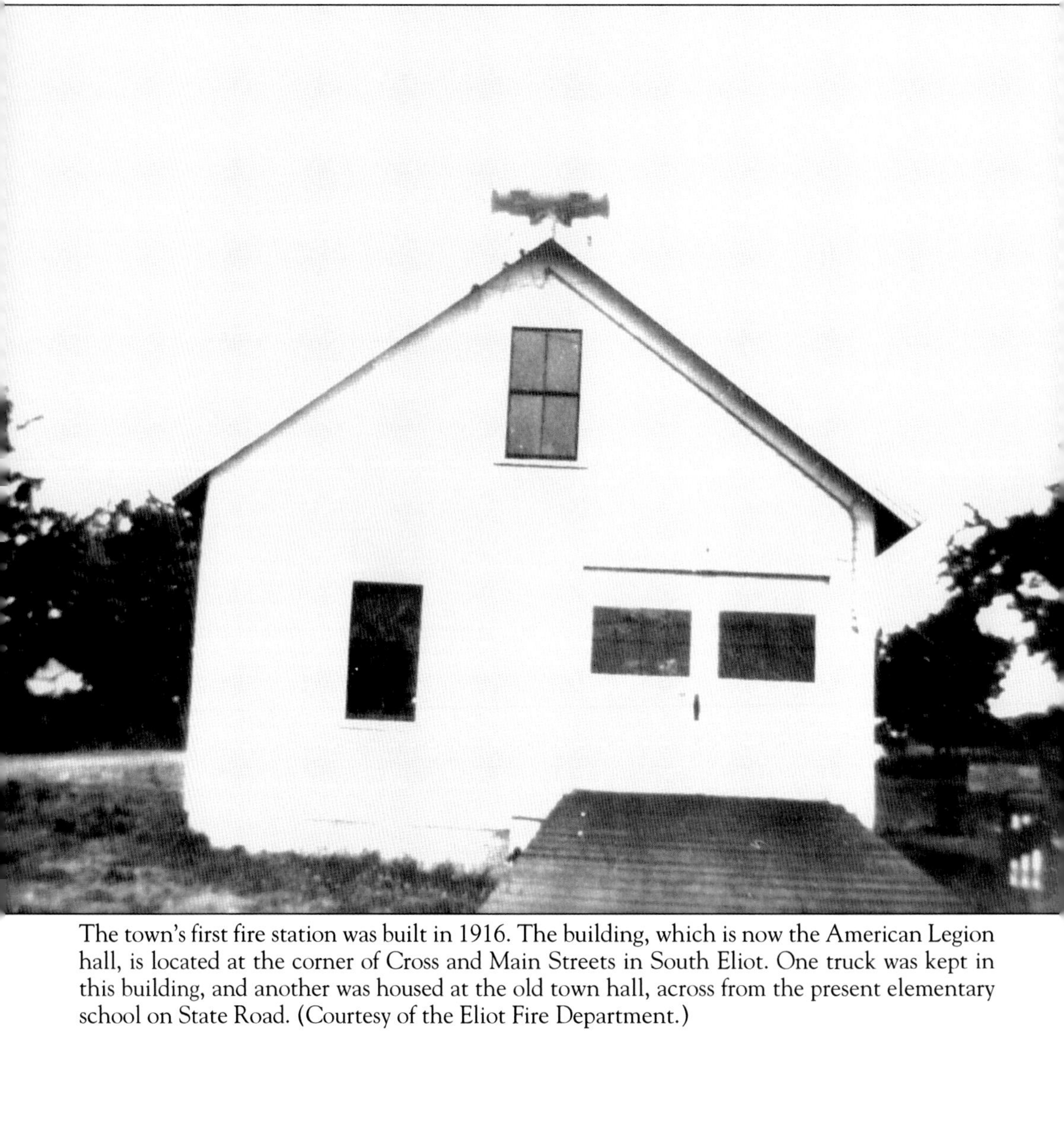

The town's first fire station was built in 1916. The building, which is now the American Legion hall, is located at the corner of Cross and Main Streets in South Eliot. One truck was kept in this building, and another was housed at the old town hall, across from the present elementary school on State Road. (Courtesy of the Eliot Fire Department.)

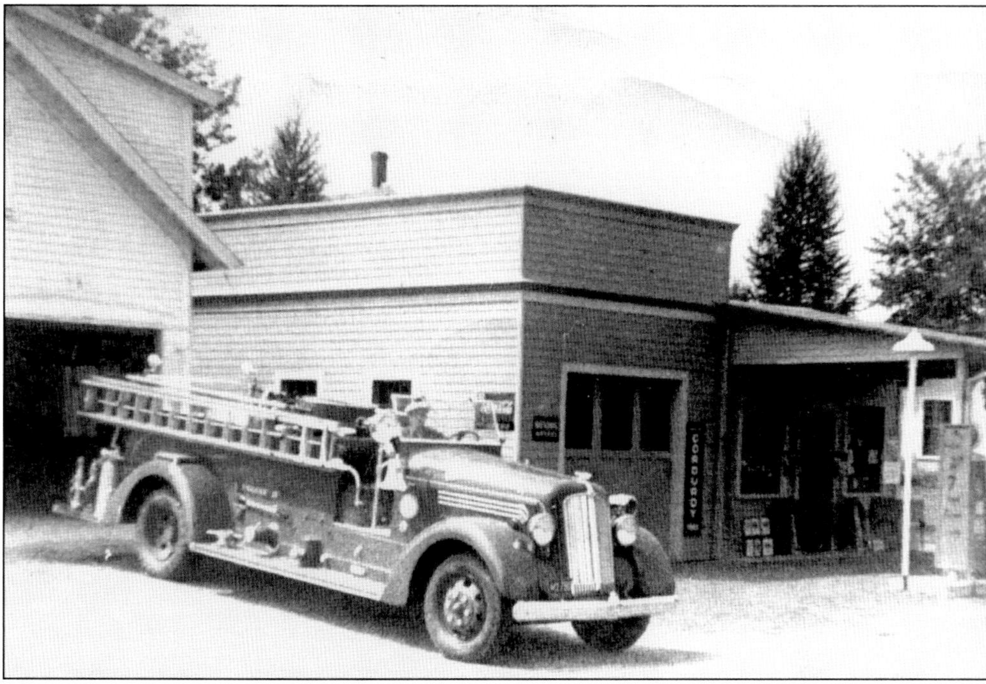

This 1939 Seagrave, the oldest Eliot fire truck still in existence, is shown here in front of the first fire station. On the right is Harold Dow's gas station. Eliot's first fire chief, Pearl Cole, is seated in the truck. (Courtesy of Donald Webber Jr.)

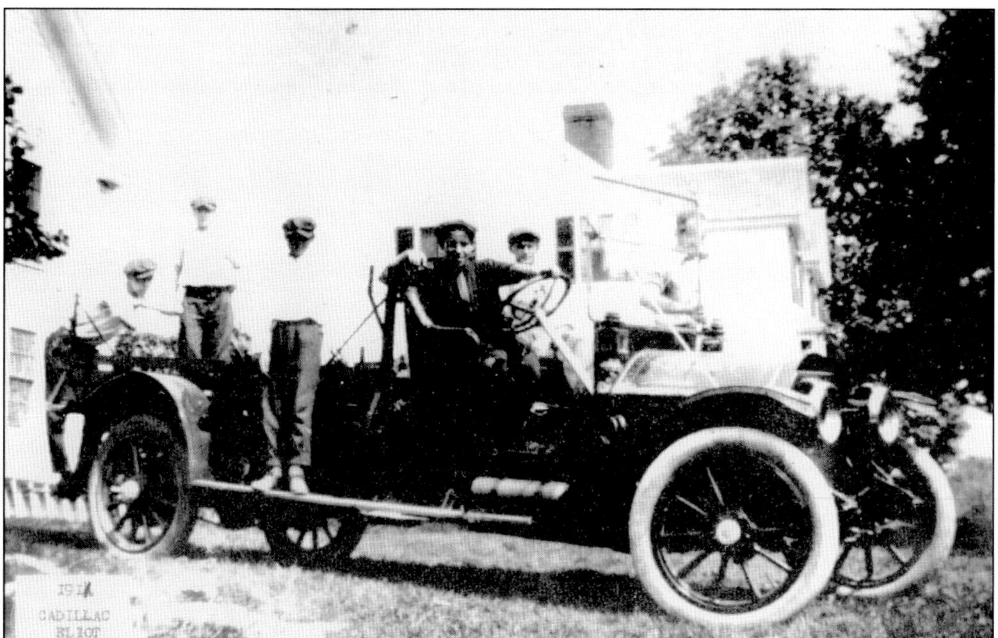

The fire department had two fire trucks built on the chassis of 1911 Cadillacs. One truck was kept at the South Eliot location, and the other was housed at the old town hall on State Road. This photograph was taken near Harlon Liebman's property. Liebman was one of the founders of the department. (Courtesy of the Eliot Fire Department.)

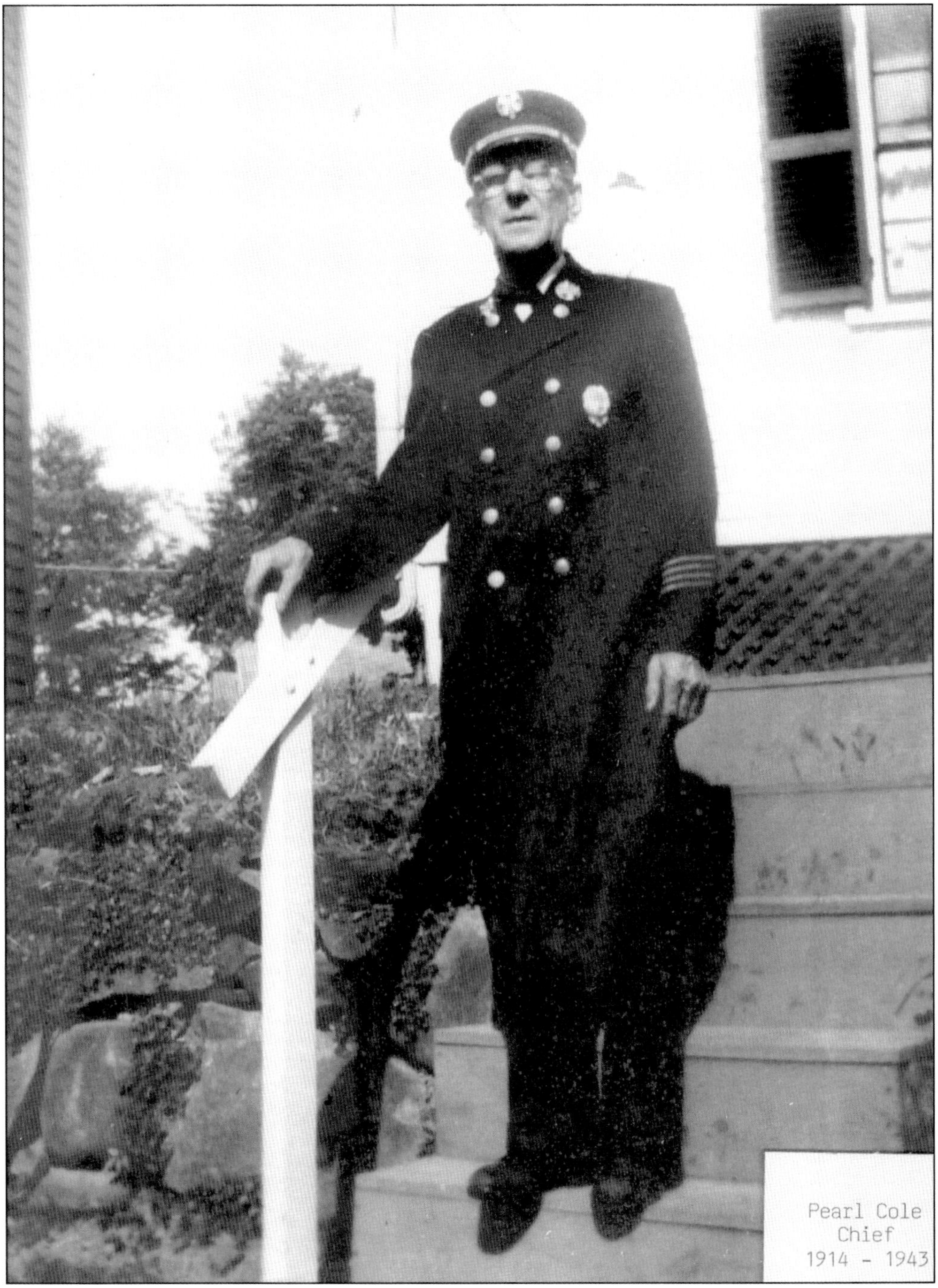

Pearl Cole, Eliot's first fire chief, served from 1914, when the fire department was formed, until 1943. From its inception, the department had 45 firefighters, and that number continued until the late 1970s, when the number dropped. For a while, there was a waiting list of volunteers. Now the number is almost back to 45. Since its formation, the fire department has had six chiefs. (Courtesy of the Eliot Fire Department.)

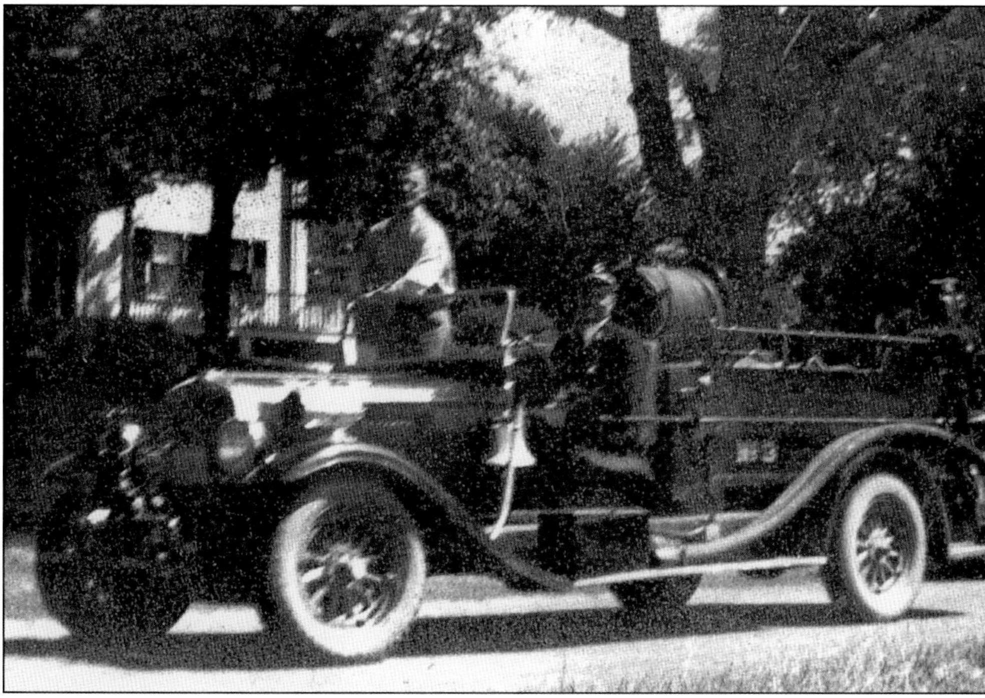

In 1948, after the arrival of a 1947 Ford, this 1930 Fargo truck was used only in summer. A door was added to the former School House No. 8 on Greenwood Street, and the Fargo spent winters there. The Fargo was cut up for scrap in 1958. In this 1950s photograph, Donald Webber Sr. is in the uniform. The other man is Howard "Pickles" Dixon. (Courtesy of the Eliot Fire Department.)

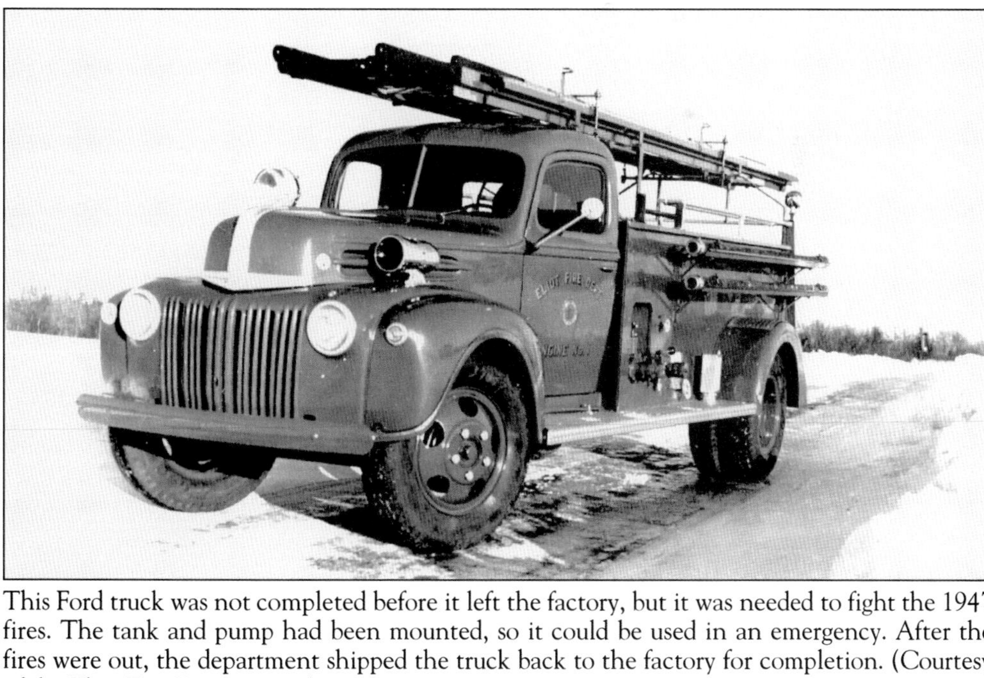

This Ford truck was not completed before it left the factory, but it was needed to fight the 1947 fires. The tank and pump had been mounted, so it could be used in an emergency. After the fires were out, the department shipped the truck back to the factory for completion. (Courtesy of the Eliot Fire Department.)

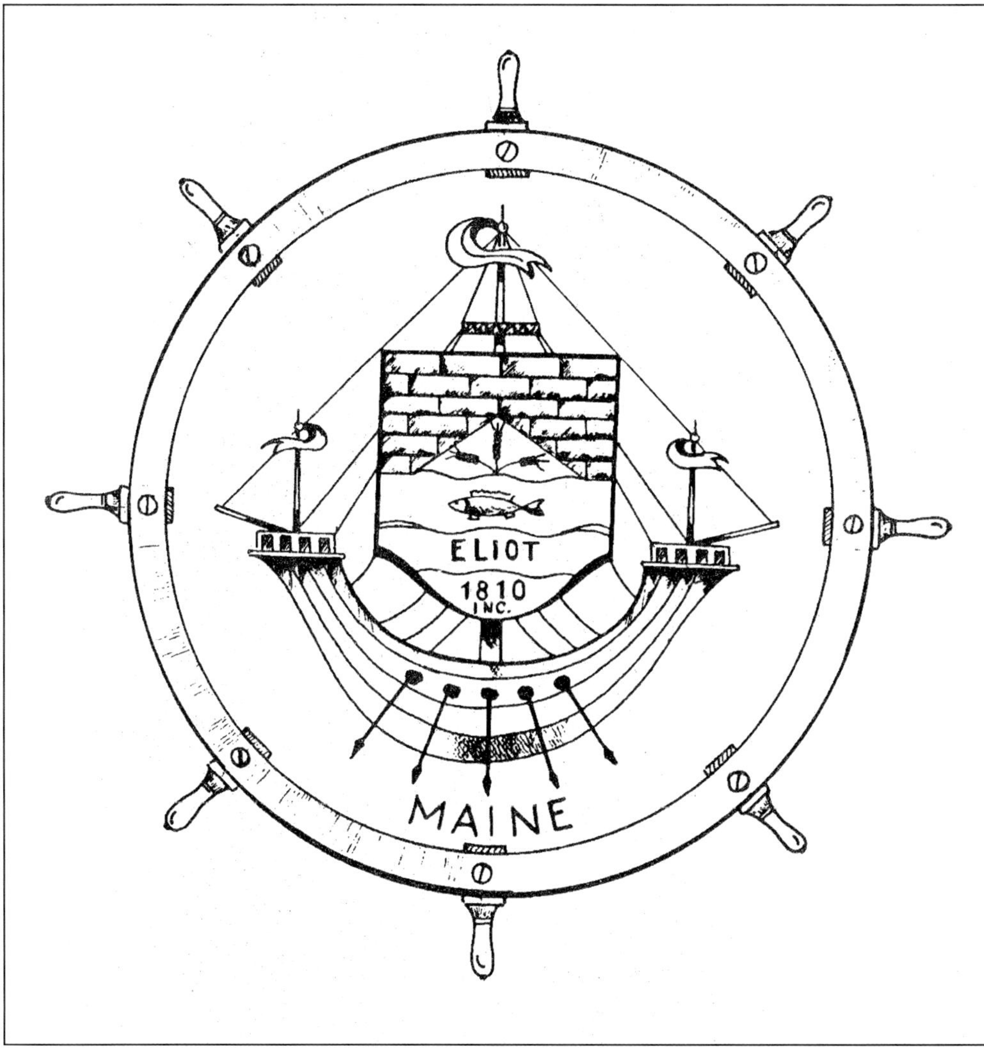

In 1985, Eliot artist Jules Weyers designed the town seal in conjunction with Eliot's 175th anniversary celebration. The seal's images encompass much of the town's history, including shipbuilding, brickmaking, fishing, and farming. The five oars represent the town's five selectmen.

Three

ARCHITECTURE

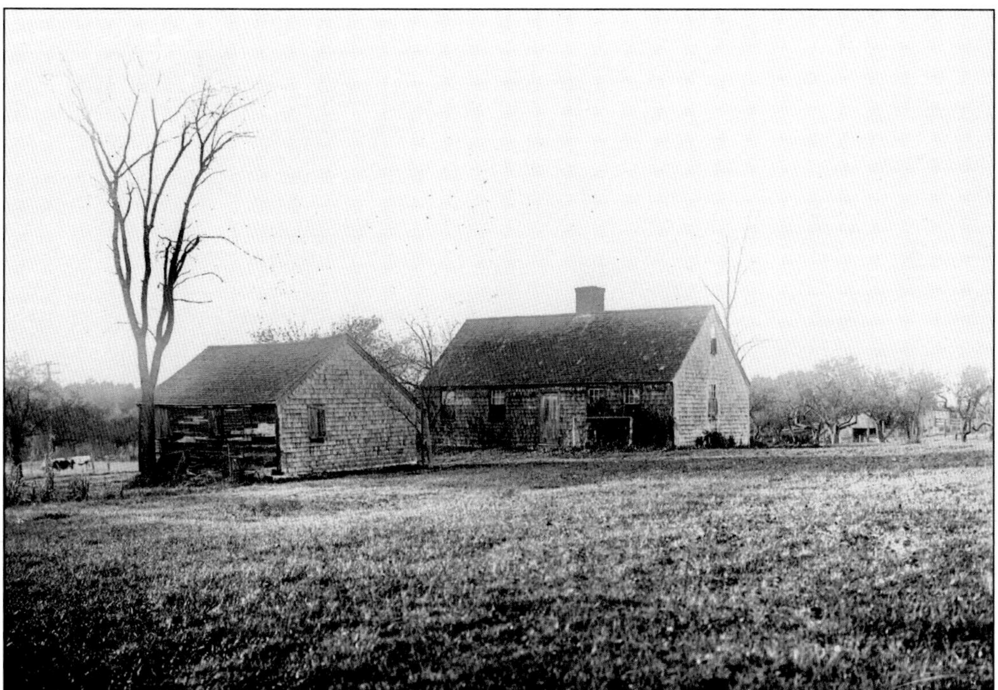

The Noah Emery House, on Goodwin Road near Gould's Corner, was built before 1722. Noah Emery (1699–1761) was the first King's Council for the province of Maine. Emery's woodshed housed an early school. (Courtesy of the Gov. John F. Hill Collection at the William Fogg Library.)

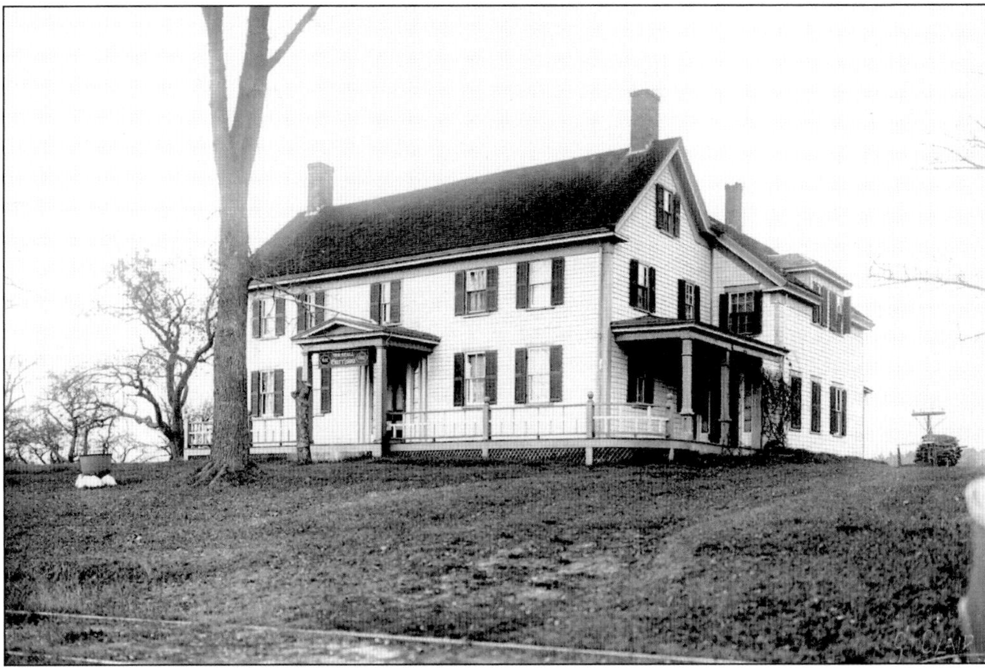

The Neal Garrison was built in the 1600s on Goodwin Road. Used as a fort where early settlers congregated during American Indian attacks, it was remodeled in 1802 and destroyed by fire on February 16, 1919. This photograph was taken in 1910. (Courtesy of the Gov. John F. Hill Collection at the William Fogg Library.)

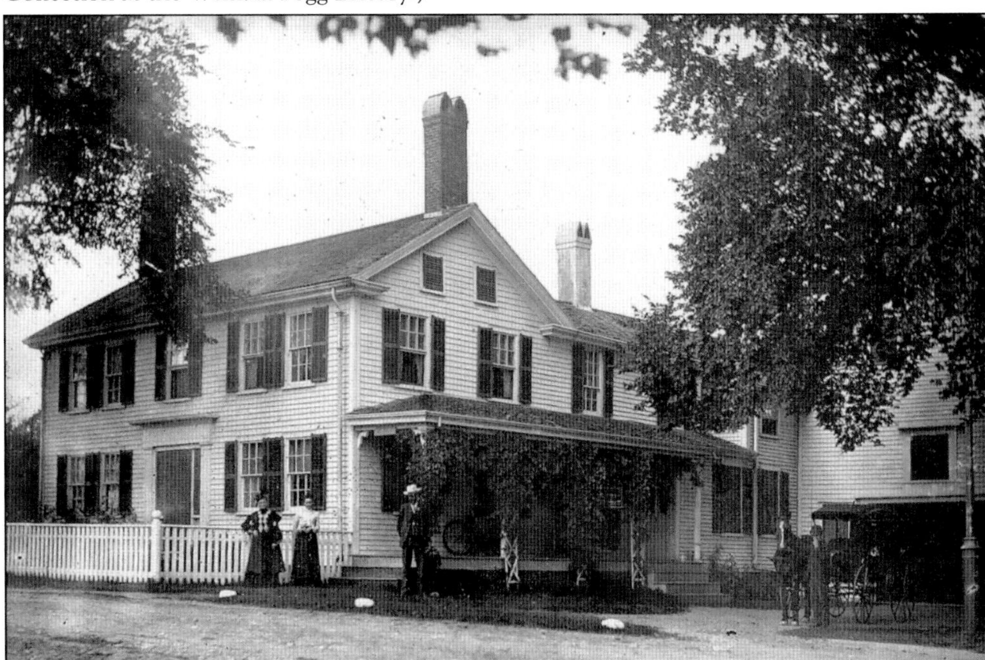

Dr. Horace Stacey built this home on State Road around 1840 in a Colonial, Greek Revival style. The residence became the home of a series of doctors, including Dr. Mark F. Wentworth, Dr. Calvin H. Guptill, and Dr. Henry I. Durgin. (Courtesy of the Eliot Historical Society.)

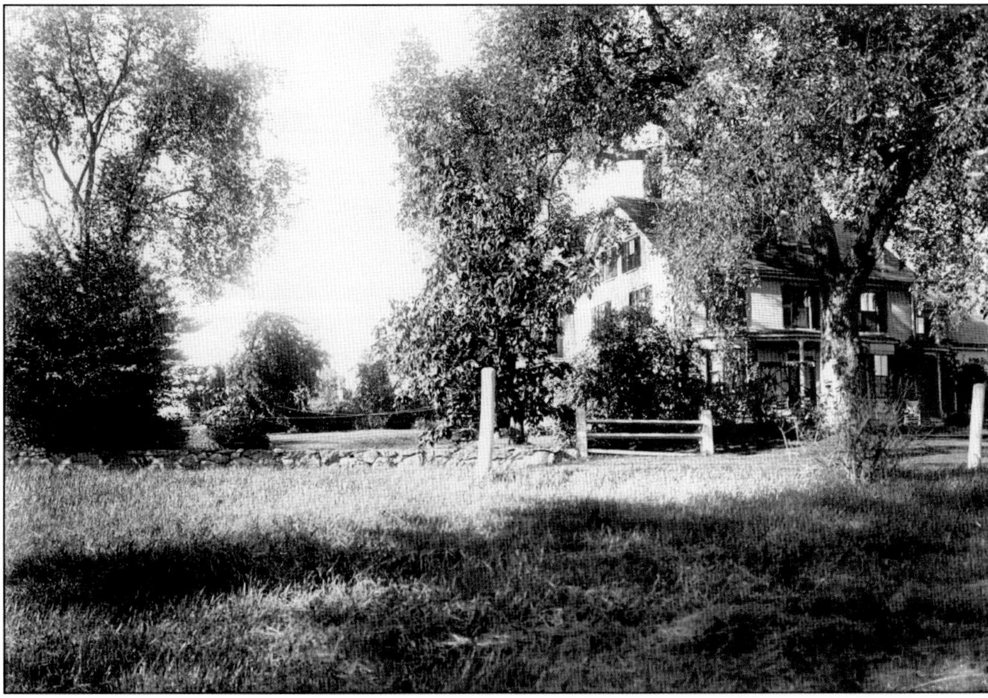

Dr. John L. M. Willis, founder of the Eliot Historical Society, lived in the Daniel Fogg house on Old Road. The home was originally built as a Cape around 1725. John Fogg Jr. made additions in 1815. Dr. Willis's mother was Paulina H. Fogg, John Fogg's daughter. (Courtesy of the Gov. John F. Hill Collection at the William Fogg Library.)

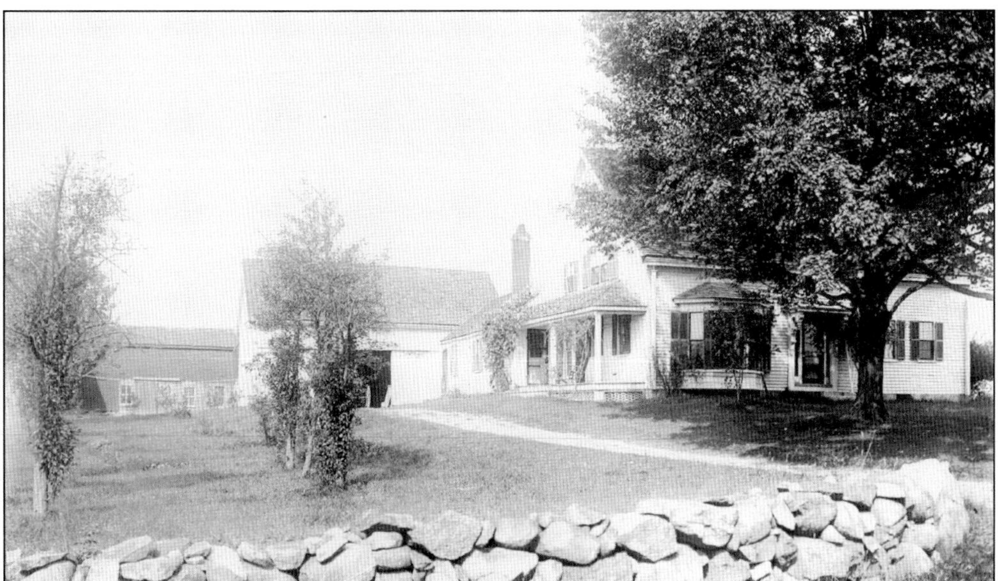

The birthplace of Gov. John Fremont Hill (1855–1912), on Governor Hill Road, burned to the ground on May 17, 1932. Governor Hill's mother was Miriam Leighton Hill. John F. Hill presided as governor of Maine from 1901 until 1905. (Courtesy of the Gov. John F. Hill Collection at the William Fogg Library.)

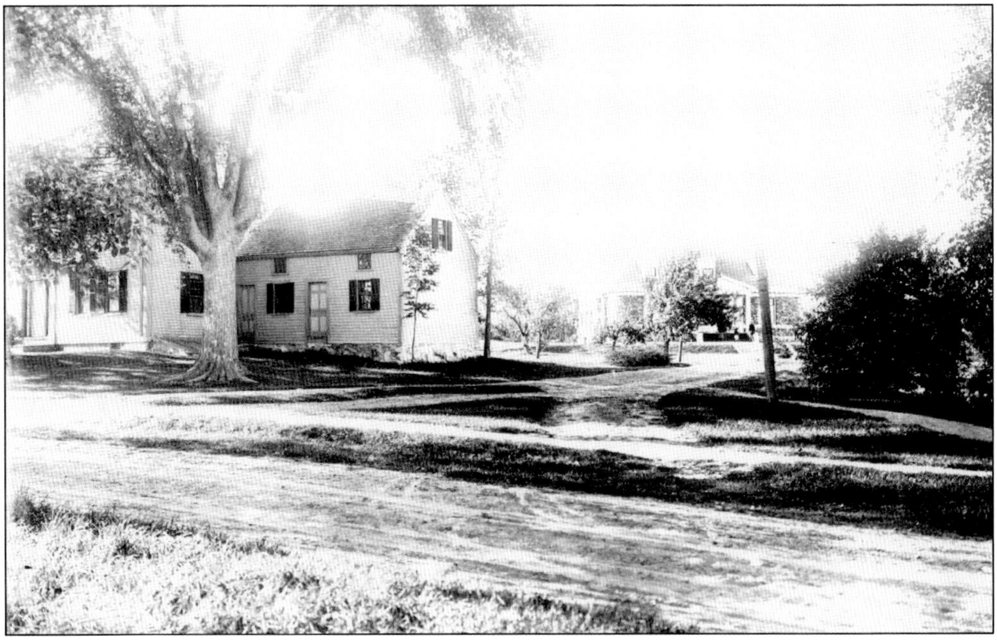

The William Fogg House, on Old Road, housed a post office for 30 years. William Fogg was postmaster from 1817 to 1847. William Fogg's son, Dr. John S. H. Fogg, was born at the house. Dr. Fogg donated the adjacent land for construction of the William Fogg Library in memory of his father. The library is on the right. (Courtesy of the Gov. John F. Hill Collection at the William Fogg Library.)

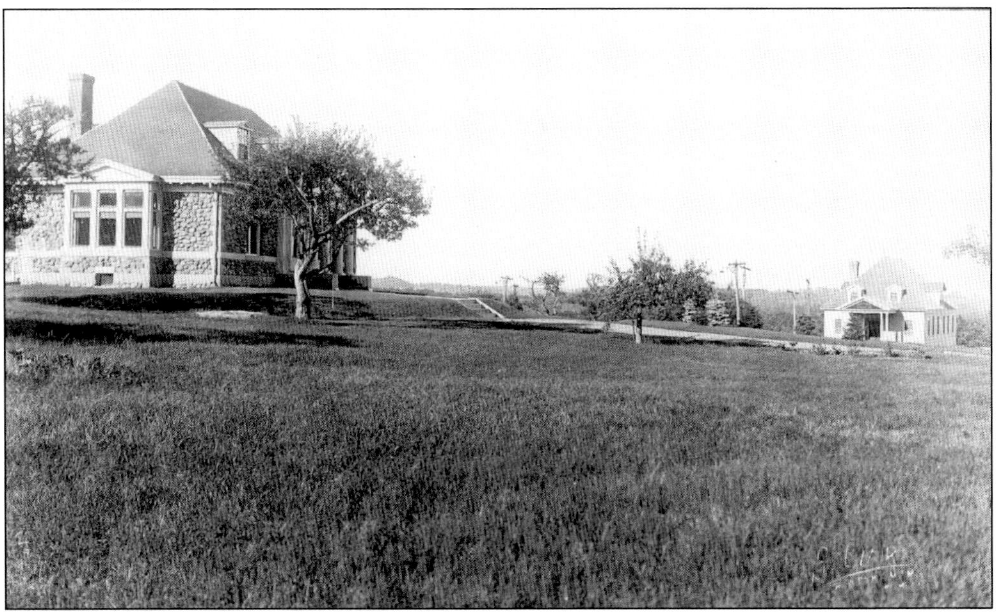

The William Fogg Library, on Old Road, was dedicated on May 21, 1907. Boston architect C. Howard Walker designed the building. Sarah Jane Farmer helped raise money for the project. Her friend John Greenleaf Whittier donated many of his books to the original collection. The building is on the National Register of Historic Places. (Courtesy of the Gov. John F. Hill Collection at the William Fogg Library.)

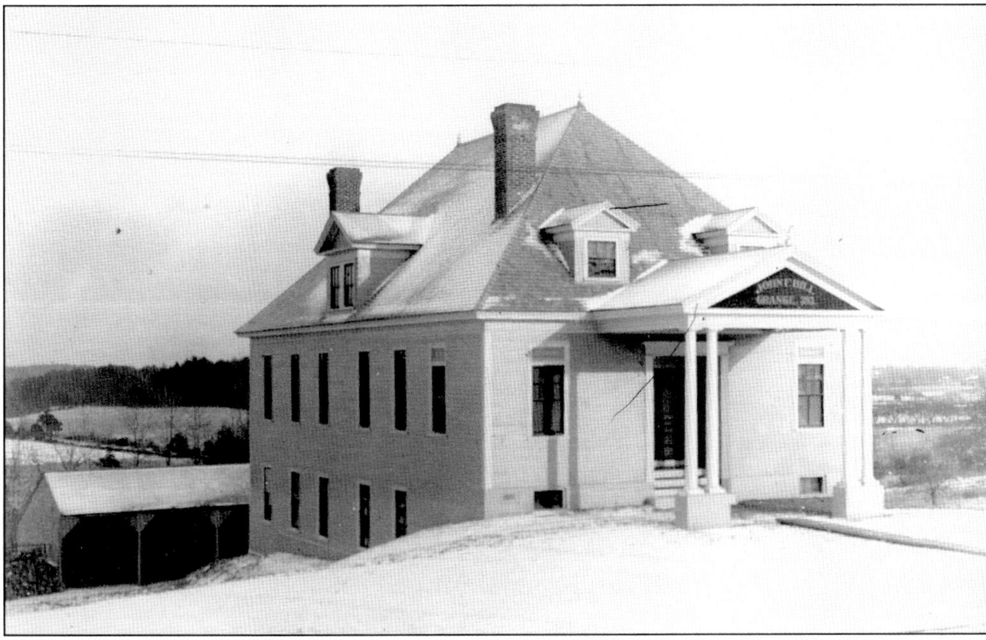

The John F. Hill Grange was organized in 1902 and named for Eliot native son Governor Hill. The Grange hall was built at Kennard's Corner in 1910. (Courtesy of the Gov. John F. Hill Collection at the William Fogg Library.)

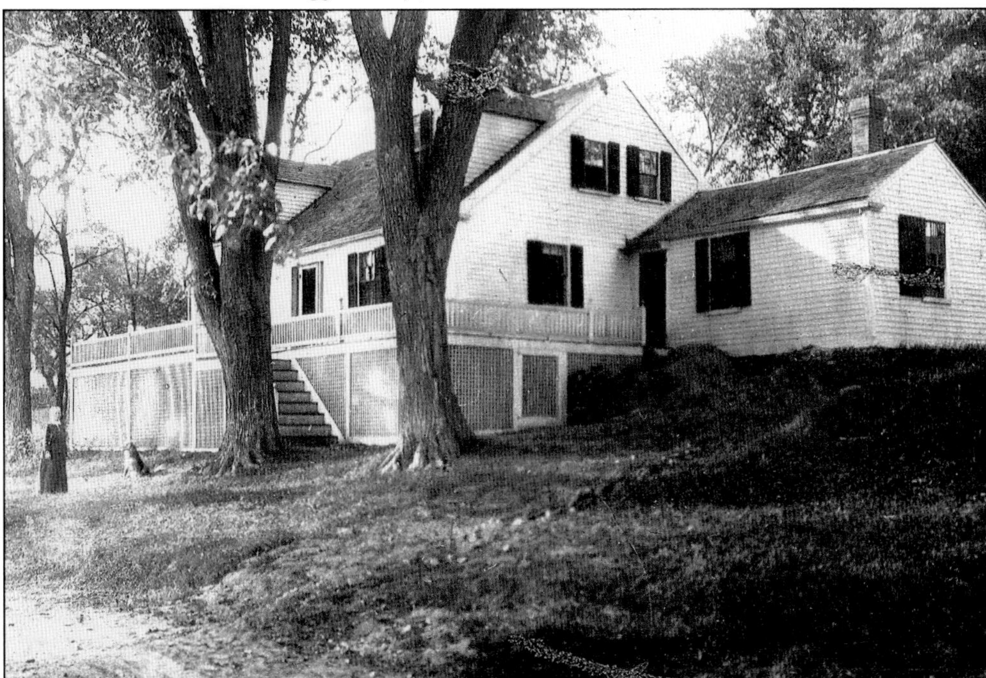

The Betsy Green Cottage, on Old Road, was built on land originally granted to John Green in 1648. Betsy Kennard, daughter of Benjamin Kennard, a tavern keeper, married Stephen Green. Stephen's cobbler shop was in the cellar, and Betsy had a penny shop upstairs where she sold needles, pins, and other small notions. (Courtesy of the Estate of C. Edward Bartlett Jr.)

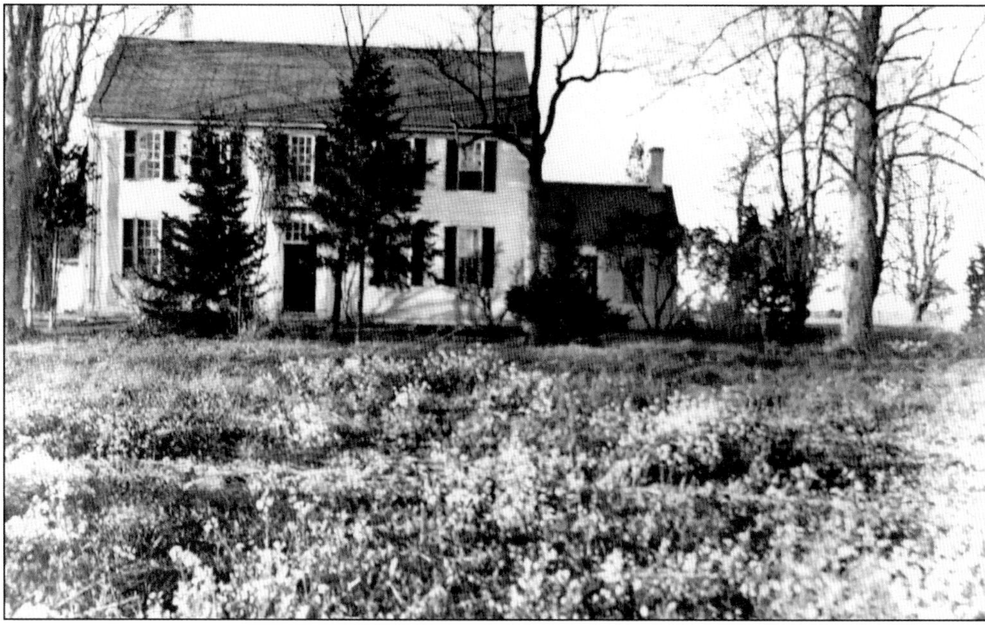

The Col. John Frost House, on Frost Hill, was built in 1732. John was the grandson of Maj. Charles Frost. The house had an addition that 20th-century family members referred to as "Grandmother's Ell." Kitchen fires heated this area, but the bedrooms in the main part of the house had no central heating. The home is on the National Register of Historic Places. (Courtesy of Mara Frost Marshall.)

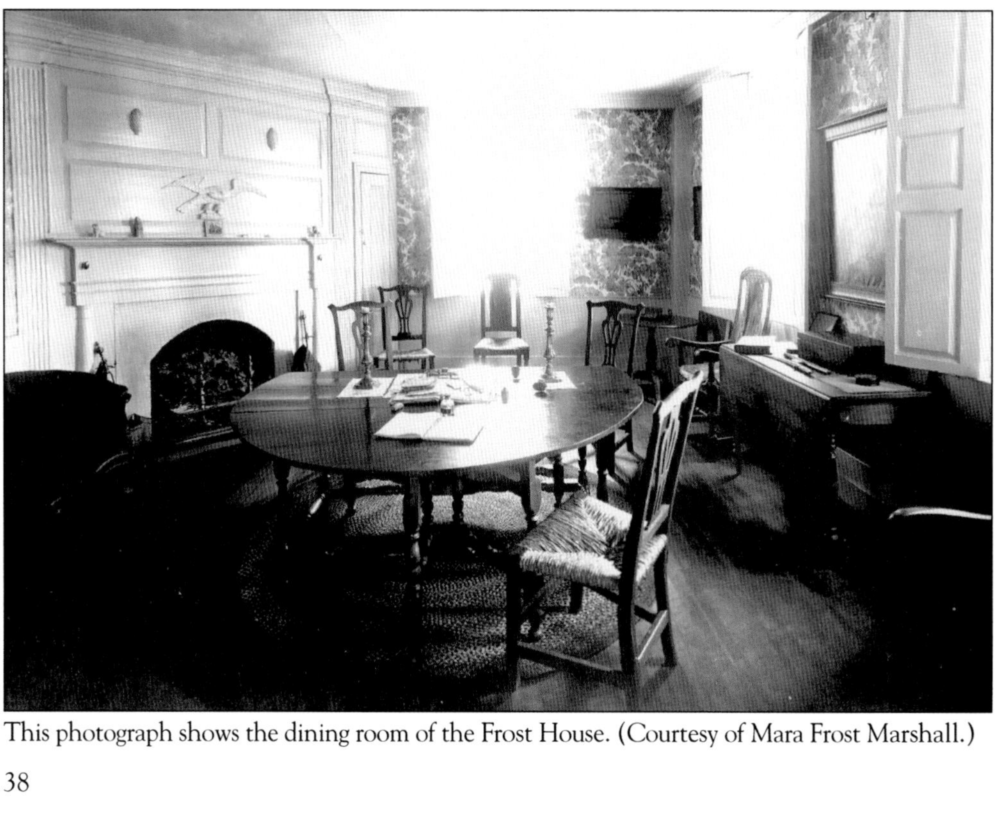

This photograph shows the dining room of the Frost House. (Courtesy of Mara Frost Marshall.)

These stairs lead to the second floor of the Frost House. (Courtesy of Mara Frost Marshall.)

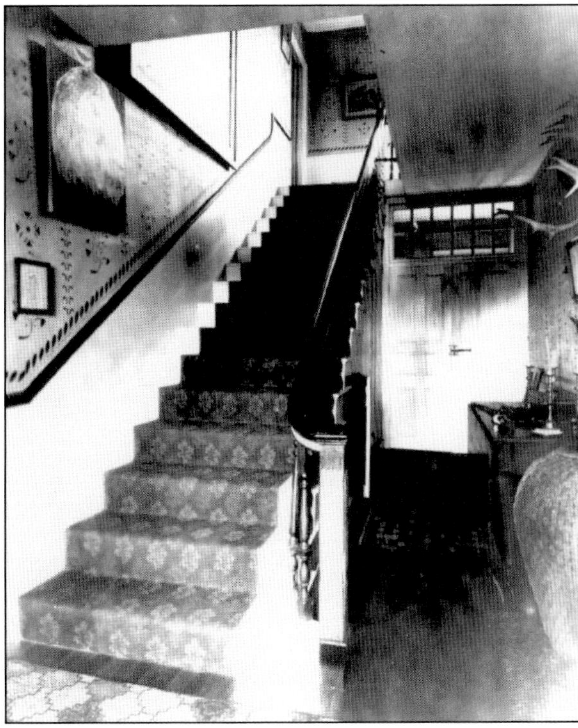

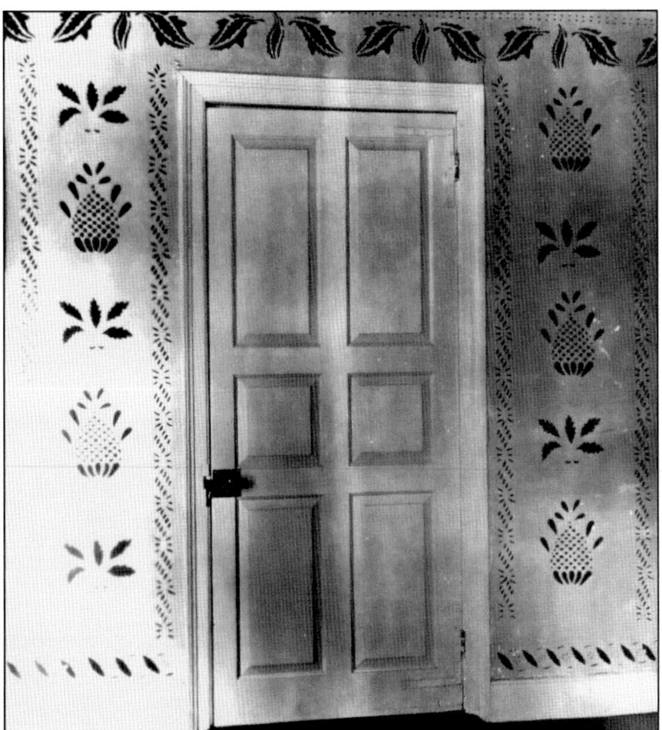

During the 1790s, itinerant painters did stenciling on the second floor of the Frost House. (Courtesy of Mara Frost Marshall.)

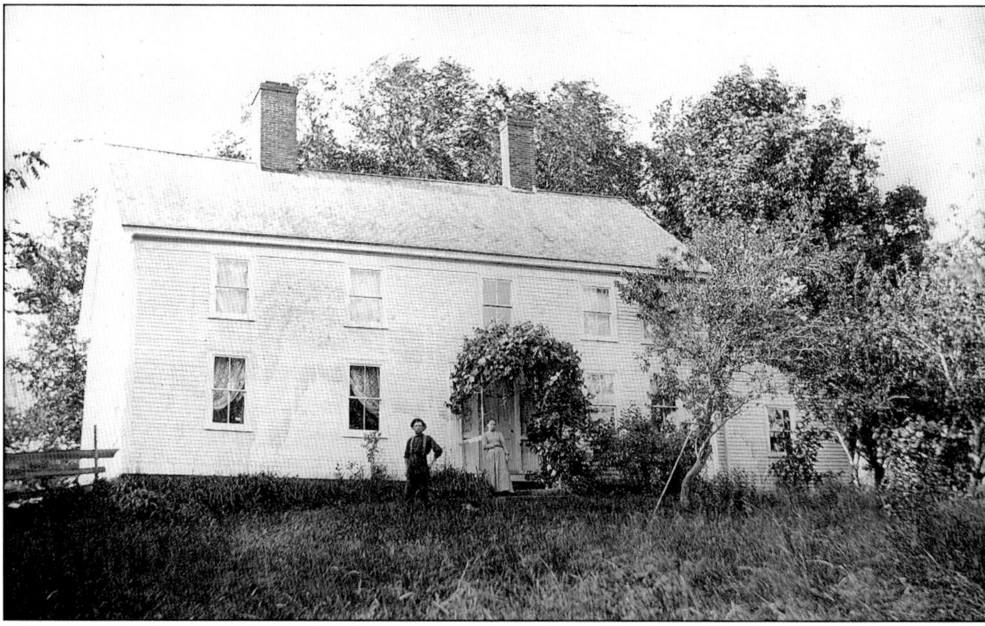

The Raitt Homestead (now the High Meadows Bed and Breakfast), at the corner of Brixham and Goodwin Roads, was constructed from a smaller house that was built around 1740 by Eliot Frost, a grandson of Maj. Charles Frost. Eliot's widow later married Alexander Raitt, and thus the home became the property of the Raitt family. (Courtesy of the Estate of C. Edward Bartlett Jr.)

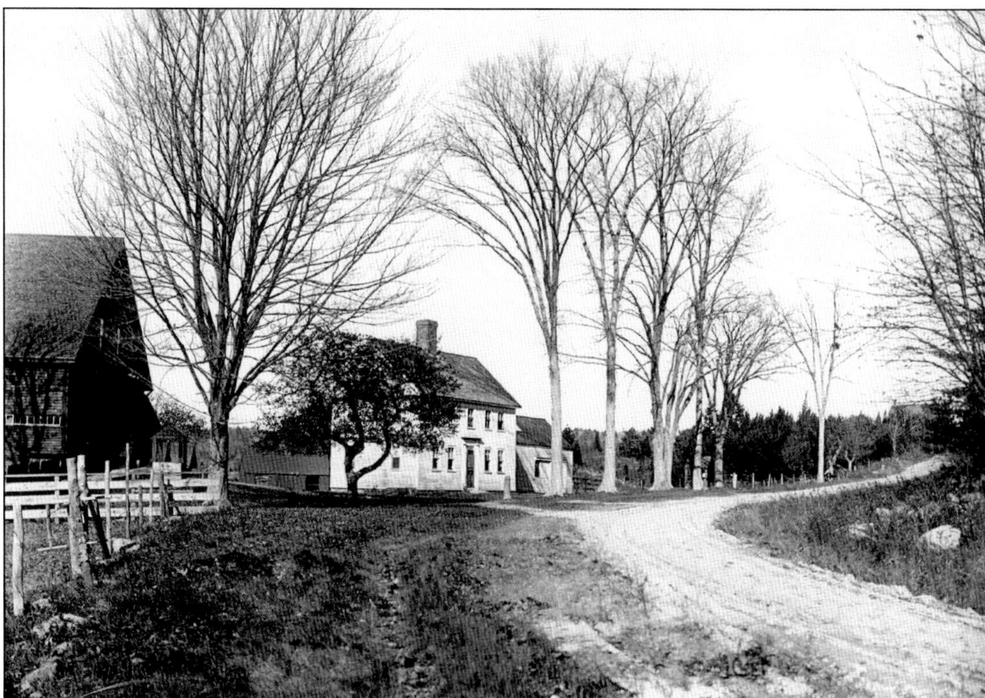

The John Frost House, on Brixham Road, dates from the 1740s. (Courtesy of the Gov. John F. Hill Collection at the William Fogg Library.)

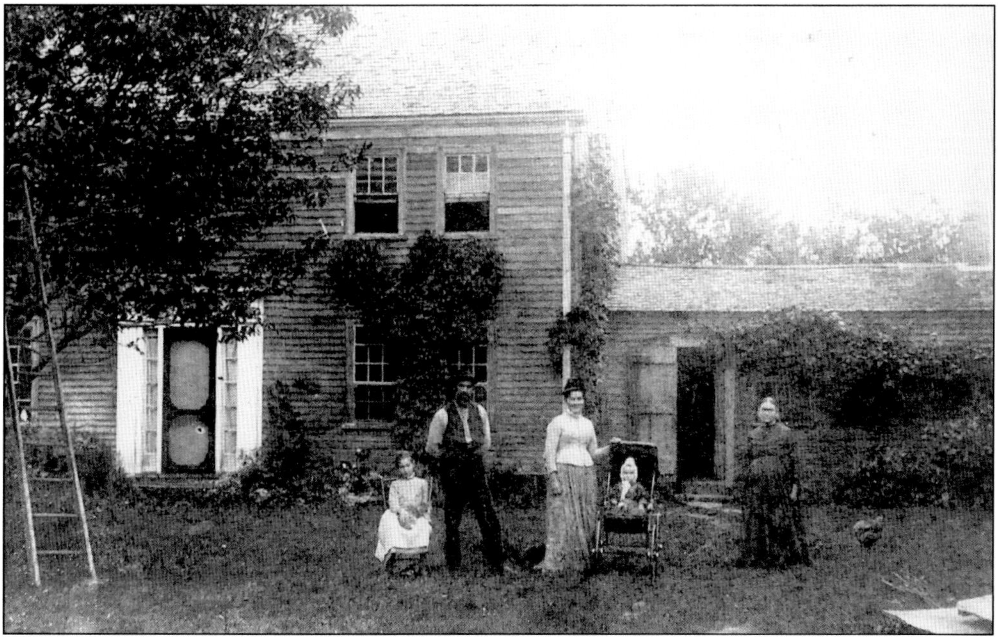

Here Civil War veteran Moses Paul and his family stand in front of their home at the corner of Depot and Goodwin Roads. Moses's father, Hugh, built the house in 1804. Pictured, from left to right, are Edna, Moses, his wife Ida, baby Dorcas, and Moses's mother, Sarah Jane (Remick) Paul. The home's chimney bricks were made at a brickyard on Goodwin Road. The building is on the National Register of Historic Places. (Courtesy of the Paul Family Association.)

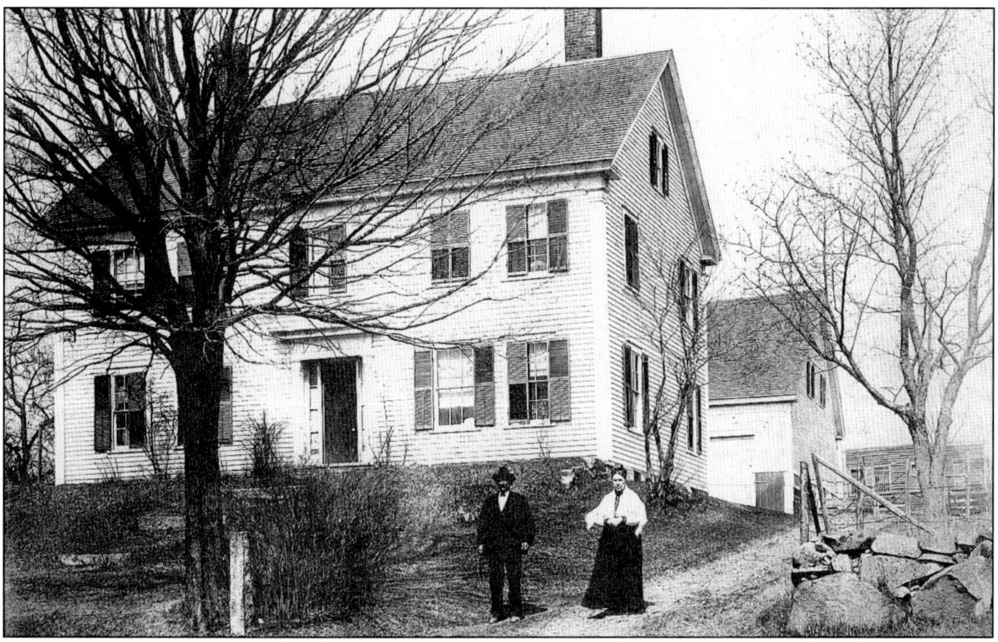

Originally the home of Maj. Samuel Leighton (who fought in the Revolutionary War), this dwelling was built around 1765, but changes have been made over the years. Located on Goodwin Road, it later became known as the Hanscom House. Clifford Trefethern and his wife lived in the house at the time of this photograph. (Courtesy of the Estate of C. Edward Bartlett Jr.)

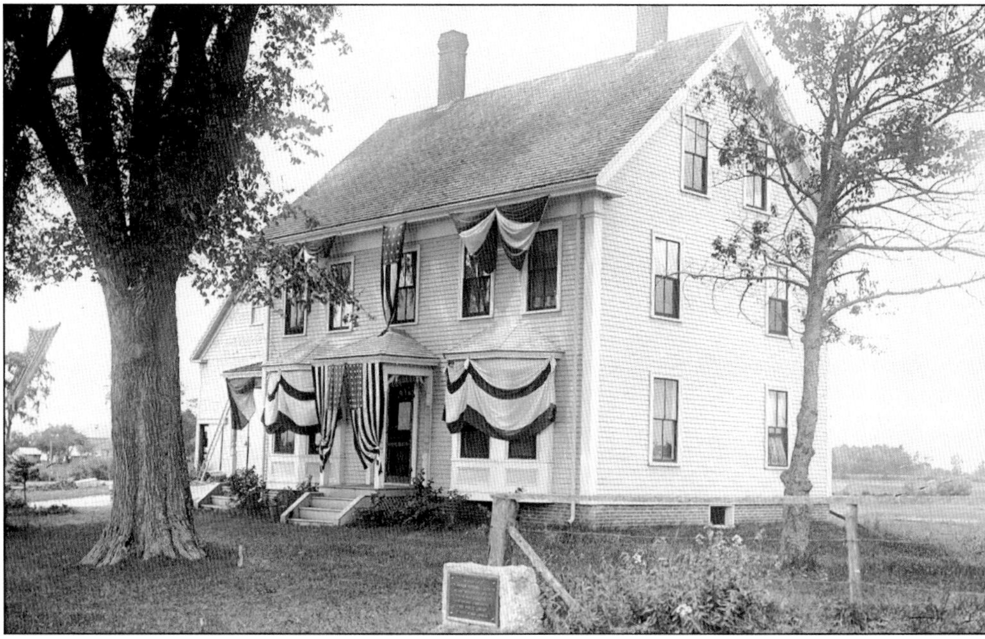

The Andrew Pepperrell Leighton homestead, on River Road, housed the town's first library. Leighton (1793–1882) was an early representative of Eliot in the Maine legislature and was the grandfather of Gov. John F. Hill. (Courtesy of the Carlton and Doris Grover Collection at the William Fogg Library.)

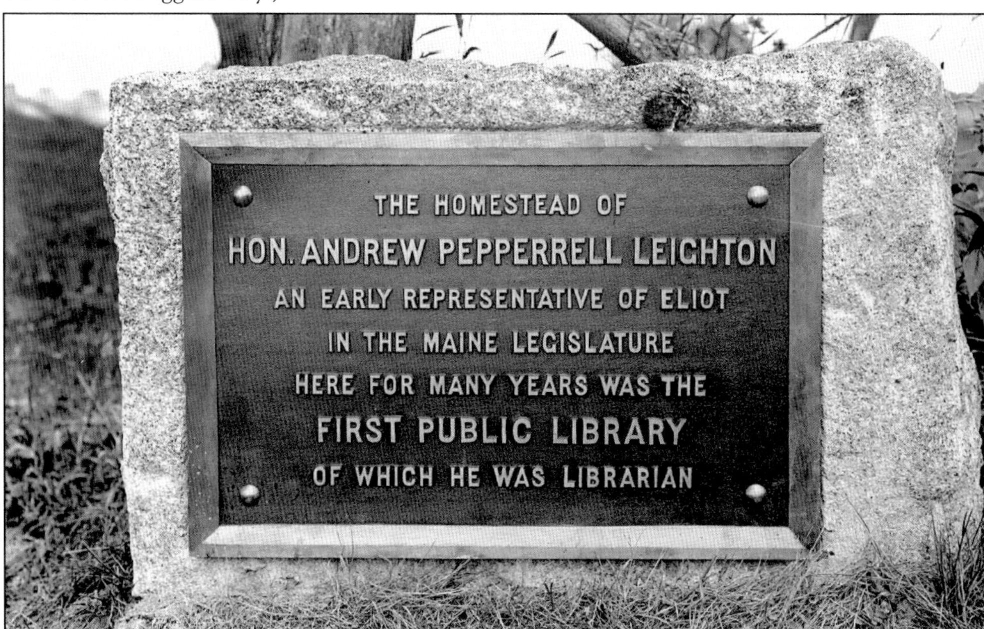

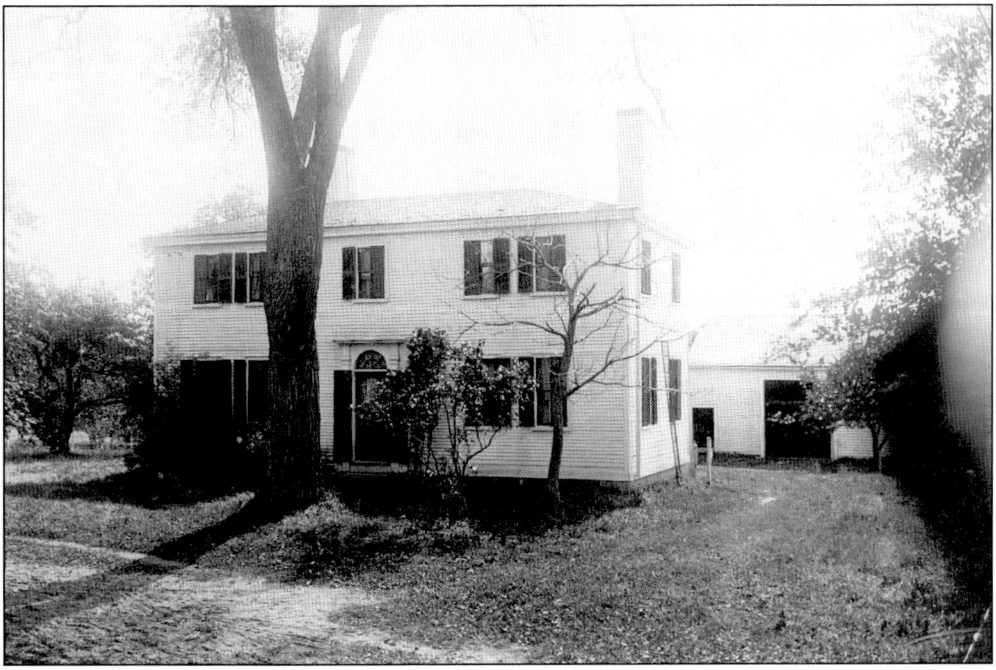

Dr. Caleb Emery, Eliot's first physician, built this house on Old Road. Emery practiced medicine in Eliot from 1809 until his death in 1831 at the age of 43. At a later time, Elizabeth Bartlett, former historian and editor, lived there. (Courtesy of the Gov. John F. Hill Collection at the William Fogg Library.)

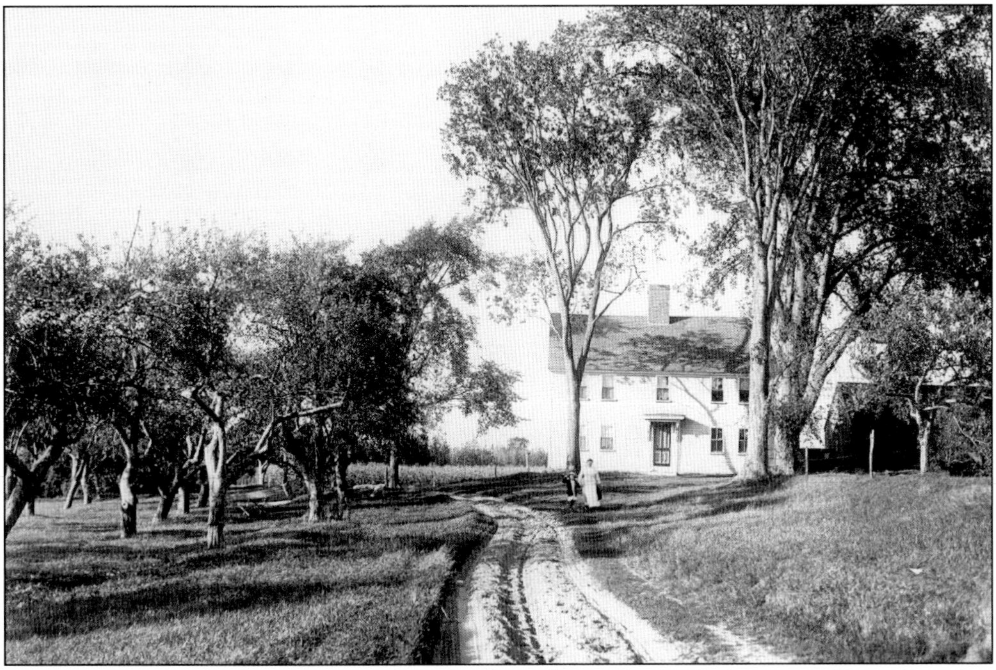

Capt. Elisha Shapleigh (1749–1822) built the Albert Shapleigh home on River Road in 1802. The property was once the site of the Kittery House. (Courtesy of the Gov. John F. Hill Collection at the William Fogg Library.)

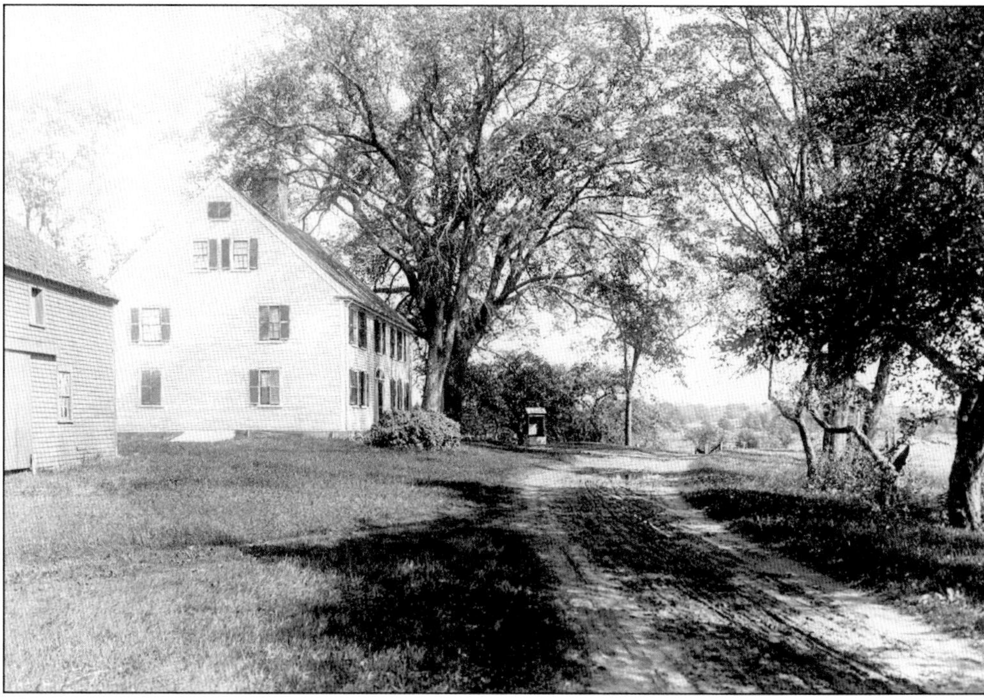

The Elisha Shapleigh House, on Governor Hill Road, was built in the 18th century and updated in the 19th century. During the American Revolution, Captain Shapleigh trained his militia in his living room. Bayonet marks are still visible on the inside walls of the house. (Courtesy of the Gov. John F. Hill Collection at the William Fogg Library.)

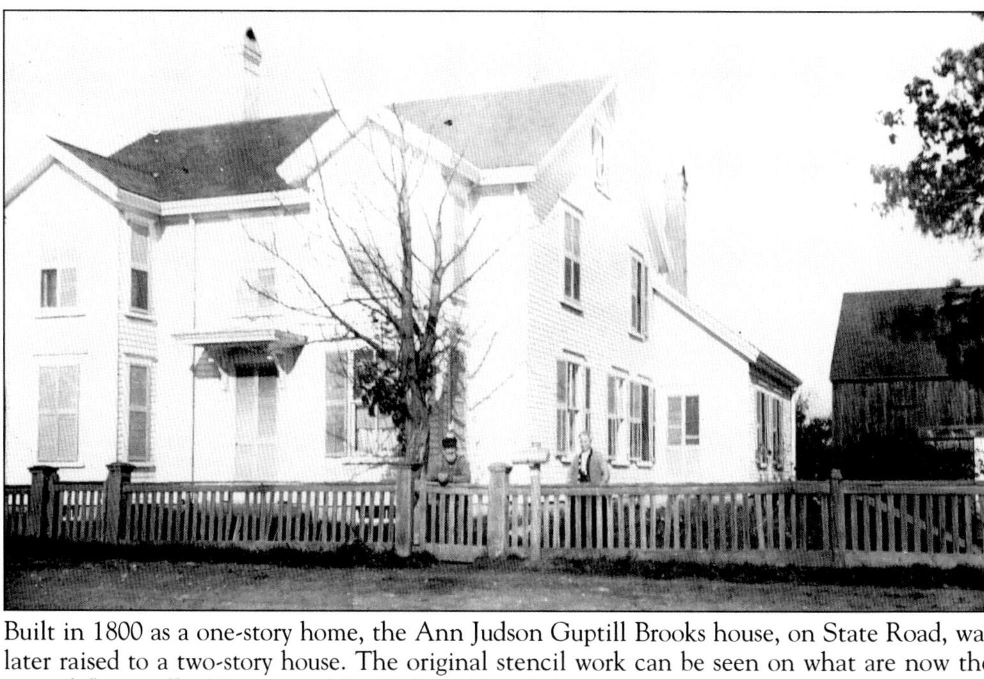

Built in 1800 as a one-story home, the Ann Judson Guptill Brooks house, on State Road, was later raised to a two-story house. The original stencil work can be seen on what are now the second-floor walls. (Courtesy of the William Fogg Library.)

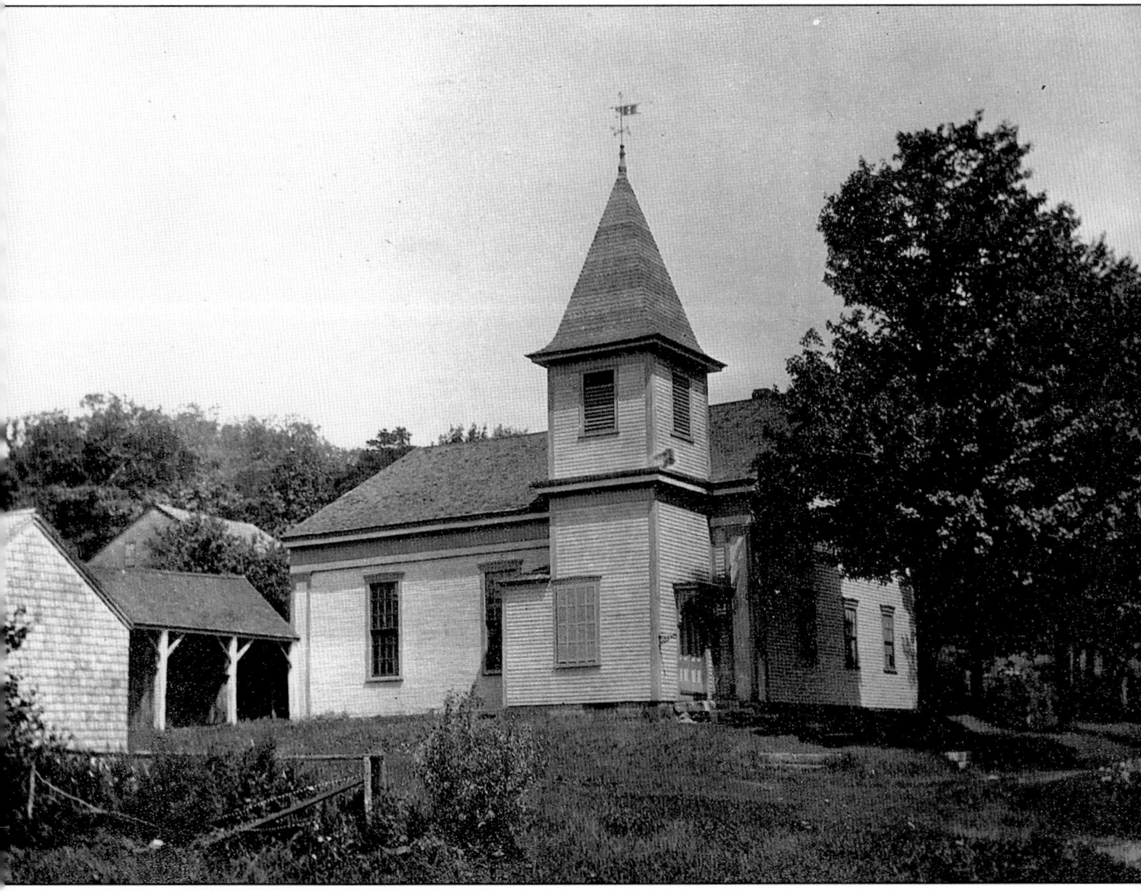

The East Eliot Methodist Episcopal Church was built on land donated by James Raitt in 1826. James Bartlett donated the church bell. It still stands at the corner of Goodwin and Brixham Roads. It is the oldest church structure in Eliot. The square tower and pyramid roof were added around 1890. (Courtesy of Kenneth Tuttle.)

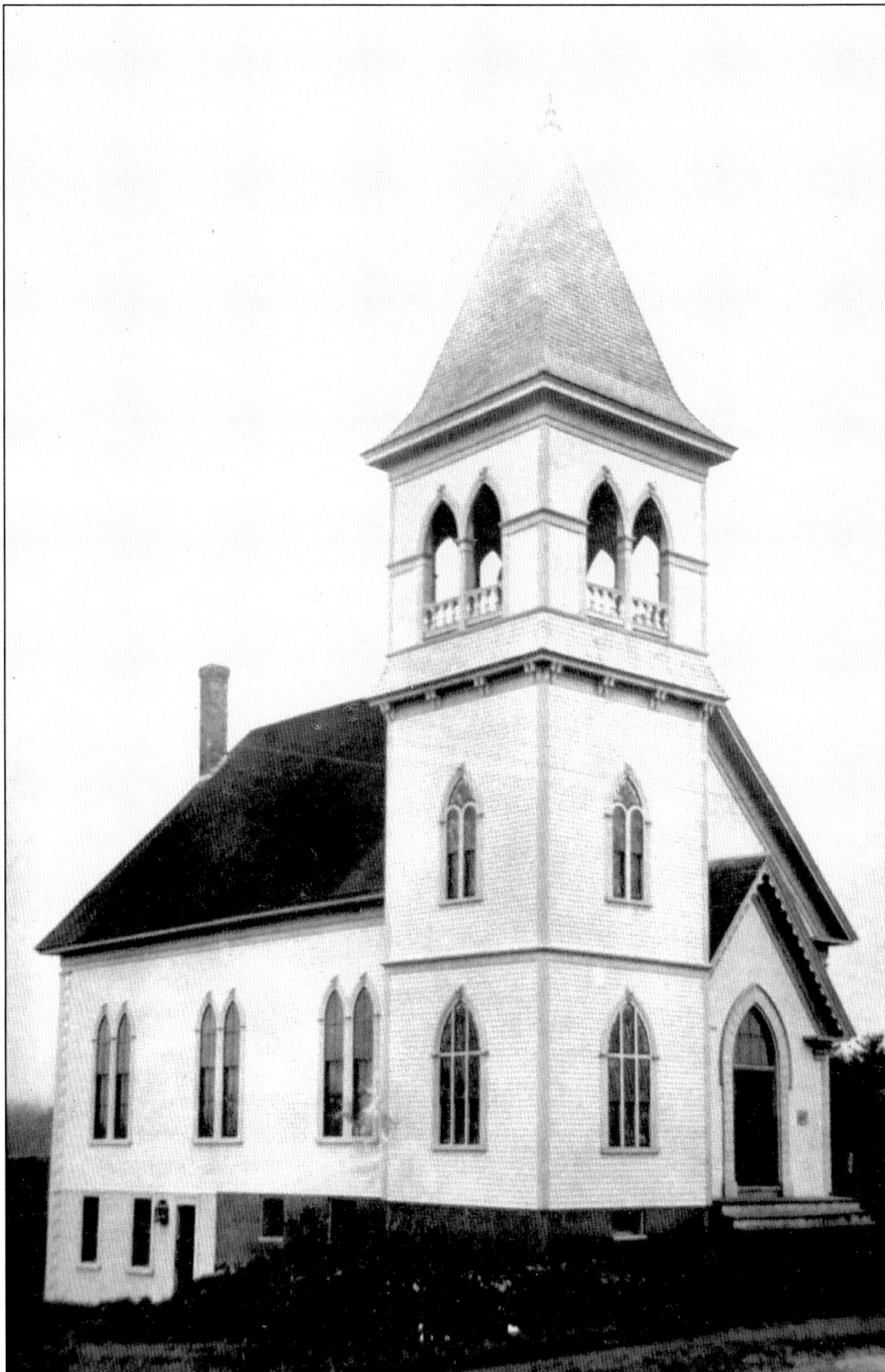

The First Congregational Church, on State Road, opened in 1881, replacing an earlier structure, which burned in 1880. The Congregational church in Eliot was organized in 1714. Its first minister was Rev. John Rogers, who served as pastor for almost 60 years. (Courtesy of Jeanette Paul.)

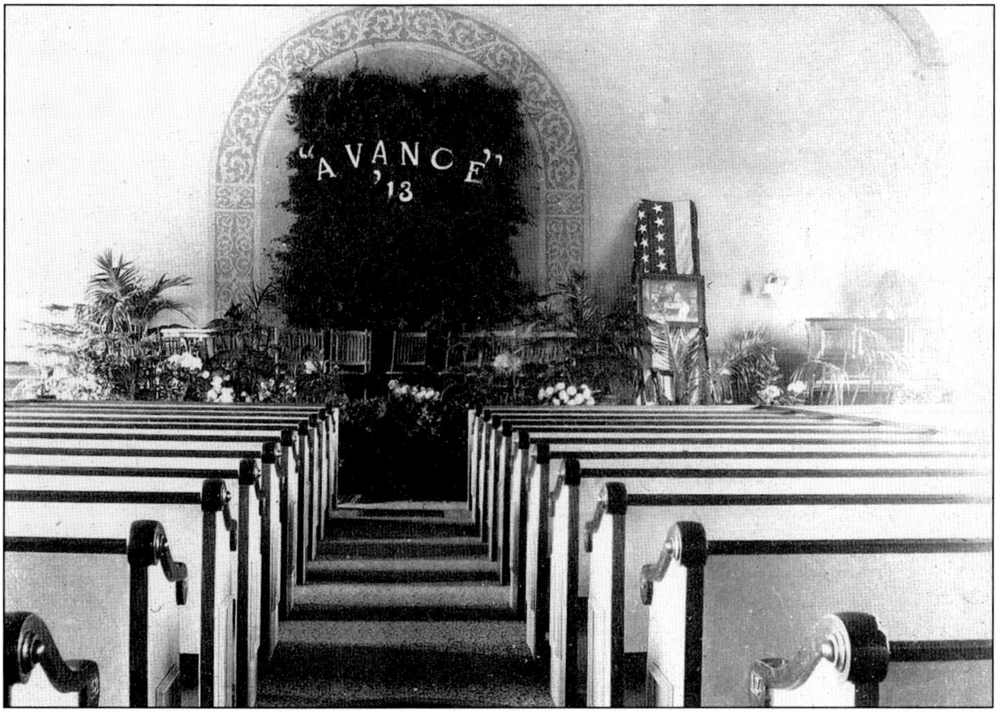

The interior of the First Congregational Church is shown decorated for graduation in 1913. (Courtesy of Jeanette Paul.)

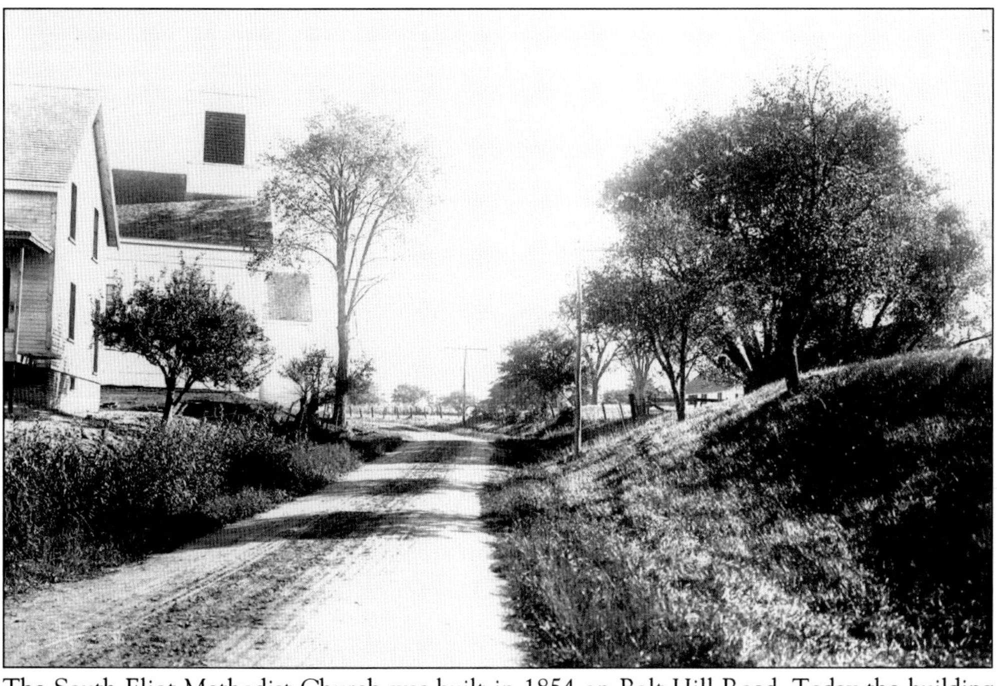
The South Eliot Methodist Church was built in 1854 on Bolt Hill Road. Today the building houses the Sanctuary Arts Studio. (Courtesy of the Gov. John F. Hill Collection at the William Fogg Library.)

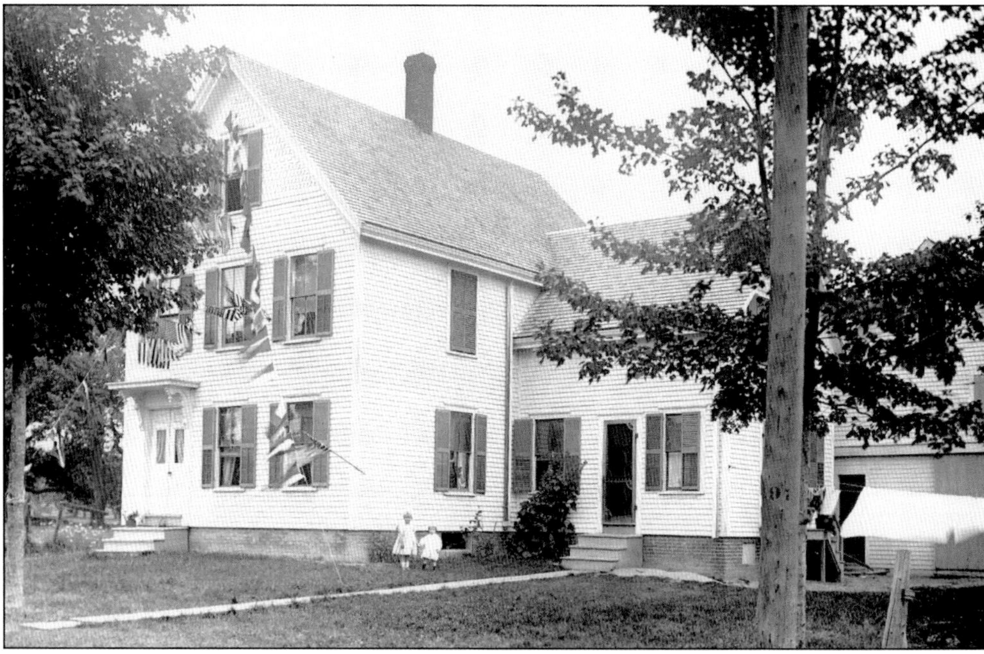

The South Methodist Parsonage was the original church. After the new church was built on Bolt Hill Road, this structure was moved to Main Street. (Courtesy of the William Fogg Library.)

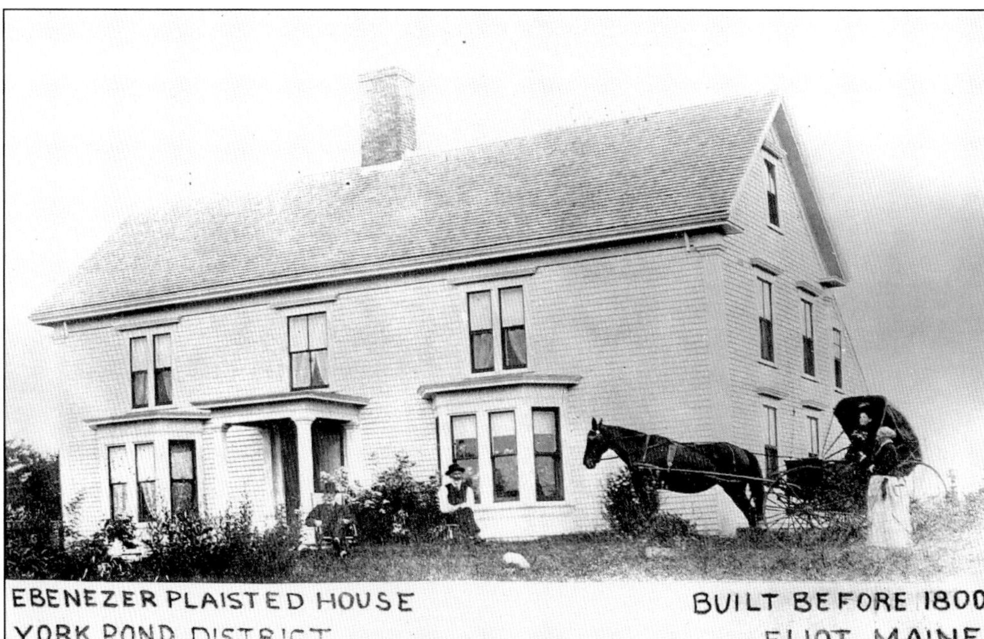

The Ebenezer Plaisted House was built before 1800 in the York Pond district of Eliot. This area was known as Emery Town and later Punkintown. A 1916 fire burned several houses in the area. Later, in 1922, a tuberculosis epidemic plagued the district. (Courtesy of the Estate of C. Edward Bartlett Jr.)

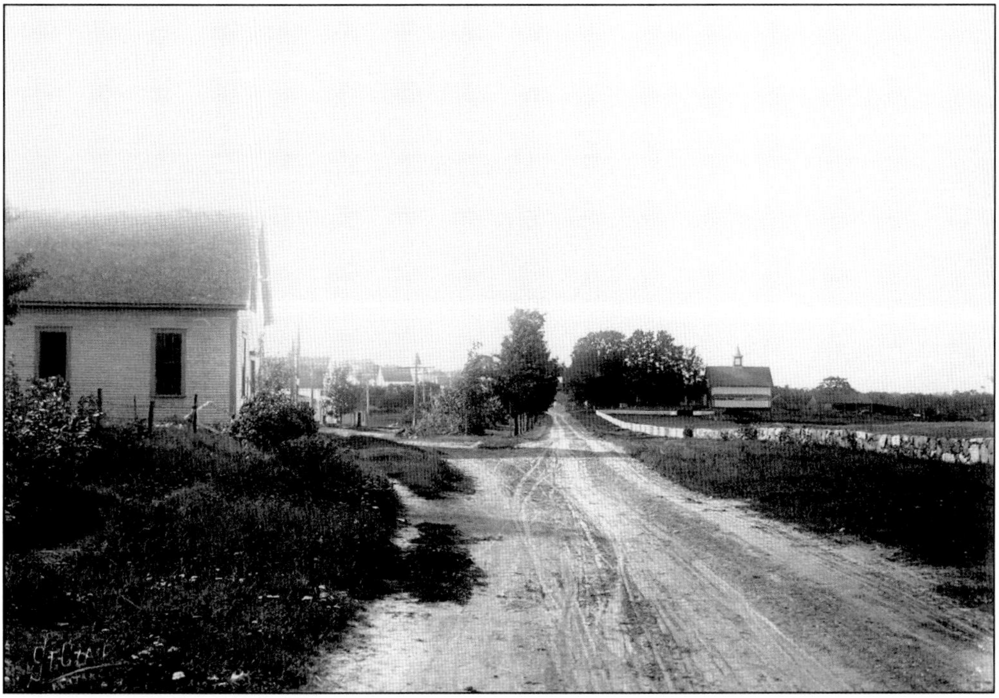

George W. Shapleigh helped build the old town hall in 1880. It stood across from the present elementary school on State Road. In the early days, it was used intermittently for high school classes. Beginning in 1901, it became a more permanent high school until the town's first high school was built several years later. The old town hall was torn down in the 1970s. (Courtesy of the Gov. John F. Hill Collection at the William Fogg Library.)

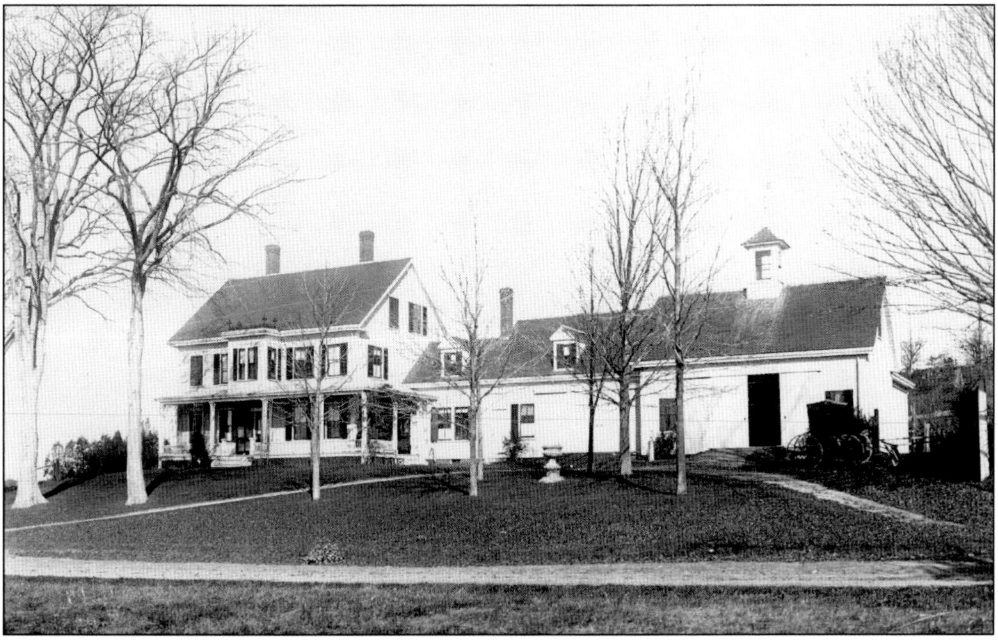

Frank E. Kennard's home on Old Road is just before the River Road turnoff. (Courtesy of the Gov. John F. Hill Collection at the William Fogg Library.)

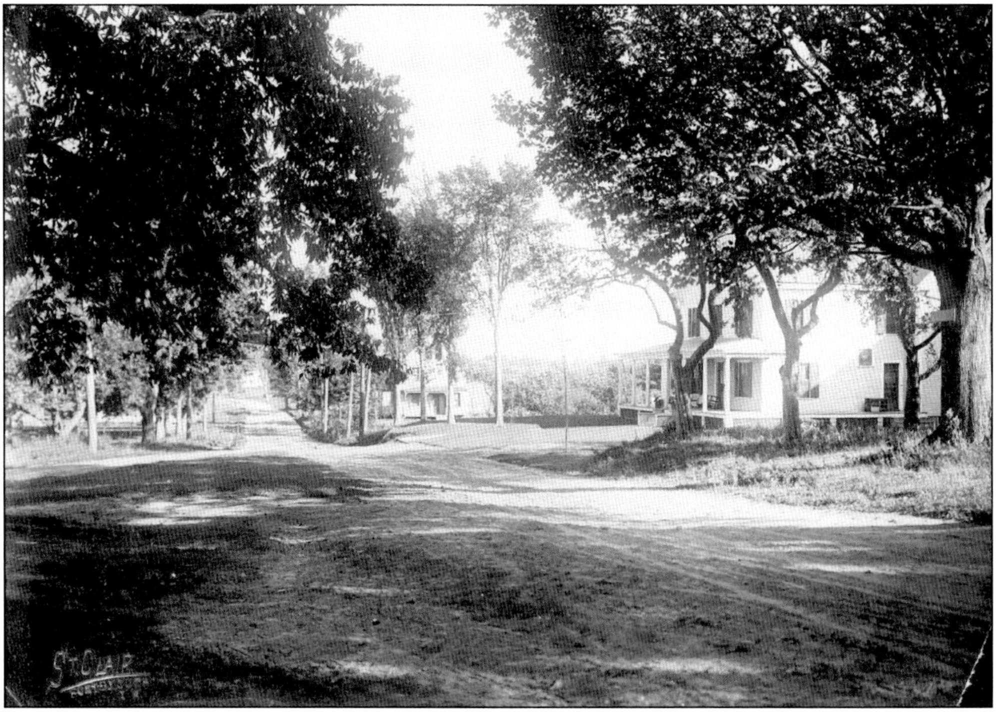

George F. Kennard lived in this house on the corner of State and Old Roads. (Courtesy of the Gov. John F. Hill Collection at the William Fogg Library.)

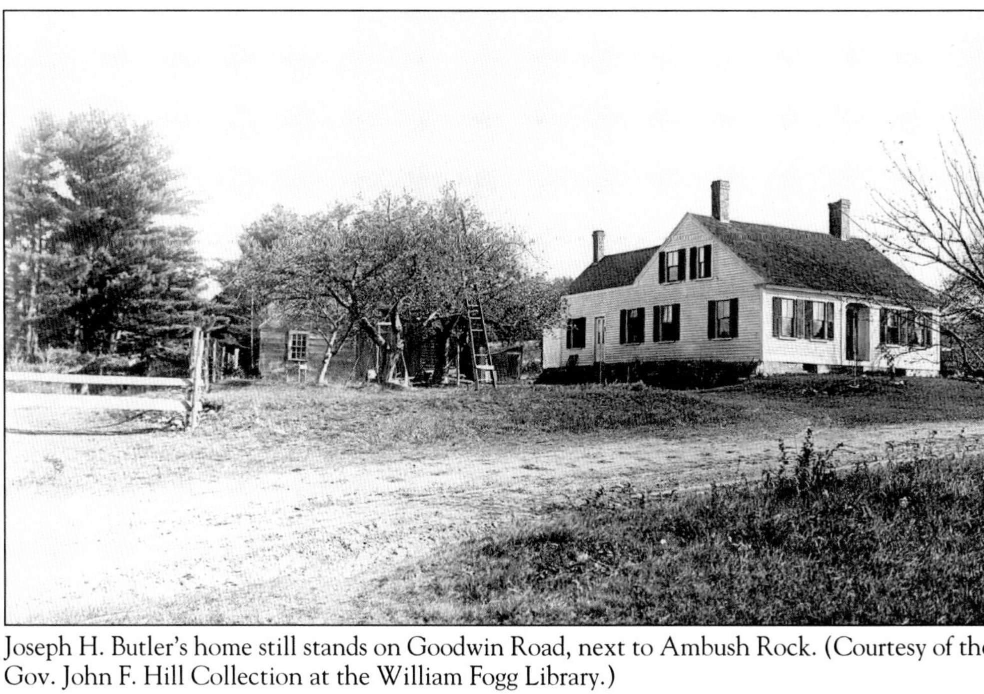

Joseph H. Butler's home still stands on Goodwin Road, next to Ambush Rock. (Courtesy of the Gov. John F. Hill Collection at the William Fogg Library.)

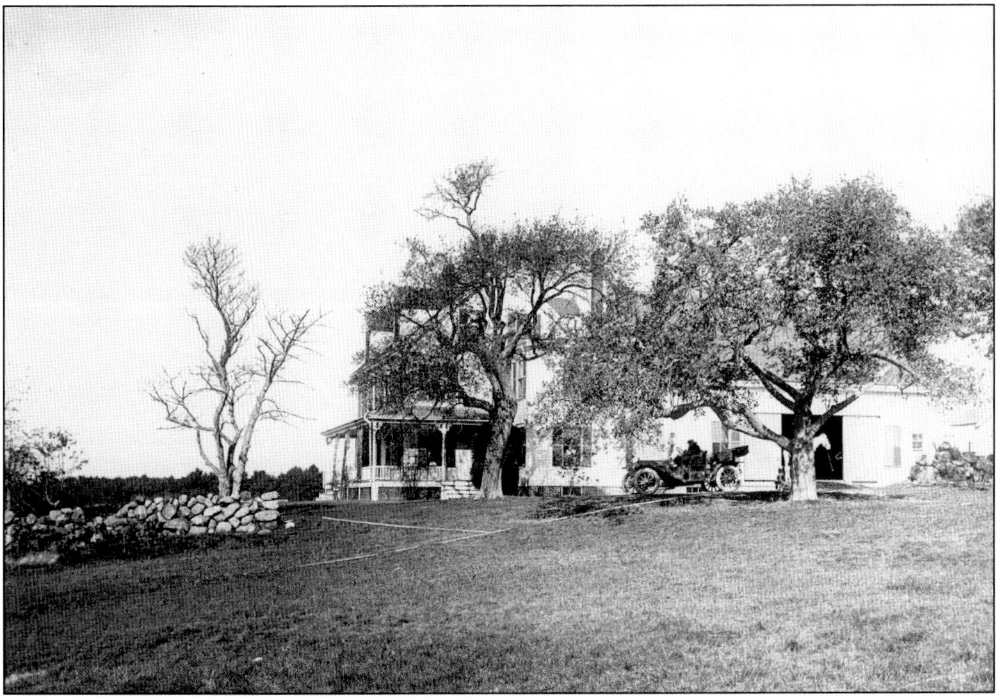

Samuel Adlington lived in this home on Adlington Road off Mast Cove Road. (Courtesy of the Gov. John F. Hill Collection at the William Fogg Library.)

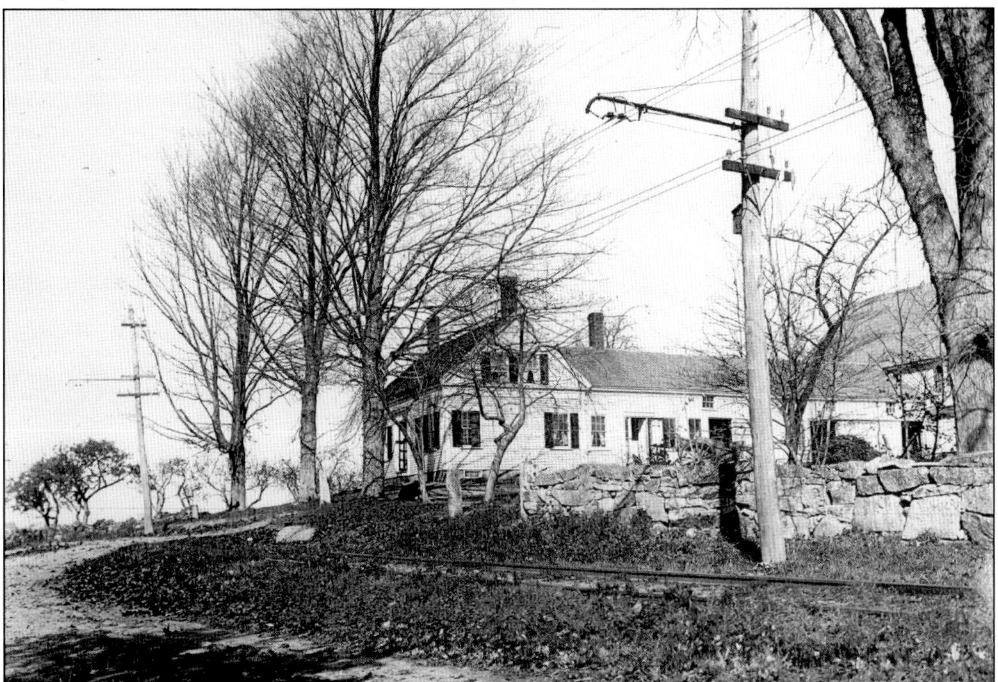

Chester Frost's home on Goodwin Road looks the same today. Chester Frost was a farmer. The electric streetcar tracks running in front of the house no longer exist. (Courtesy of the Gov. John F. Hill Collection at the William Fogg Library.)

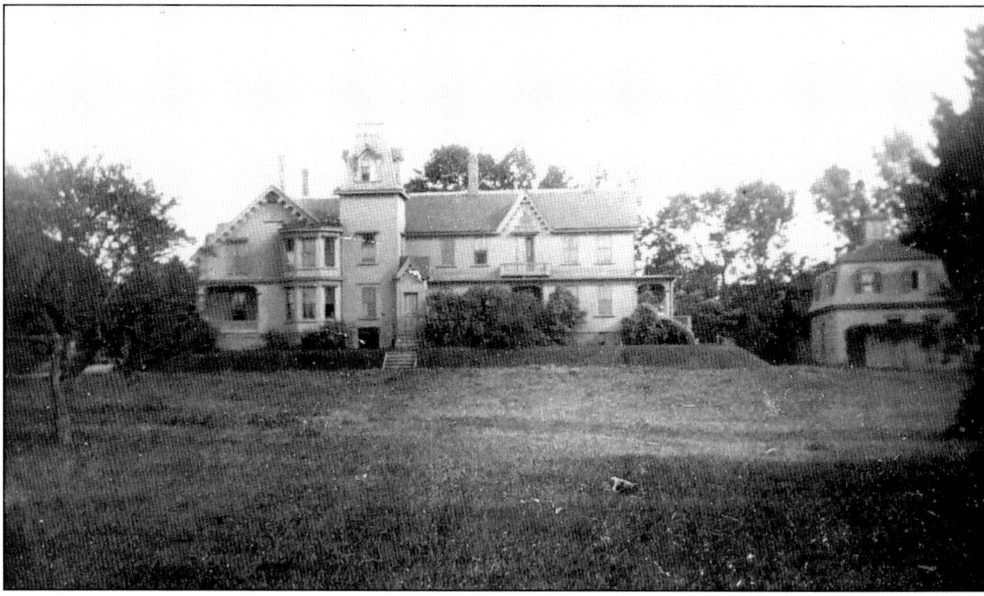

Built in the 1840s, Bittersweet-in-the-Fields, on State Road, had been in Hannah Farmer's family. She and her husband, Moses Gerrish Farmer, updated the home in the 1880s, when they returned to Eliot after living in Rhode Island. The smaller building on the right was Professor Farmer's laboratory and workshop. Later moved, it was made into a home. Bittersweet-in-the-Fields burned in February 1904. (Courtesy of the Estate of C. Edward Bartlett Jr.)

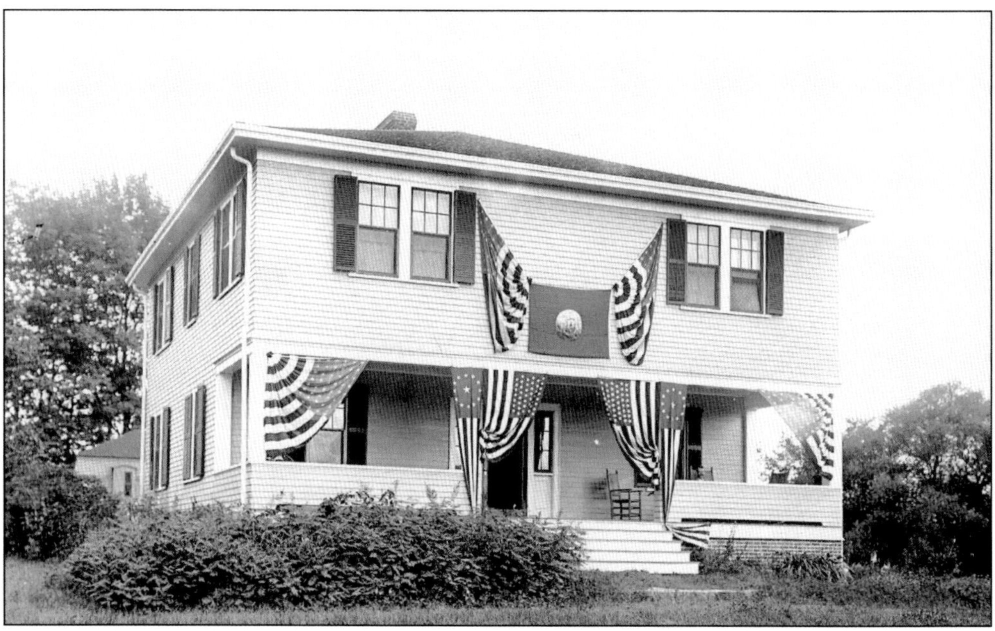

A smaller home was built on the property of the original Bittersweet. The Green Acre Fellowship erected this house for Sarah Jane Farmer (Moses and Hannah's daughter) in 1908. (Courtesy of the Carlton and Doris Grover Collection at the William Fogg Library.)

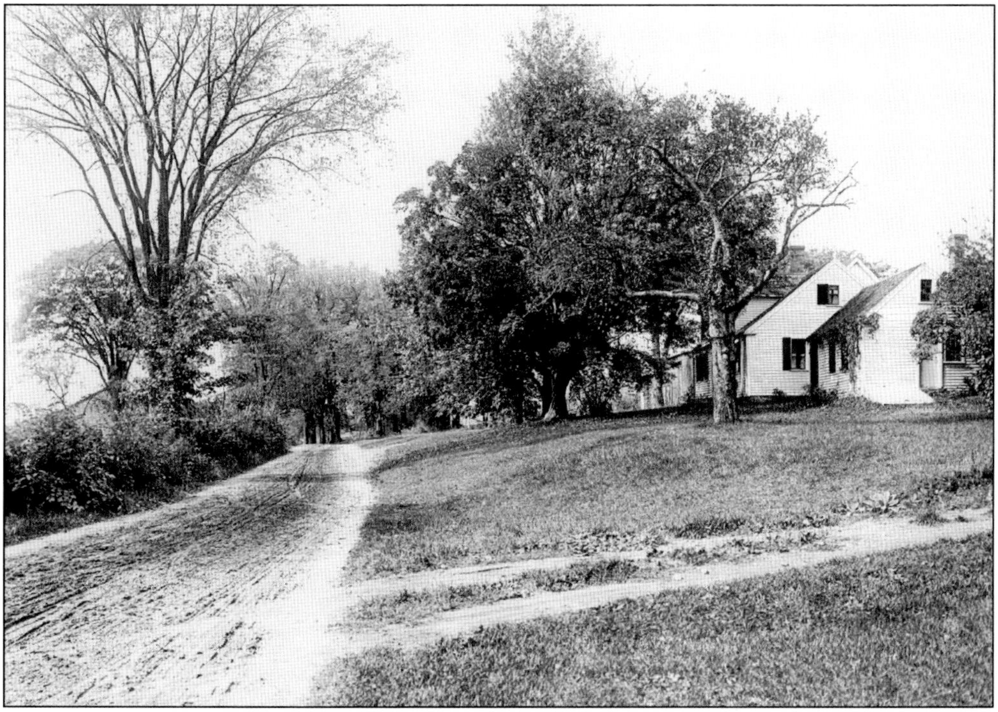

Joseph Hammond lived in this house on Old Road. At one time, Mrs. Joseph Hobbs, sister of Gov. John F. Hill, resided here. (Courtesy of the Gov. John F. Hill Collection at the William Fogg Library.)

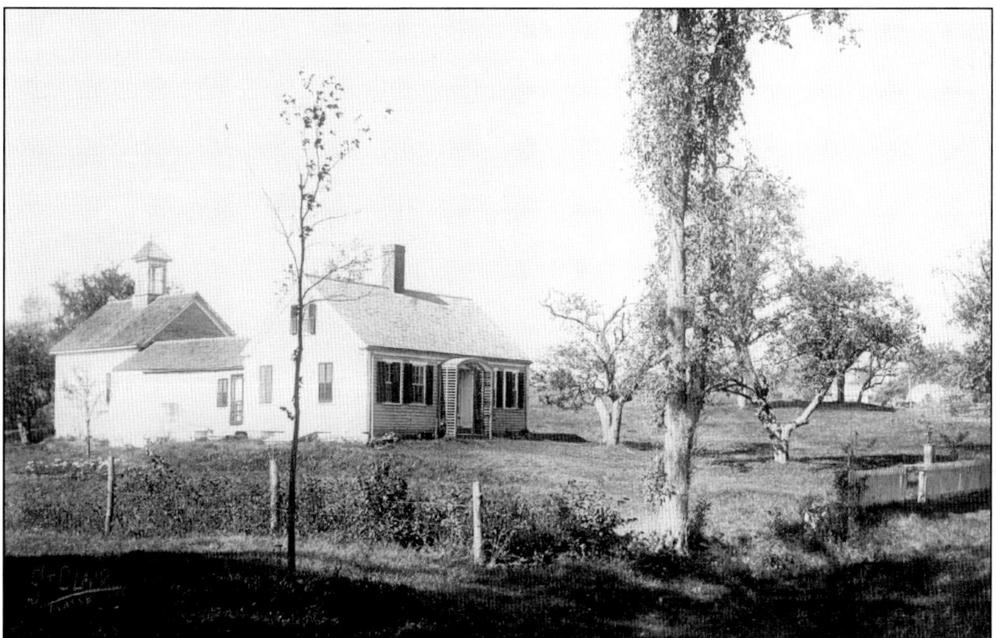

Edward Hanscom's cottage is on Goodwin Road. Hanscom later moved to Philadelphia, where he successfully started several bakeries. (Courtesy of the Gov. John F. Hill Collection at the William Fogg Library.)

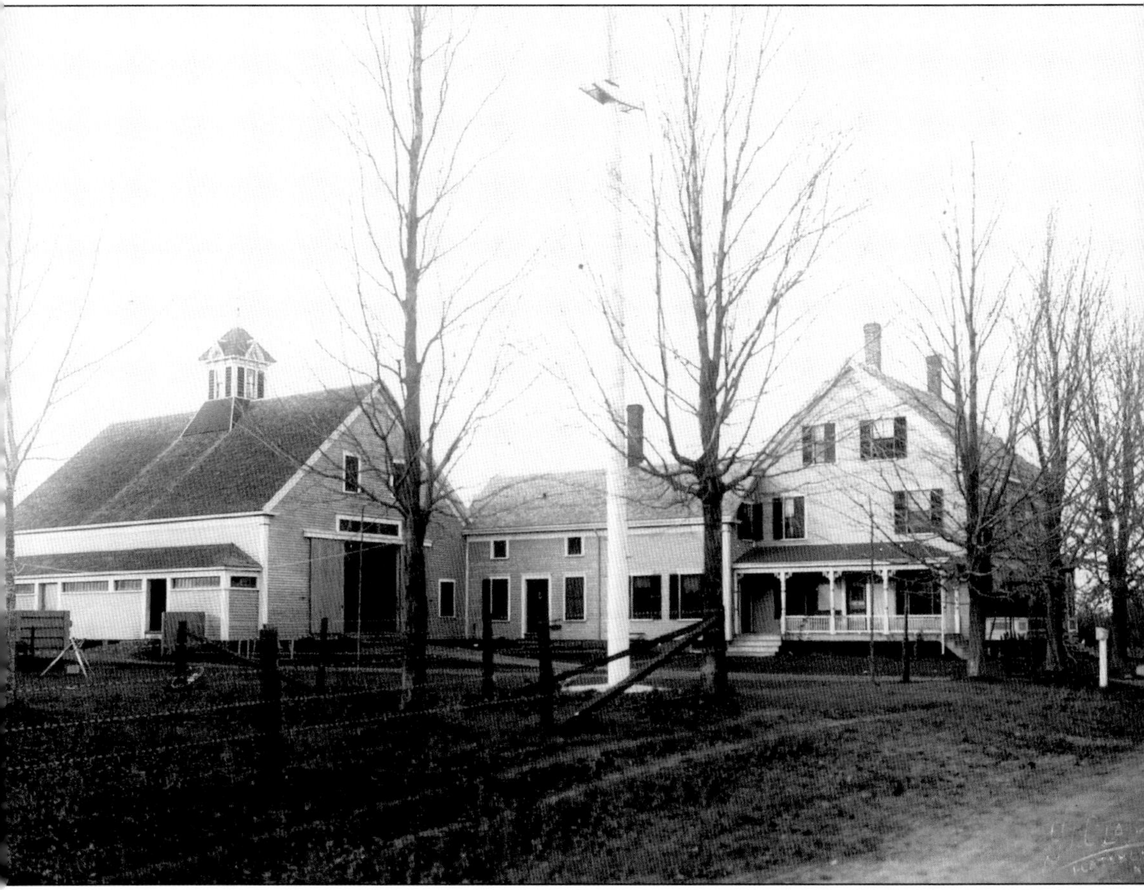

Charles A. Raitt built this farm on State Road in 1898. Raitt also ran a brickyard off Houde Road on the Piscataqua River. He was involved in many enterprises, including apple orchards, a lumbermill, and harvesting ice. Today the Eliot Antique Tractor and Engine Association oversees the property, where the annual tractor and engine show takes place. (Courtesy of the Gov. John F. Hill Collection at the William Fogg Library.)

Four

BUSINESS AND INDUSTRY

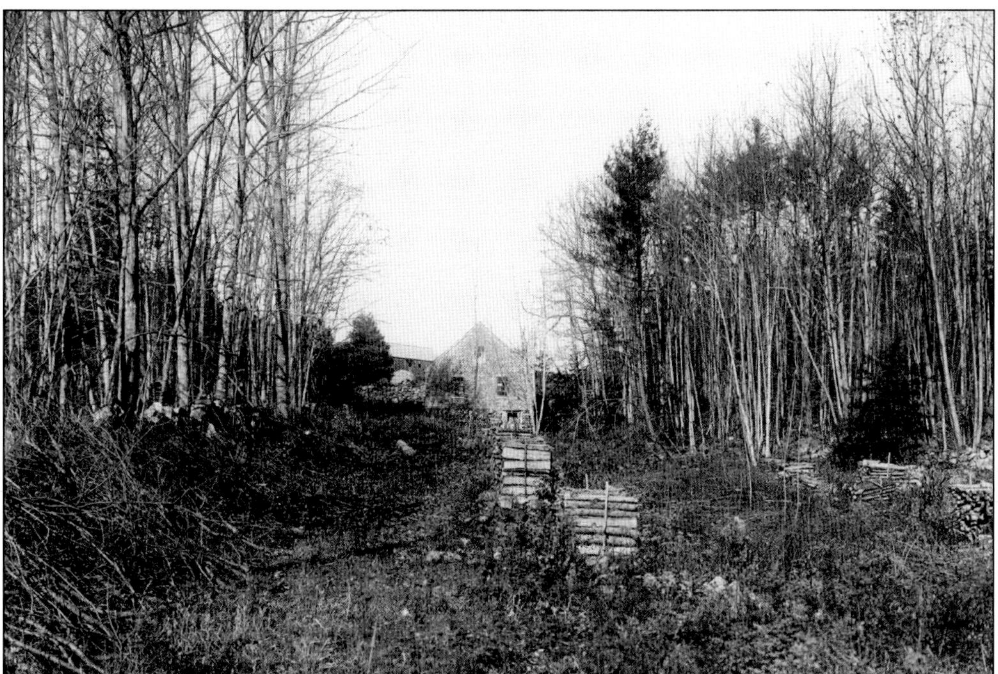

Along with fishing and farming, mills were one of the earliest enterprises in Eliot. (Courtesy of the Gov. John F. Hill Collection at the William Fogg Library.)

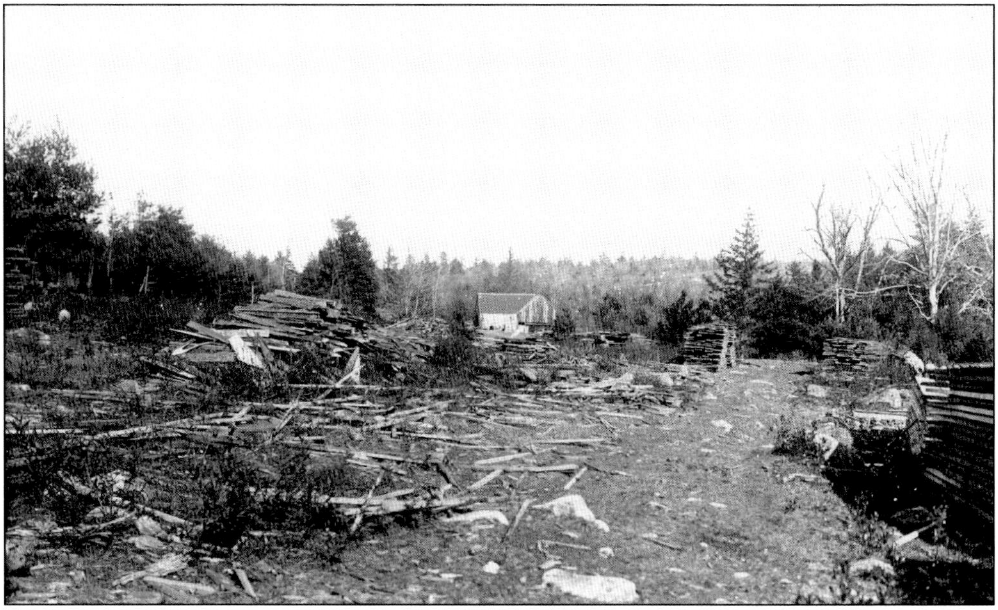

There was a sawmill on Sturgeon Creek even before 1651. A later mill in the same area ground meal only at high tide, which annoyed local farmers. (Courtesy of the Gov. John F. Hill Collection at the William Fogg Library.)

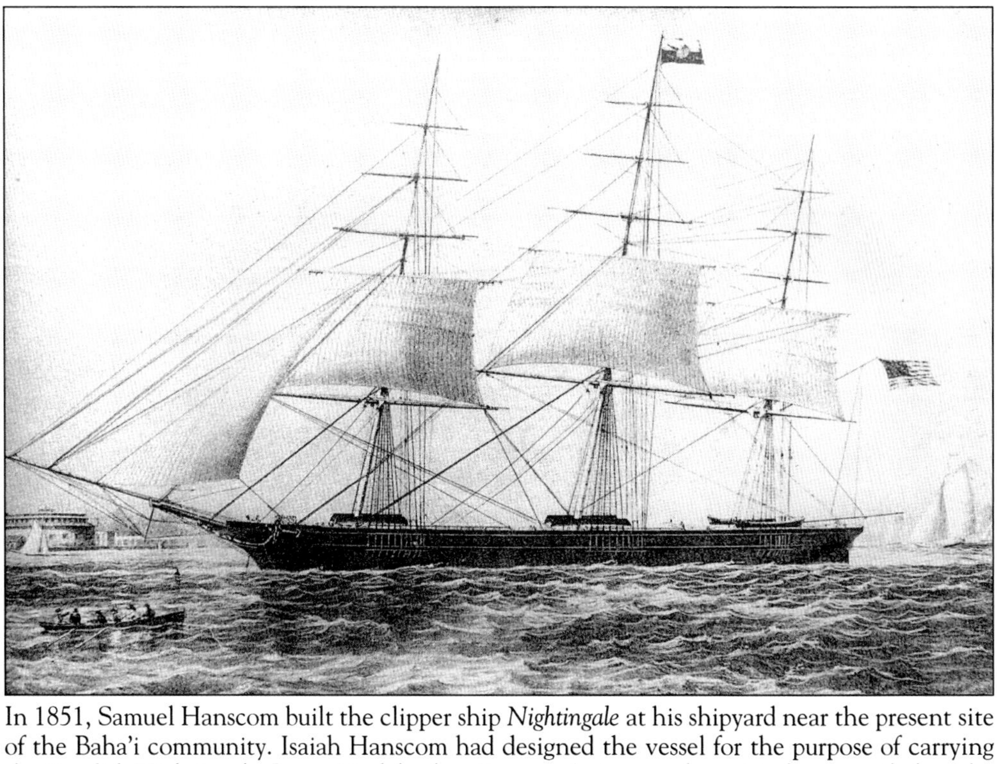

In 1851, Samuel Hanscom built the clipper ship *Nightingale* at his shipyard near the present site of the Baha'i community. Isaiah Hanscom had designed the vessel for the purpose of carrying the Swedish Nightingale, Jenny Lind, back to Europe. As it turned out, Lind never sailed on the ship. Between the years 1847 and 1855, seven clipper ships were built at the shipyard, which was the largest in Eliot. (Courtesy of Edward H. Vetter.)

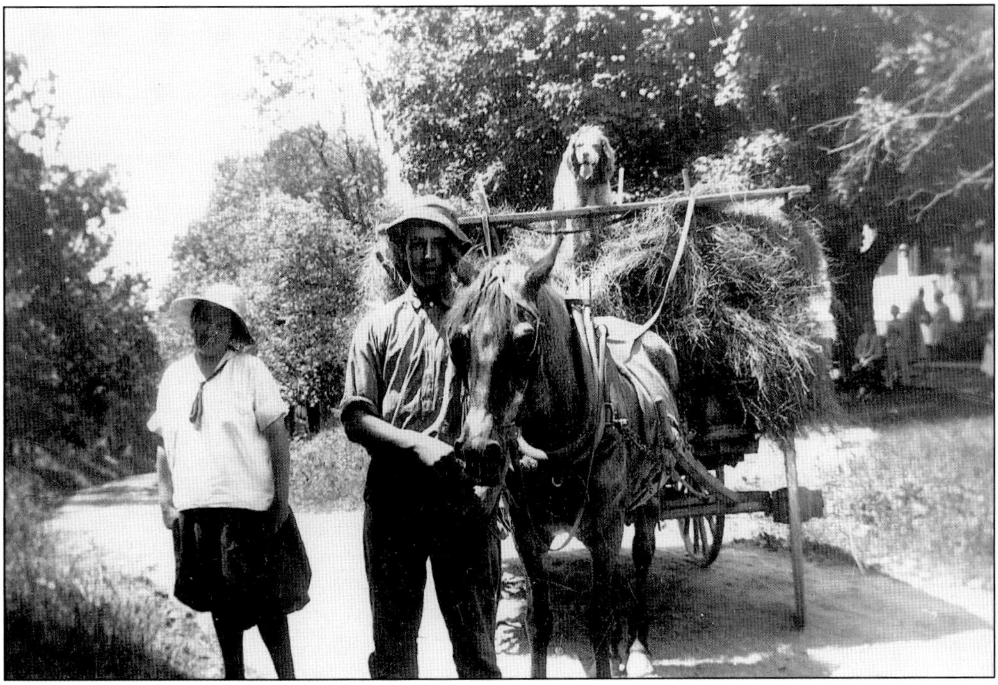

Farmers gathered hay from the salt marsh around Sturgeon Creek. Salt hay was an early export product. Farmers mixed the salt hay with meadow hay to feed their animals. This photograph was taken between 1912 and 1915. (Courtesy of the Paul Family Association.)

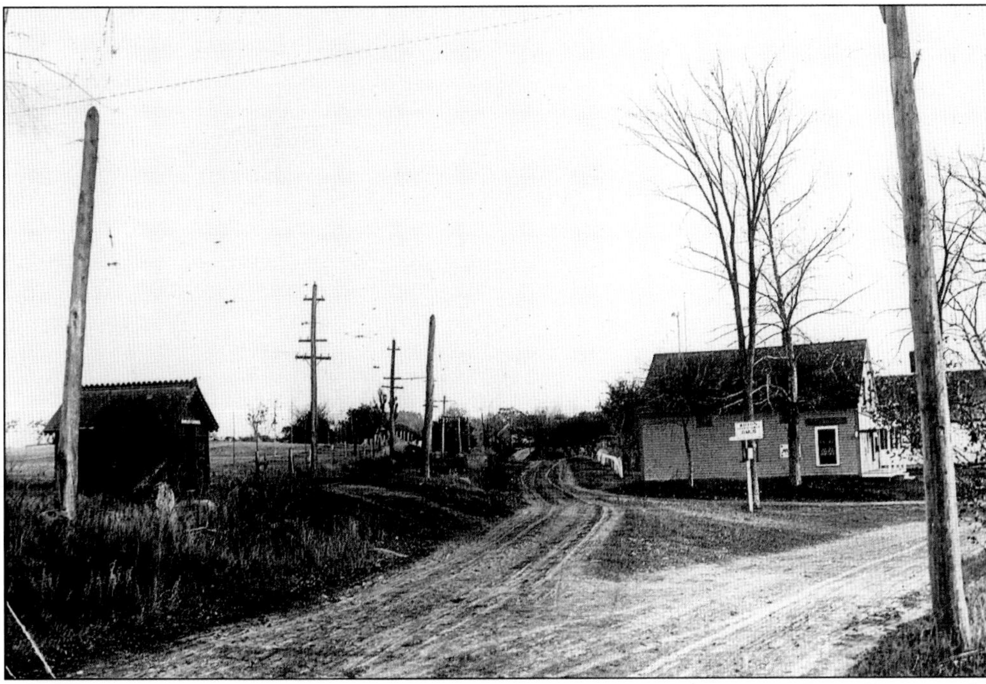

John Raitt opened a shop around 1894 at Gould's Corner. In the 1920s, Percy Day ran the business. Later, the building was remodeled and turned into apartments. This photograph was taken in 1910. (Courtesy of Kenneth Tuttle.)

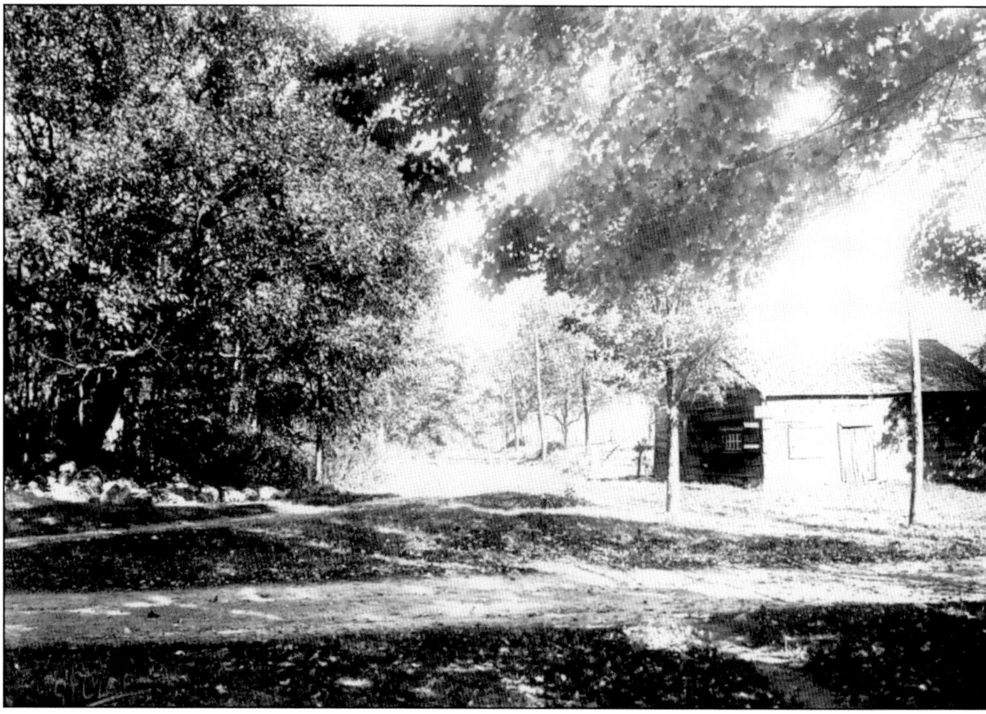

Nathaniel Knowlton owned a carriage and furniture shop at the corner of Goodwin and Frost Hill Roads. His work ledger for furniture made here may be seen at the Maine Historical Society in Portland. (Courtesy of the Gov. John F. Hill Collection at the William Fogg Library.)

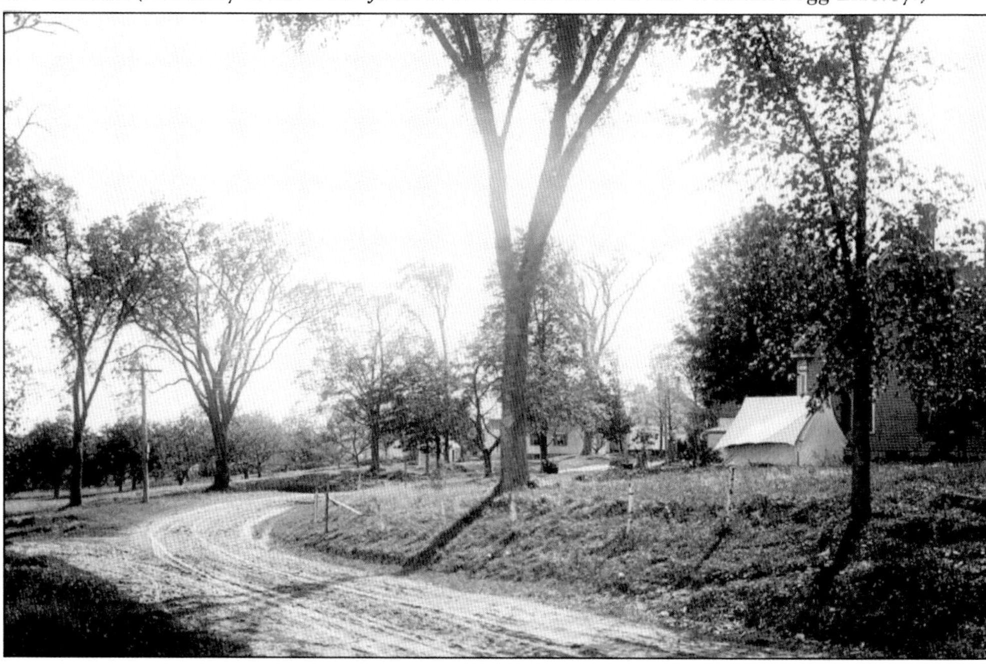

In the 1920s, George Ireland owned a store at the corner of State and Depot Roads, which sold meat and produce. Later, the Ireland's Corner building became a home. (Courtesy of the Gov. John F. Hill Collection at the William Fogg Library.)

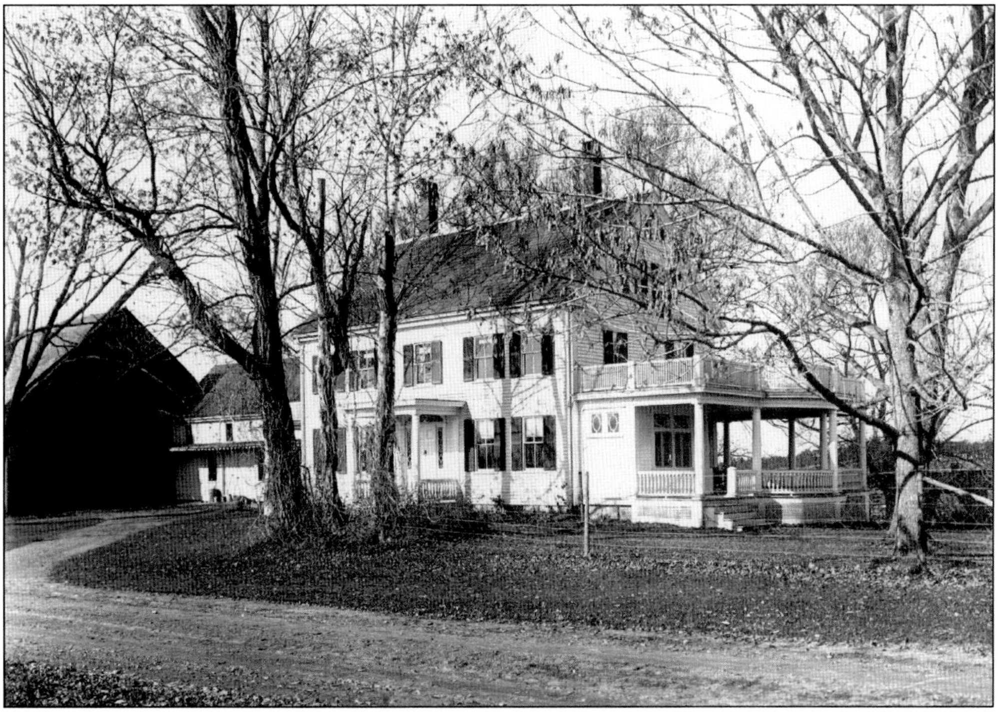

Sylvester Bartlett owned this farm on Depot Road. Beginning in 1855, he and his brother, James, ran a meat trade business for 20 years. James owned an adjacent farm. Sylvester married Clementine Raitt. (Courtesy of the Estate of C. Edward Bartlett Jr.)

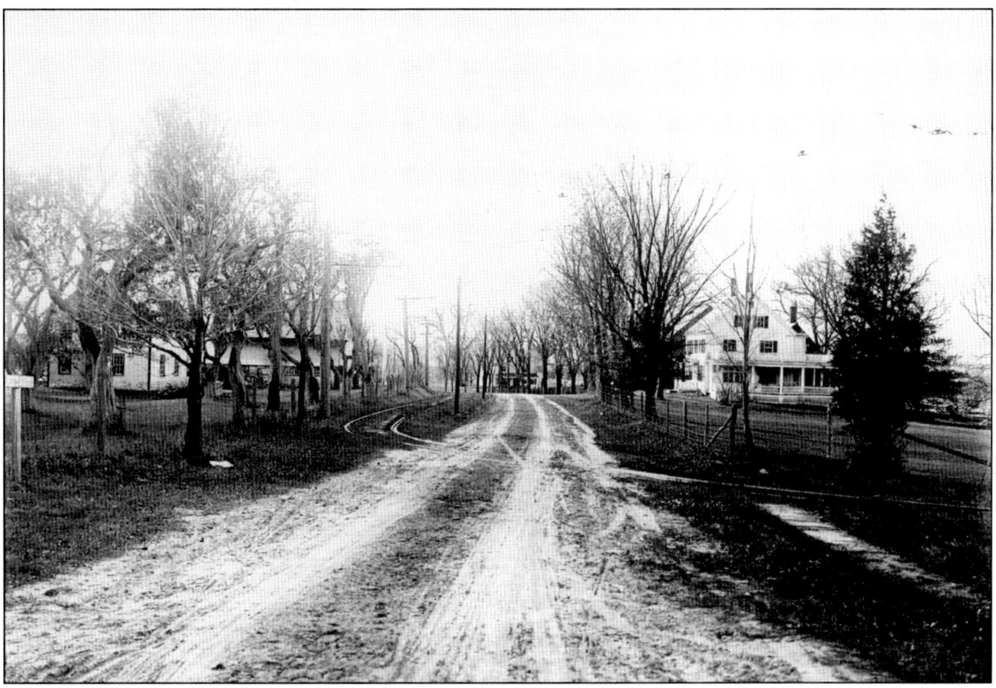

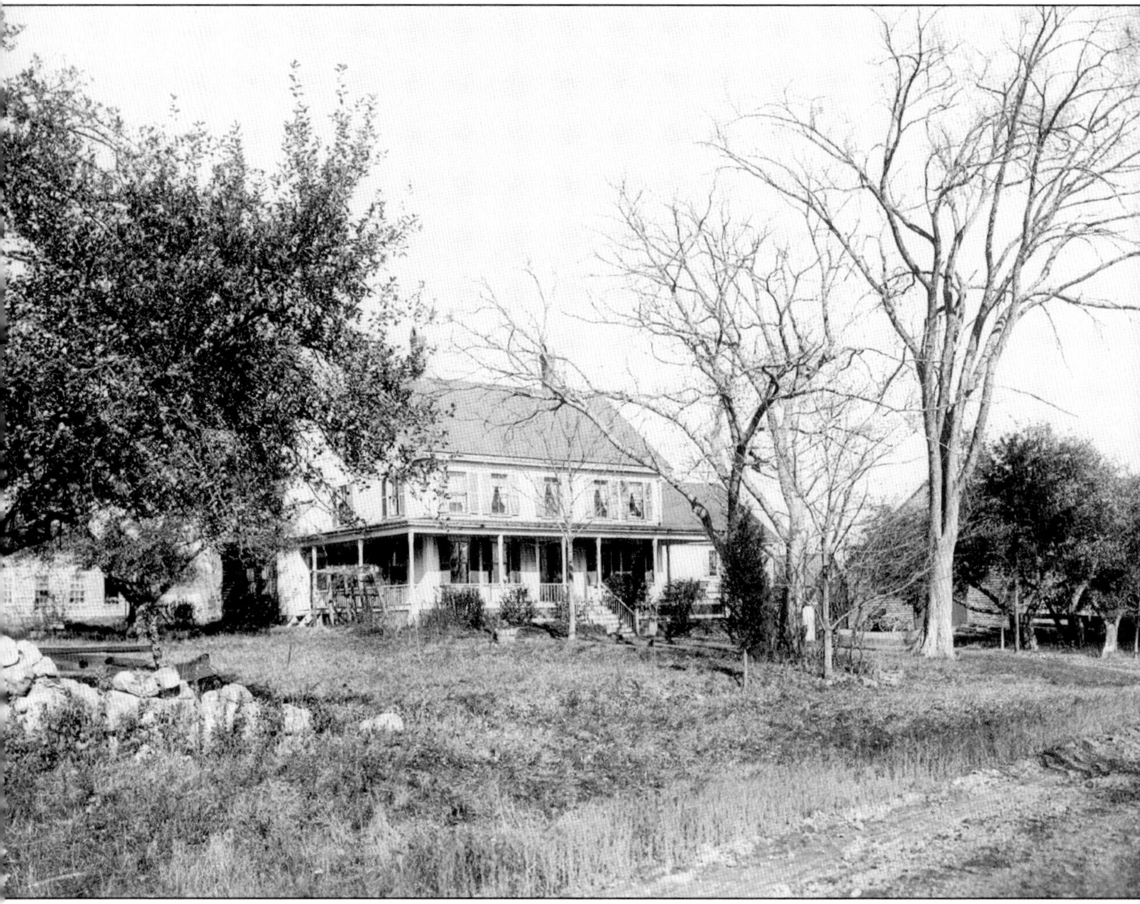

William Bartlett's Third Hill Farm on Brixham Road, Eliot's largest 20th-century dairy farm, still stands today. Built in the 18th century, it was remodeled in the 19th century. The dairy closed about 20 years ago. (Courtesy of the Gov. John F. Hill Collection at the William Fogg Library.)

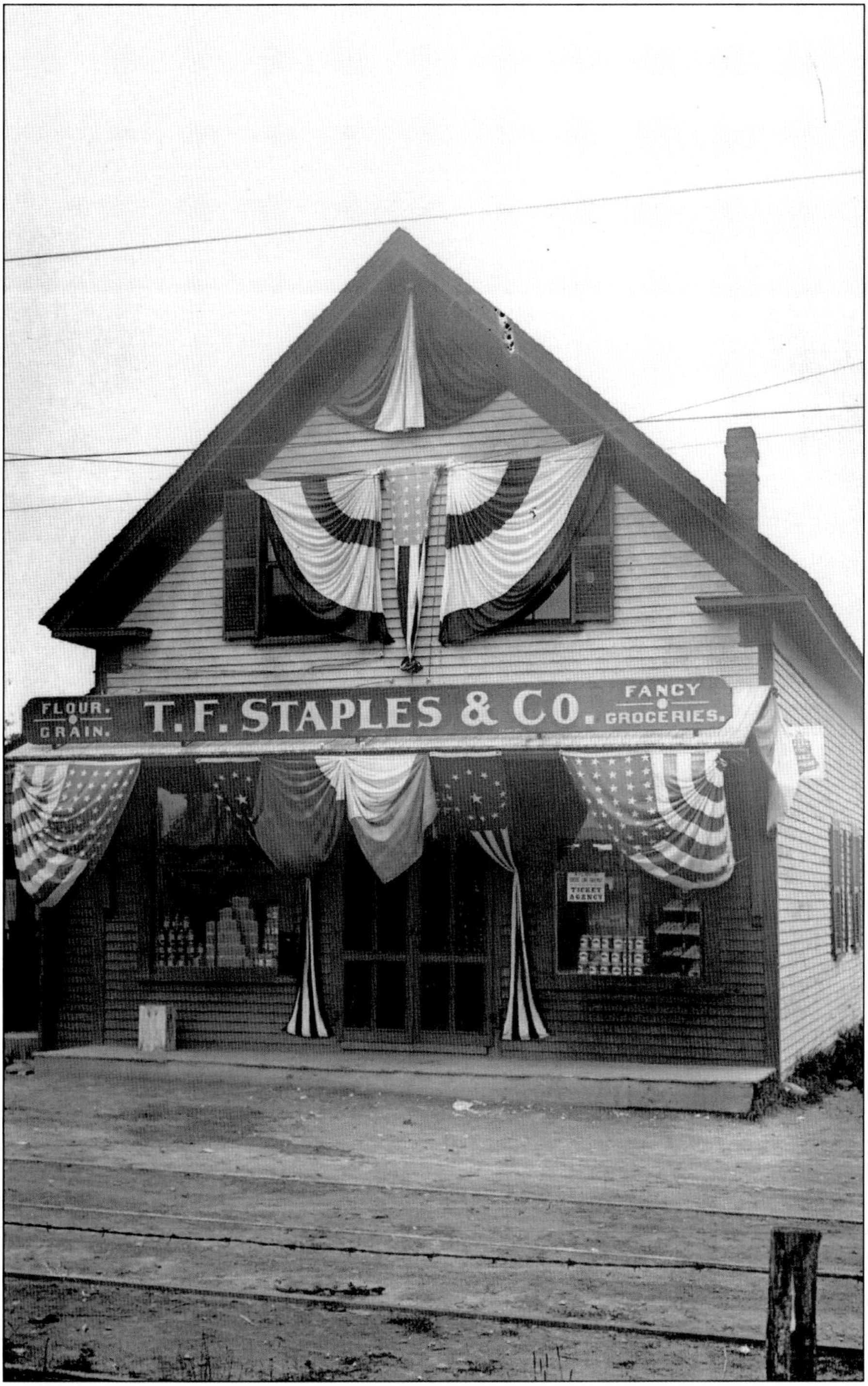

Ed and Harry Staples ran a grocery store in South Eliot on Pleasant Street. Remaining a family business for several generations, it later became Goodwin's Market and, after that, the Eliot House of Pizza. The post office was located here from 1847 until 1962. (Courtesy of the Gov. John F. Hill Collection at the William Fogg Library.)

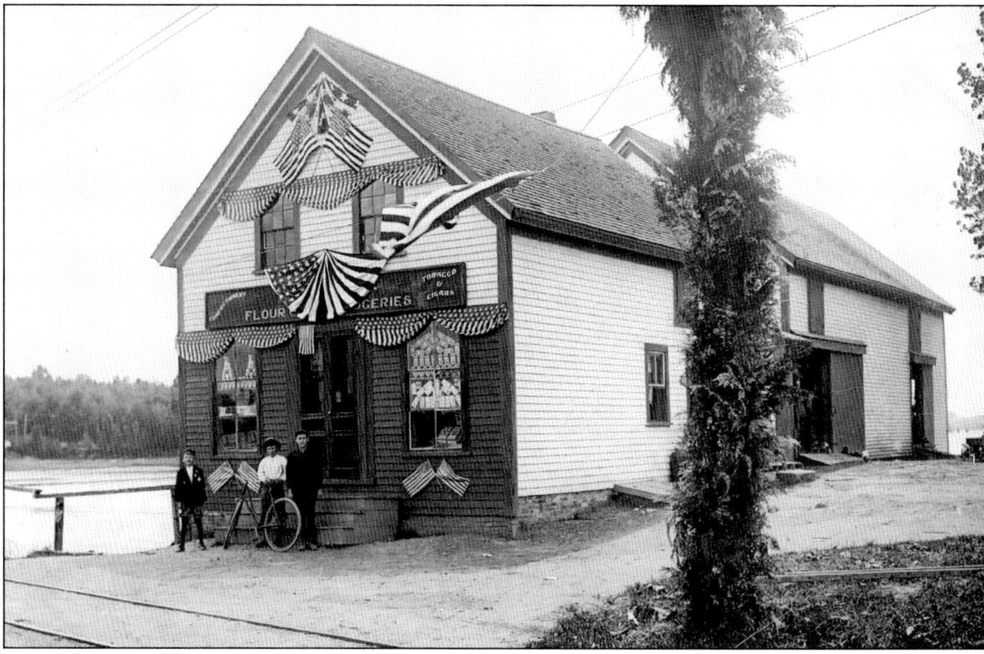

The Harris Spinney grocery was located on Main Street in South Eliot, next to the Spinney Creek Bridge. A marina is now at this location. (Courtesy of the William Fogg Library.)

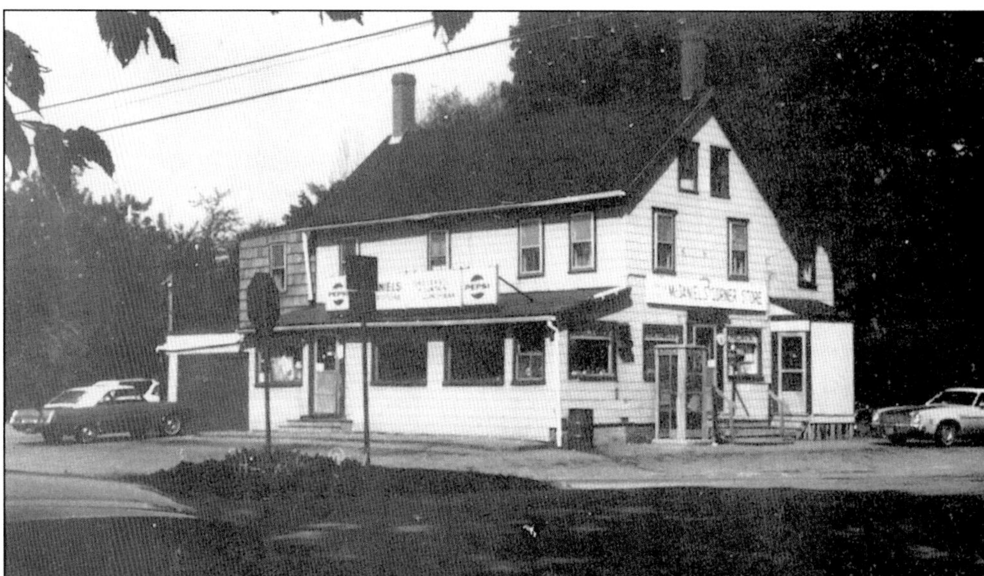

McDaniel's Corner Store, built in 1860, is now the Eliot Meat Market, at the corner of State and Moses Farmer Roads. The building has had many owners, including Sanders Liebman. (Courtesy of the Eliot Historical Society.)

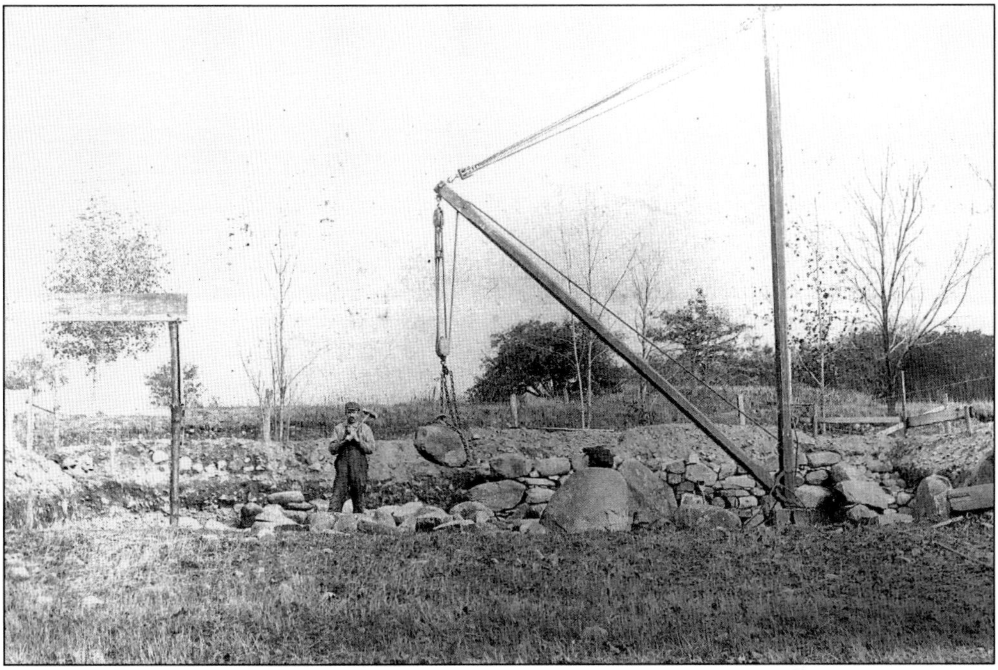

Here Bertram A. Tuttle is laying stone in the cellar hole of John Lord Emery's house on Goodwin Road. (Courtesy of Kenneth Tuttle.)

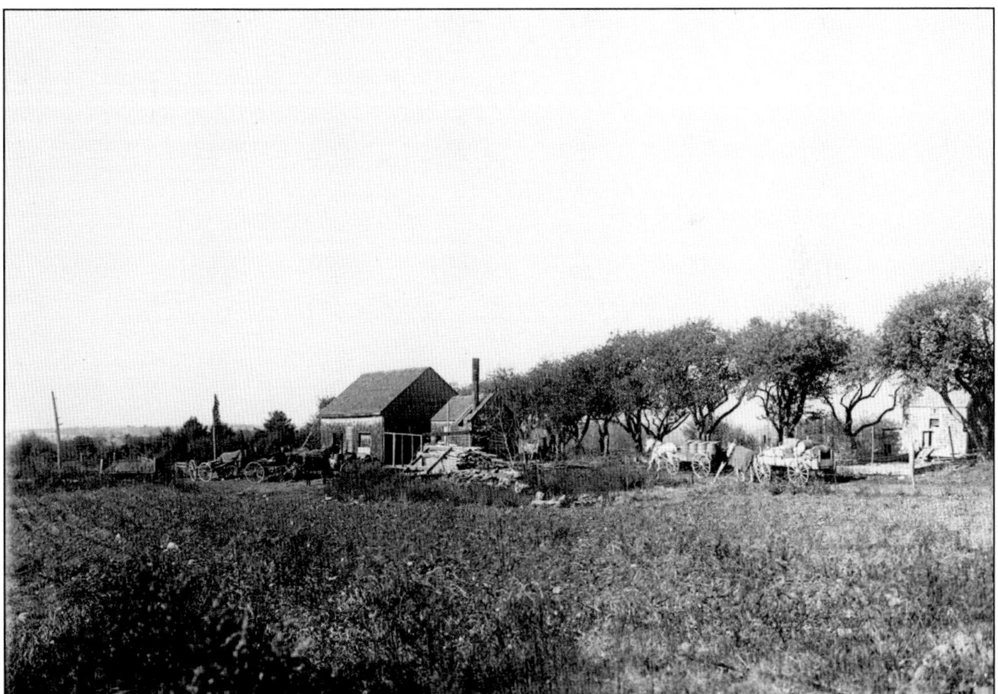

Bertram Tuttle opened Tuttle's Cider Mill on Goodwin Road in 1903. His son, Charles "King Tut," ran the business until 1975. Now Charles's son, Kenneth, is in charge. (Courtesy of the Gov. John F. Hill Collection at the William Fogg Library.)

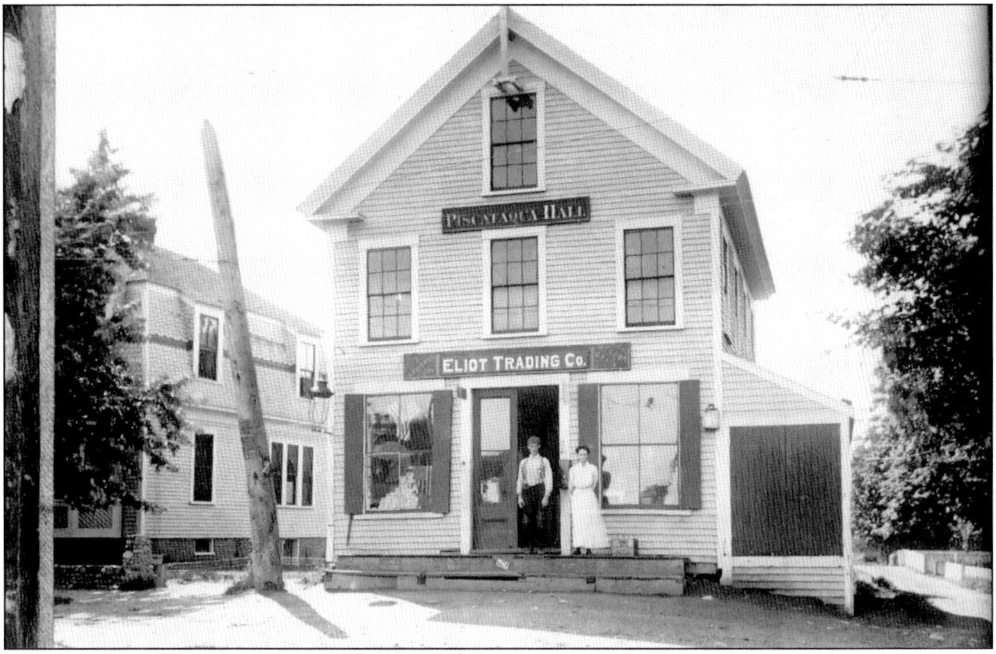

The Eliot Trading Company was on the corner of Maple Avenue and Pleasant Street in South Eliot. Mary Buck ran the business. A general store was on the first floor. Upstairs was an ice-cream parlor. (Above, courtesy of the Carlton and Doris Grover Collection at the William Fogg Library; below, courtesy of the Eliot Historical Society.)

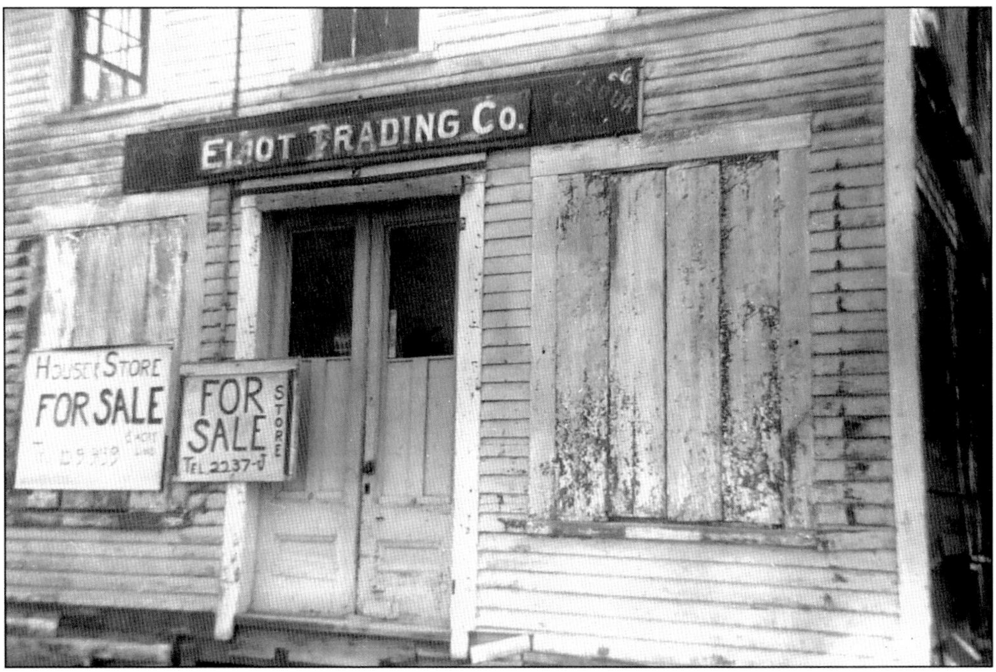

Lawrence Rowe used this tractor to smooth roads in the spring. The harsh winters left many ruts in the dirt thoroughfares. Rowe was road commissioner. Later, he became the state of Maine overseer of roads. (Courtesy of the Paul Family Association.)

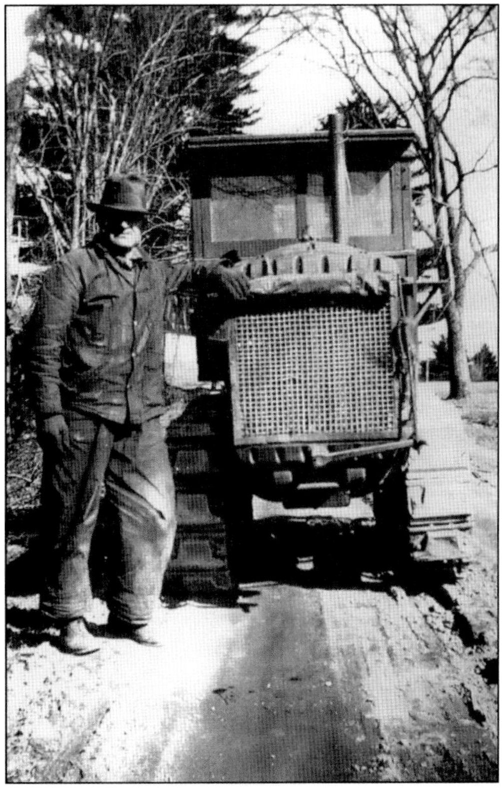

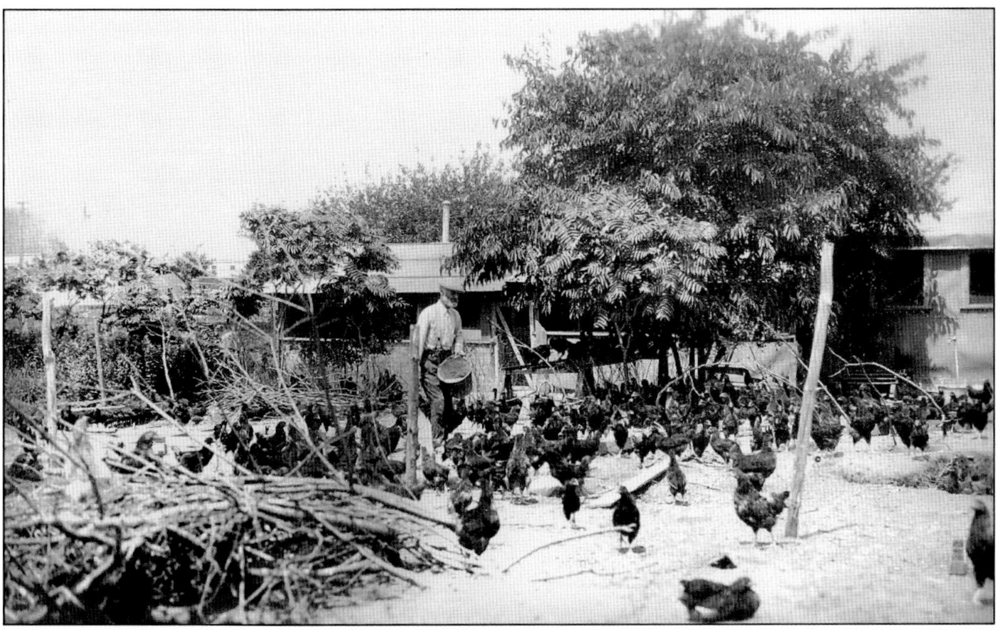

Here Ernest Wood feeds the birds on his Riverside Poultry Farm, which was located near the Laura V. Dame School in South Eliot. Poultry farming became important in Eliot in the early 20th century and continued into the 1960s. (Courtesy of Jeanette Paul.)

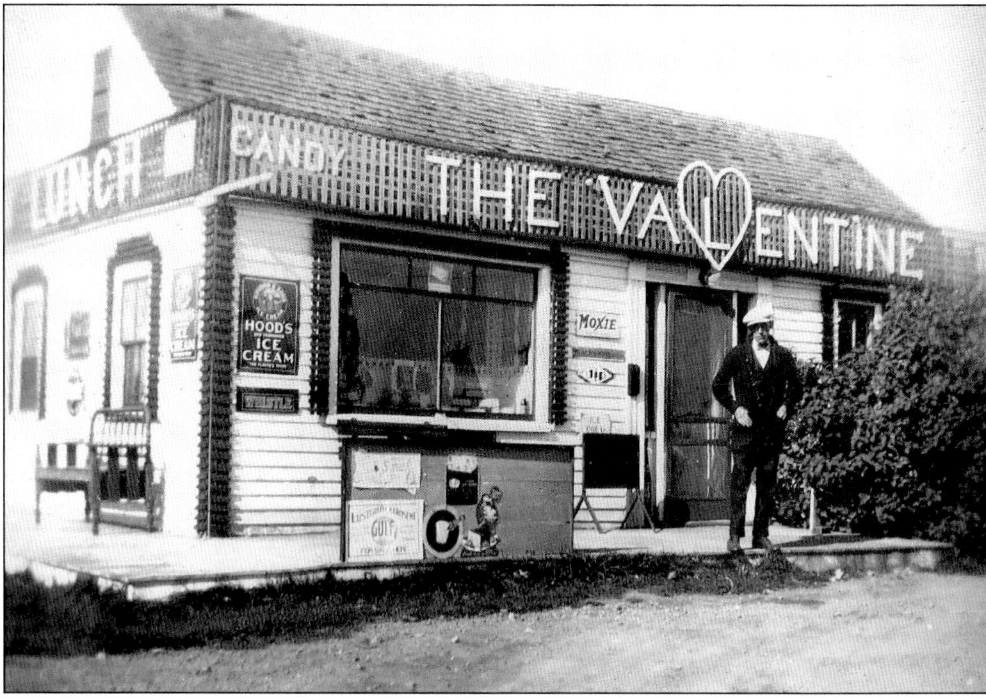

Harold Furbish, owner of the Valentine store, stands in front of his business. The store stood near the corner of what are now Route 236 and the Dover Road. This photograph was taken in the 1930s. (Courtesy of Carol Zamarchi.)

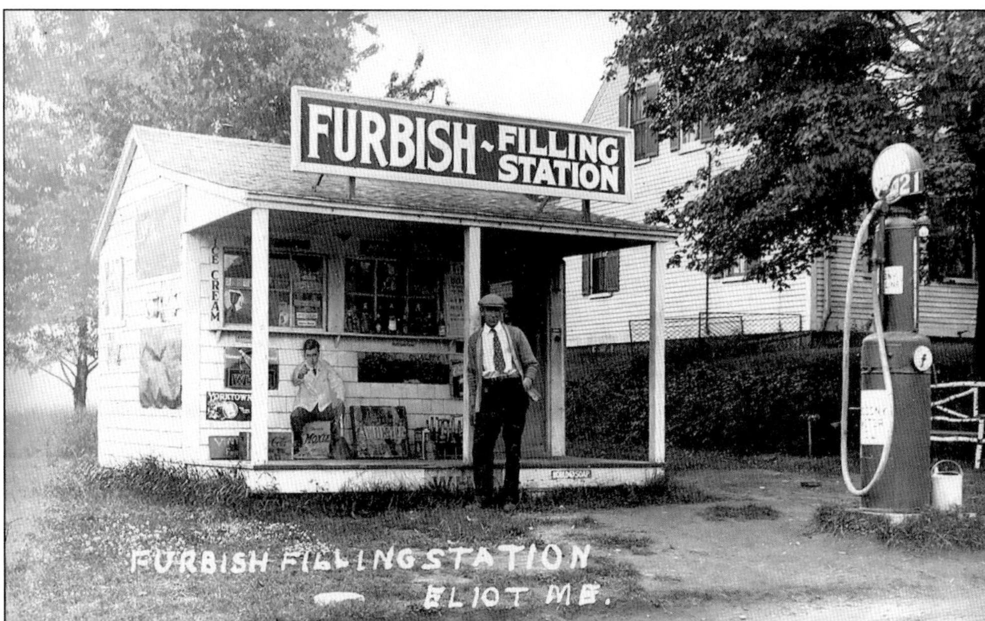

The Furbish Filling Station, on Furbish Hill, was near the Valentine store. Philip Furbish, brother of the Valentine's owner, was the proprietor of this business. Philip Furbish stands in front of the building. (Courtesy of the Estate of C. Edward Bartlett Jr.)

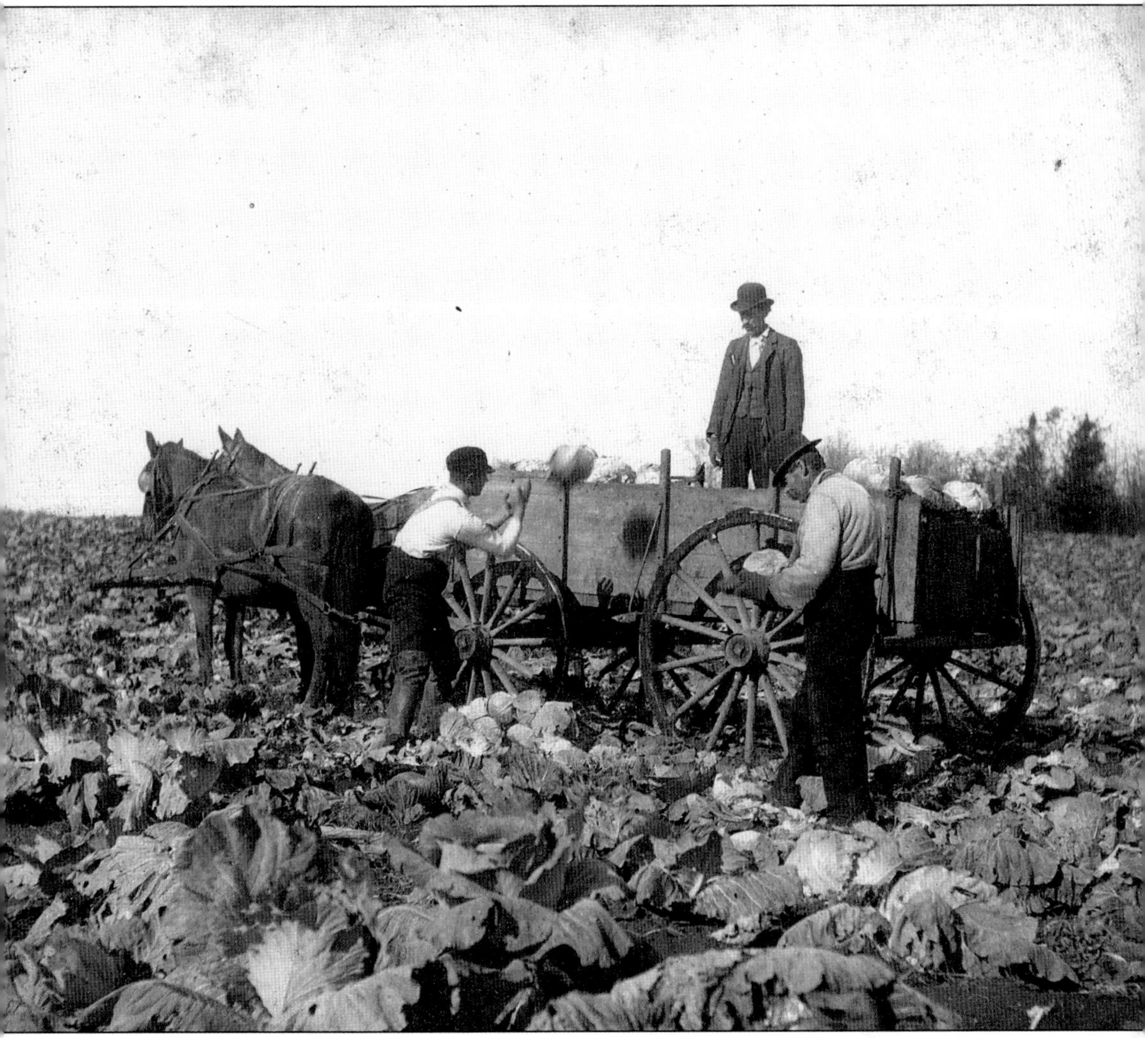

It must be harvest time in old Eliot. Until the advent of supermarkets, farming was an important occupation in town. (Courtesy of the Paul Family Association.)

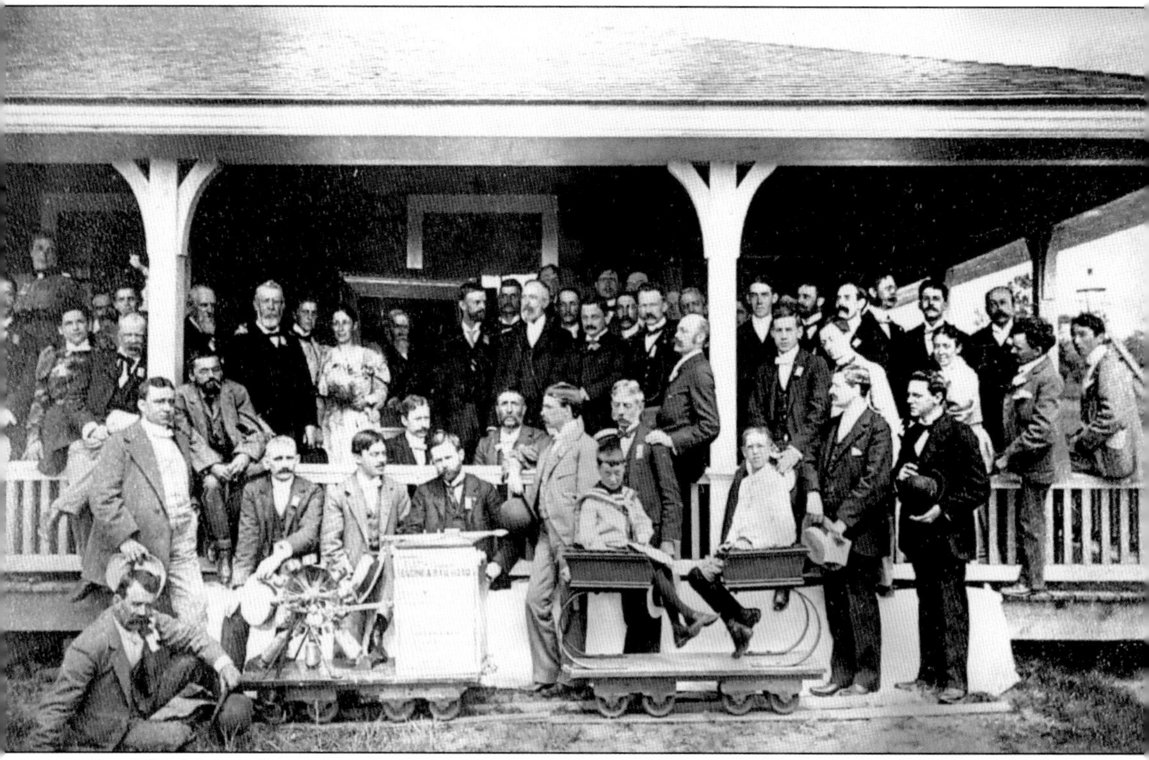

On July 26, 1897, at Green Acre, the American Institute of Electrical Engineers celebrated the 50th anniversary of the first electrically operated passenger car in the world. The original electric car was invented by Eliot resident Moses Gerrish Farmer and is now in the Smithsonian Institute. Sarah Jane Farmer stands on the porch, holding a bouquet. (Courtesy of Tom Wilson, Piscataqua History Club.)

Five

TRAVEL AND TRANSPORTATION

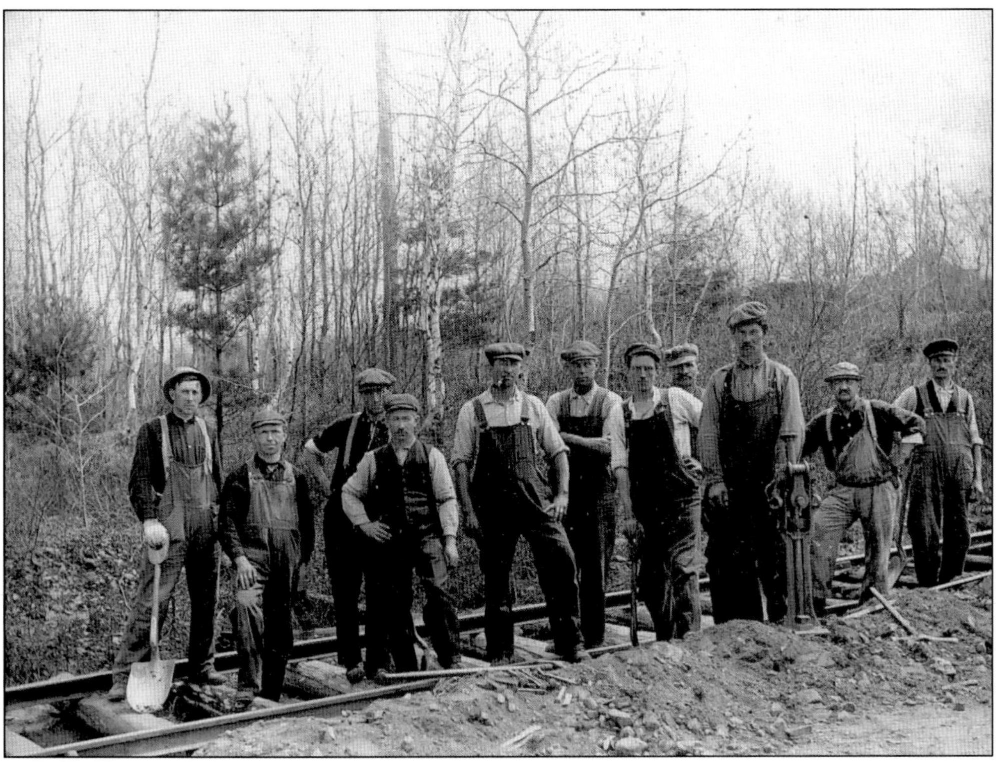

These men are working on tracks for Eliot's early transportation system. The electric railway, known as the PDY (Portsmouth, Dover, York), ran from 1902 until 1923. The Boston and Maine Railroad ran from 1842 until c. 1952 along what is now Route 236. (Courtesy of the Paul Family Association.)

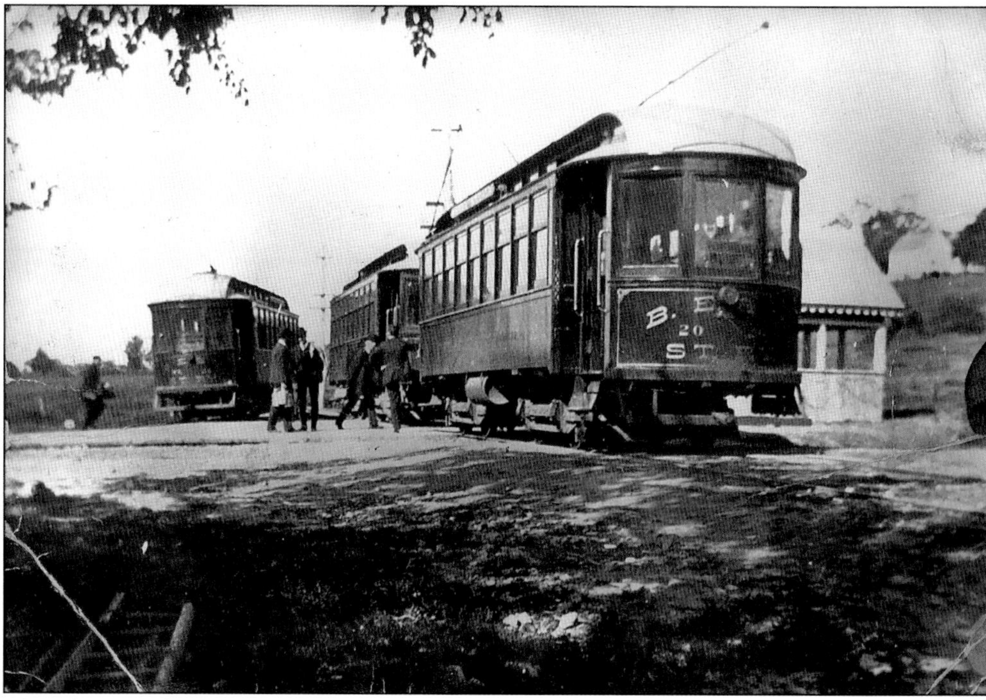

This photograph of electric cars at Rosemary Junction was taken around 1902. (Courtesy of the Estate of C. Edward Bartlett Jr.)

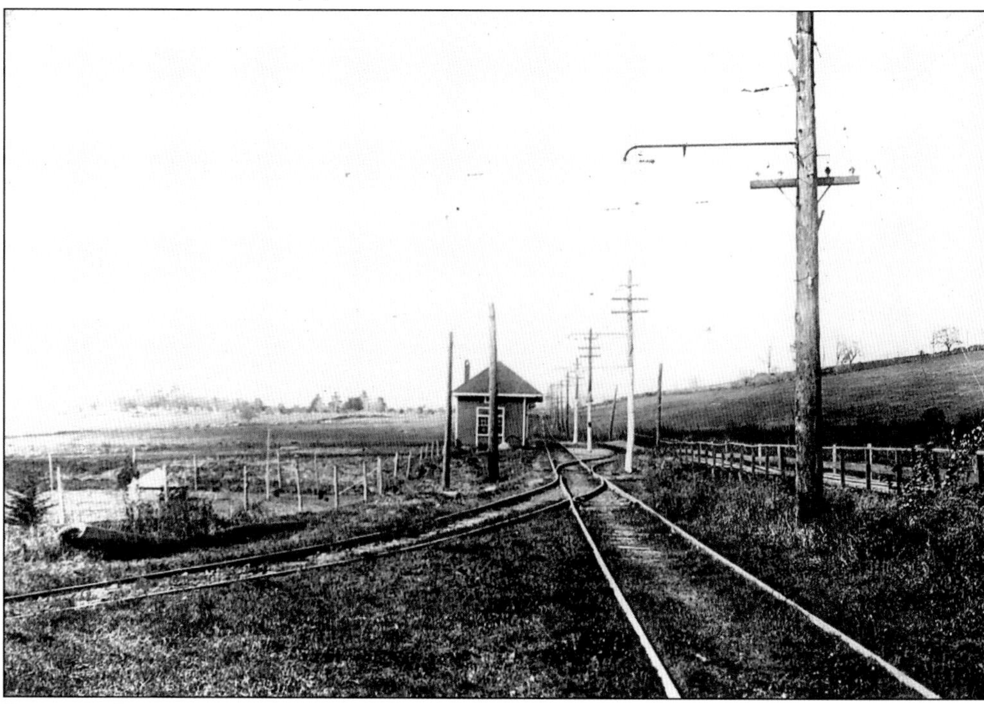

Rosemary Station was at Rosemary Junction, below Rosemary Hill on Depot Road. The building burned in 1922. Later, the Main Street electric streetcar station was moved to the Rosemary Cottage area. (Courtesy of Kenneth Tuttle.)

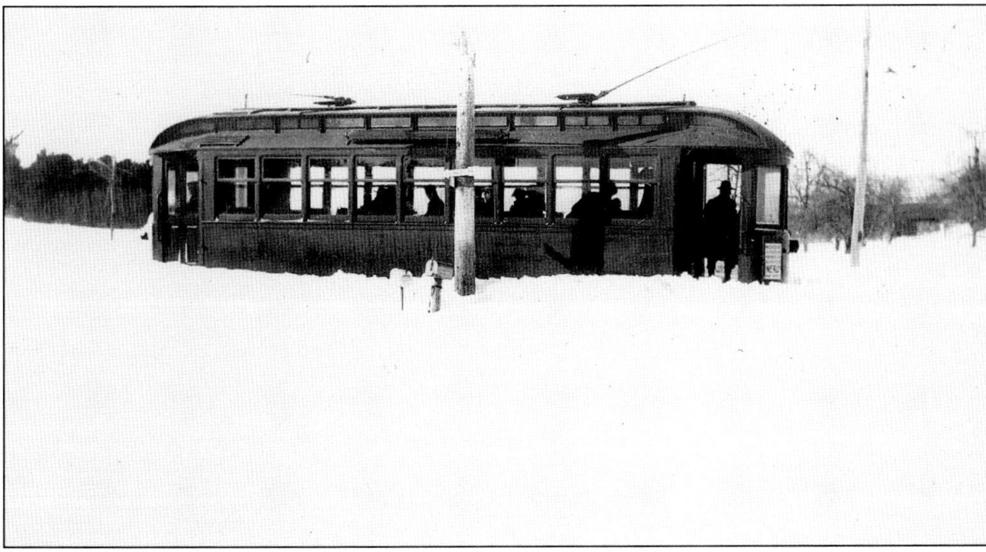

Electric cars ran through Eliot from 1902 until 1923. Eliot resident Moses Gerrish Farmer invented the electric car, which made its first run in Dover, New Hampshire, on July 25, 1847. (Courtesy of the Estate of C. Edward Bartlett Jr.)

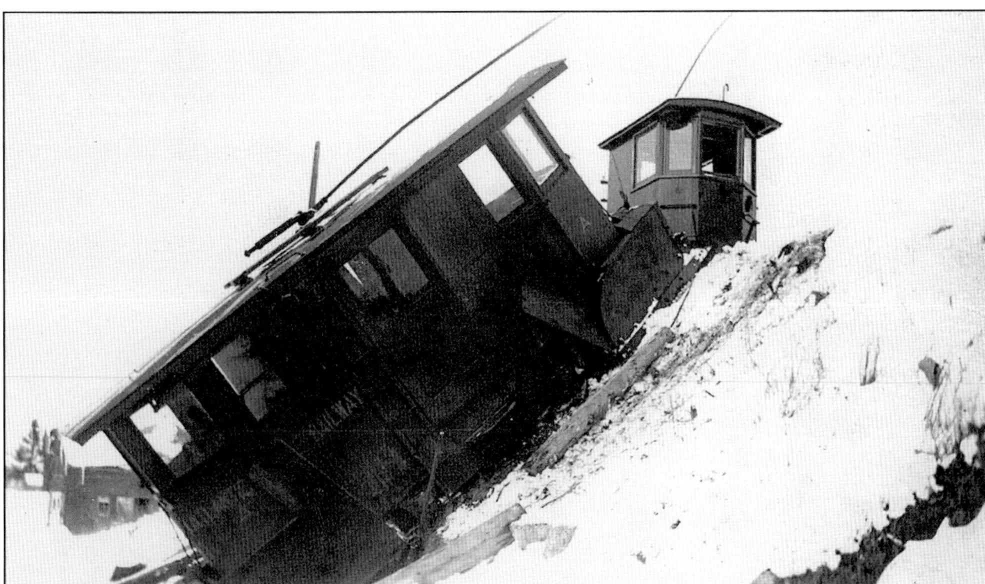

This snowplow for the electric railway derailed while plowing the electric road in 1920. (Courtesy of the Estate of C. Edward Bartlett Jr.)

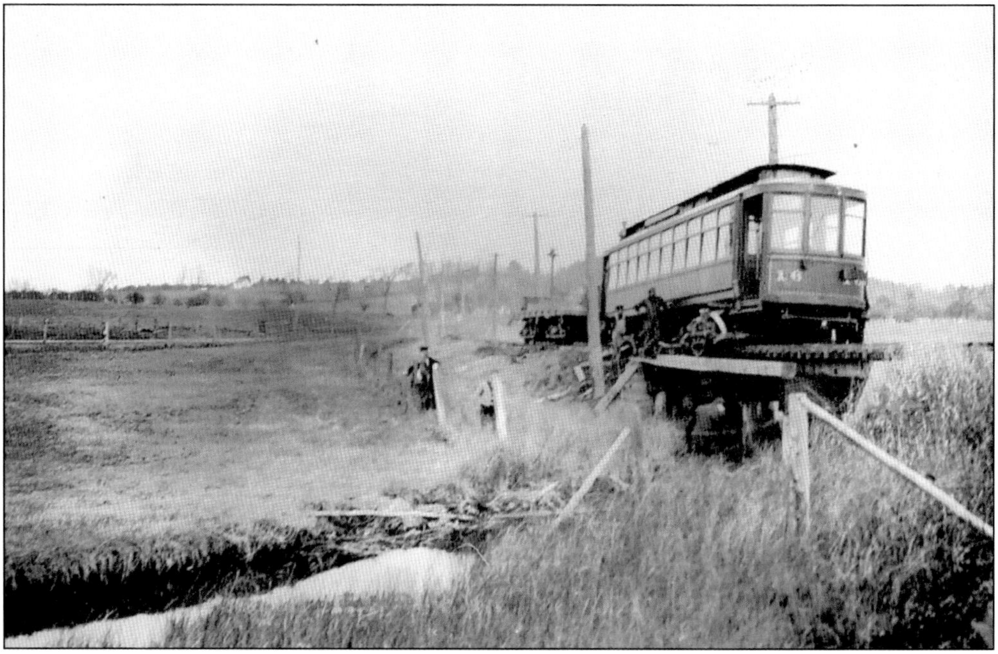

Here are two views of an electric car that derailed at the creek in Eliot. Residents often referred to the PDY as the Pull, Drag, and Yank. (Courtesy of the Estate of C. Edward Bartlett Jr.)

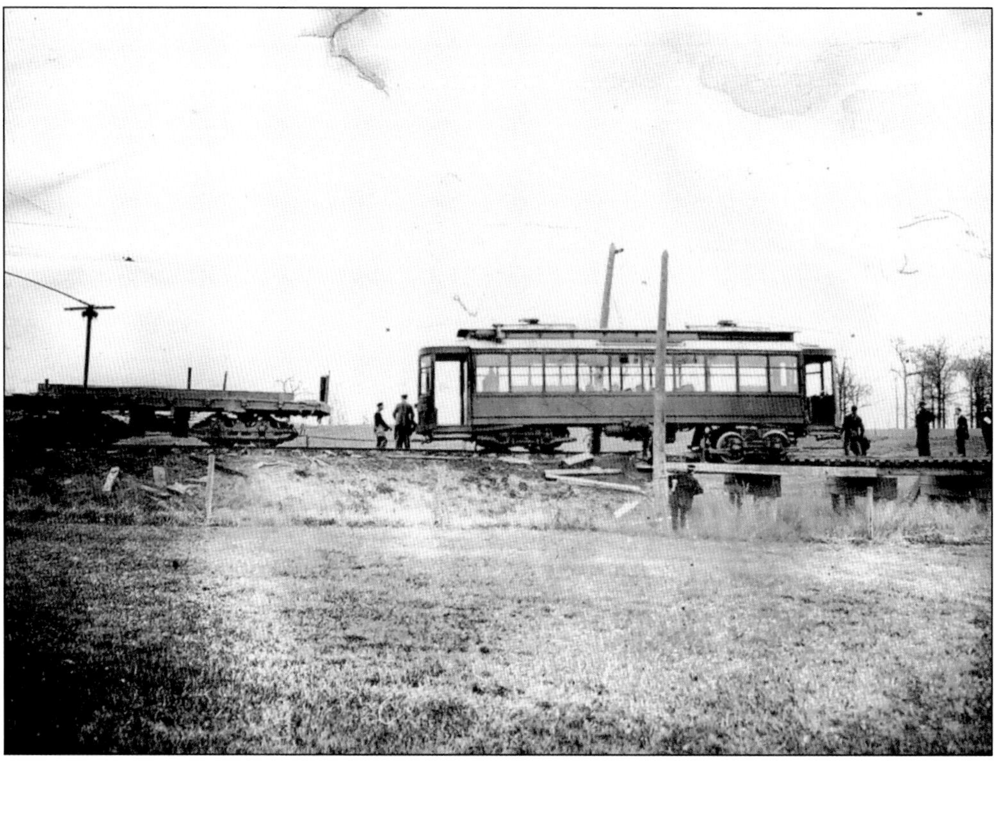

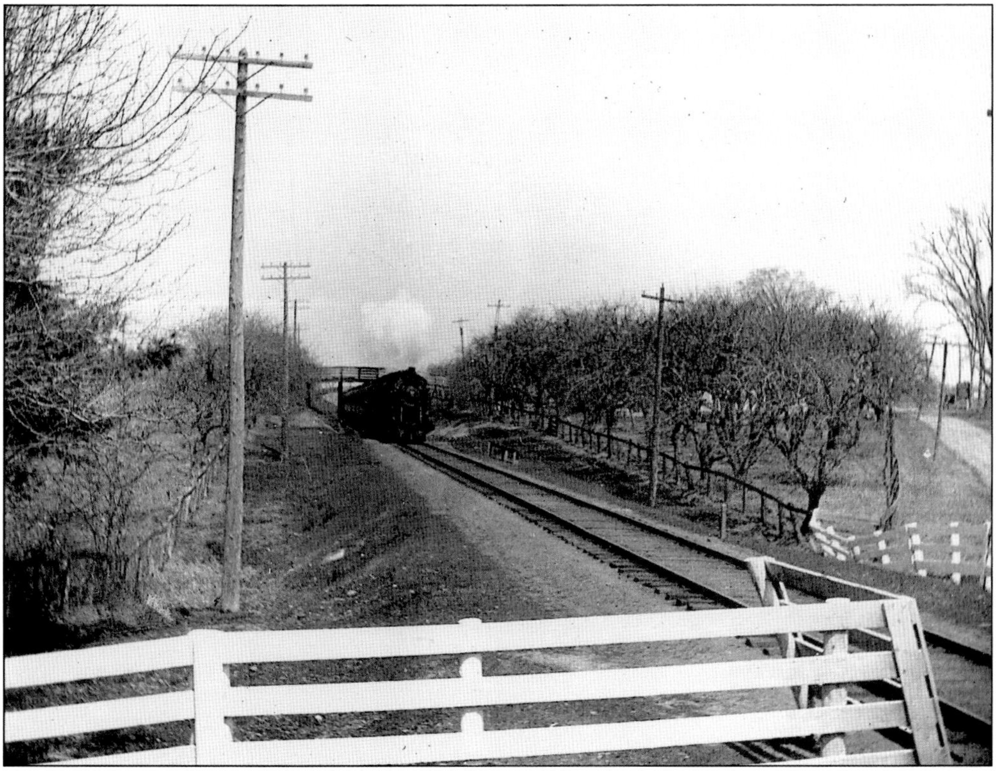

A Boston and Maine Railroad train approaches Gould's Crossing, going west, in 1904. (Courtesy of Kenneth Tuttle.)

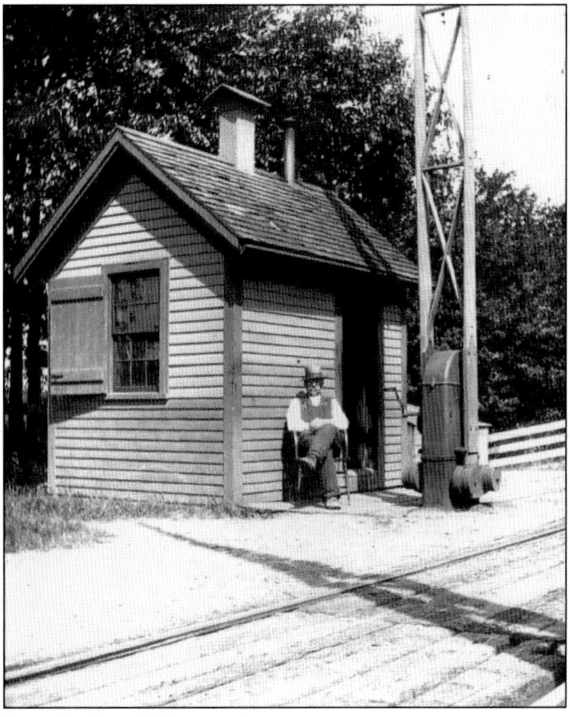

This flagman is enjoying a sunny day at Gould's Crossing in 1918. (Courtesy of Kenneth Tuttle.)

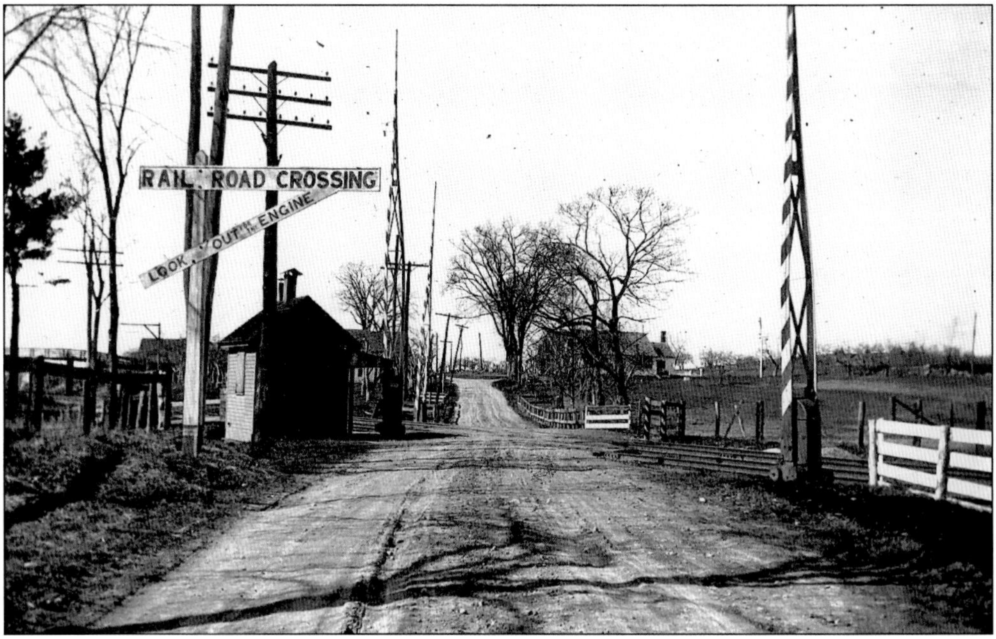

Gould's Crossing looked like this in 1910. (Courtesy of Kenneth Tuttle.)

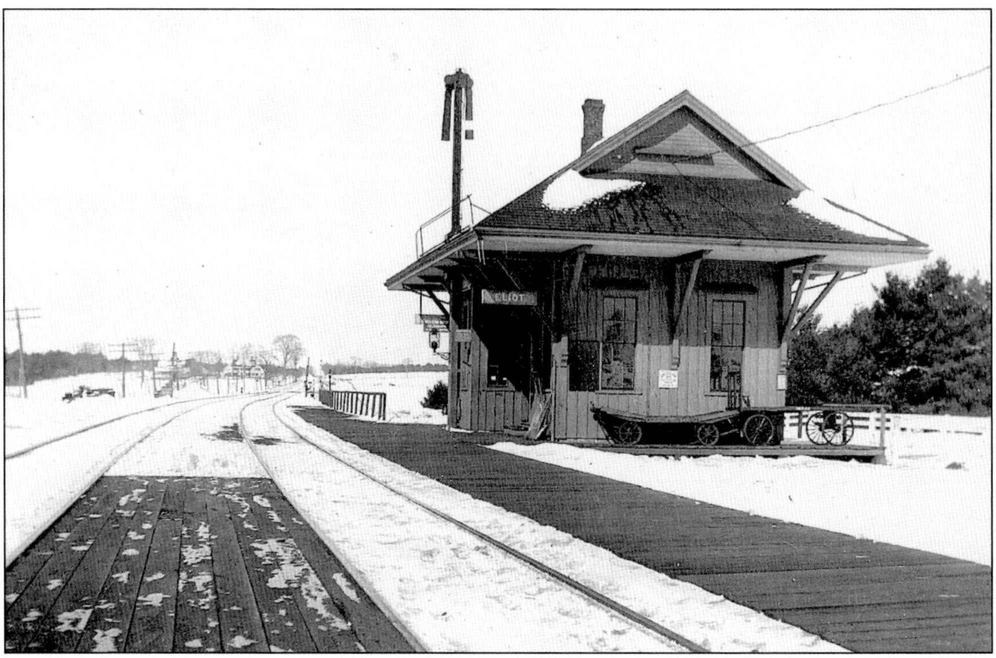

Eliot Station was located near Depot Road and the present Route 236. This photograph was taken in the winter of 1924. In 1842, tracks were laid from Kittery to South Berwick on what is now Route 236. (Courtesy of Kenneth Tuttle.)

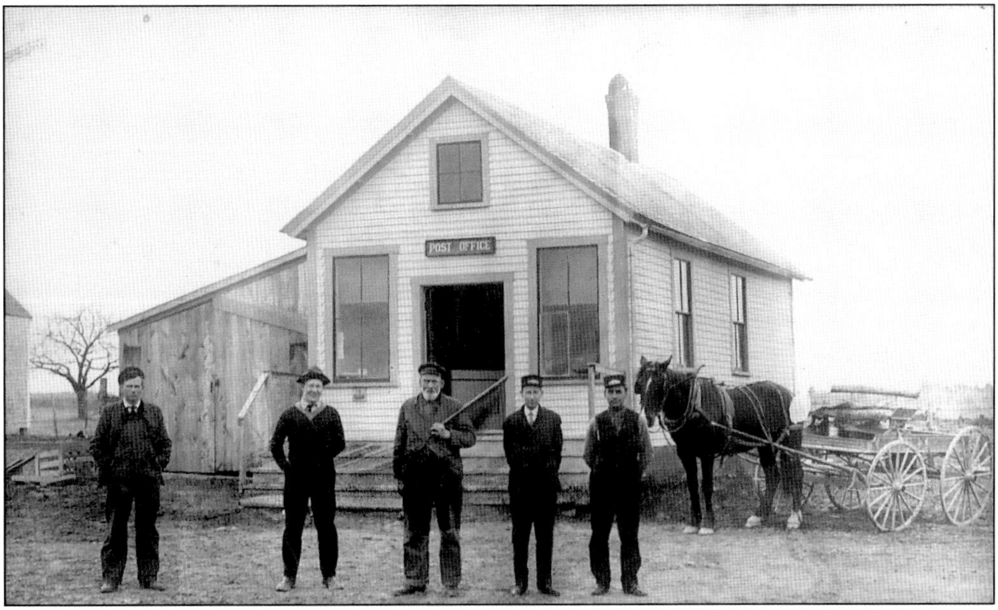

These five gents seem to have enjoyed being photographed on this particular day in 1909. In the image above, Raymond Clark, Willis Hayden, Tom Boyce, Cyrus Bartlett, and Walter Hodgdon stand in front of the post office at the corner of Depot and Cedar Roads. The Boston and Maine train dropped off Eliot's mail near this location. Below, the same men pose in front of the Eliot depot of the Boston and Maine Railroad. Standing are Tom Boyce (crossing tender), Cyrus Bartlett (station agent), and Walter Hodgdon (baggage master); Raymond Clark and Willis Hayden (assistant baggage master) are in the wagon. (Above and below, courtesy of the Libby Collection.)

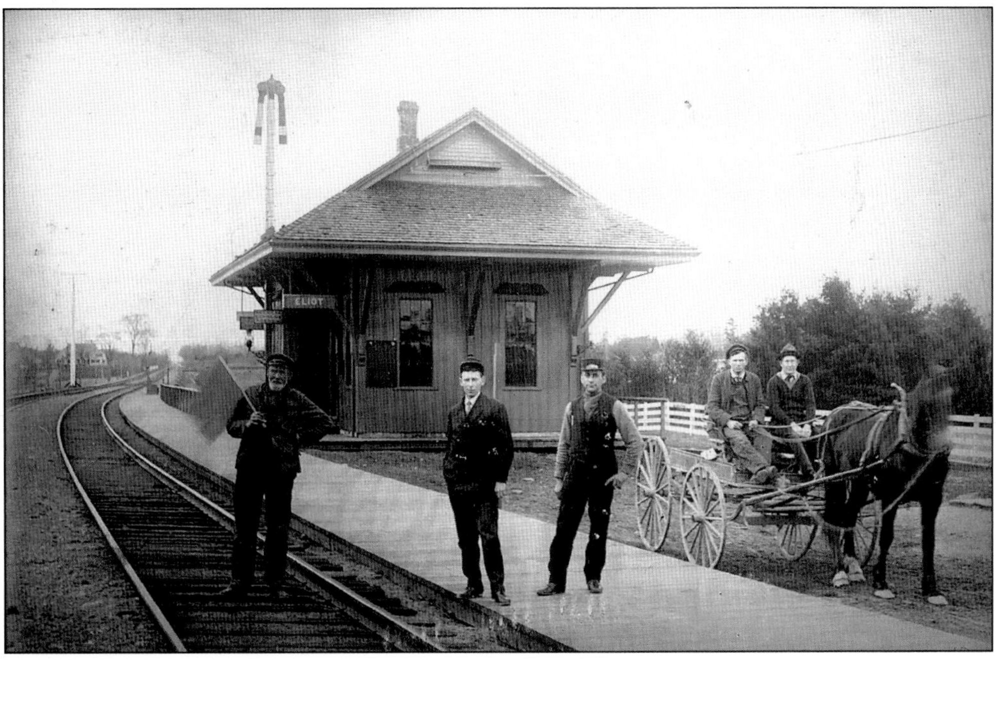

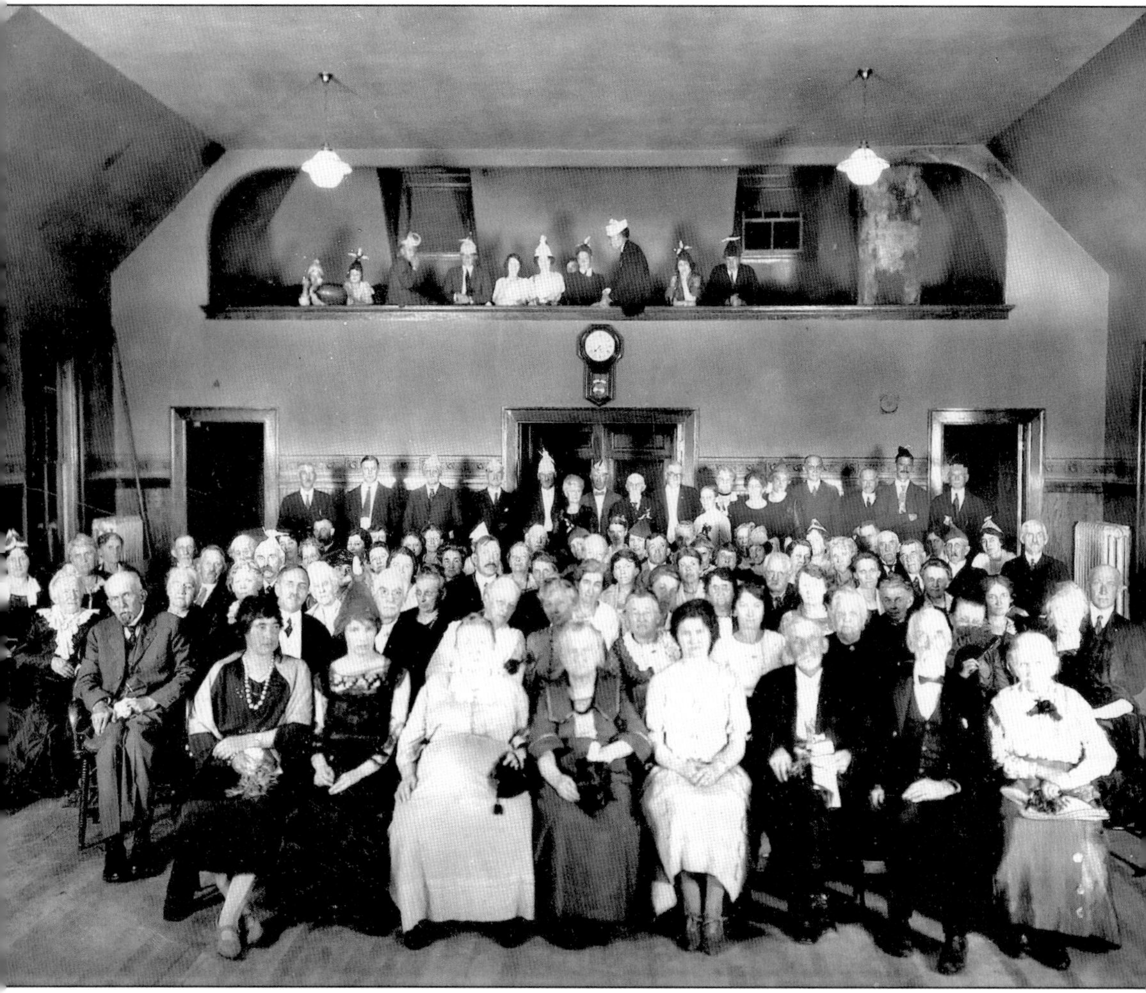

In August 1922, graduates of the Eliot Academy met at the John F. Hill Grange Hall for a reunion. The academy prepared students for college and was also a normal school. (Courtesy of the Eliot Historical Society.)

Six

School Days

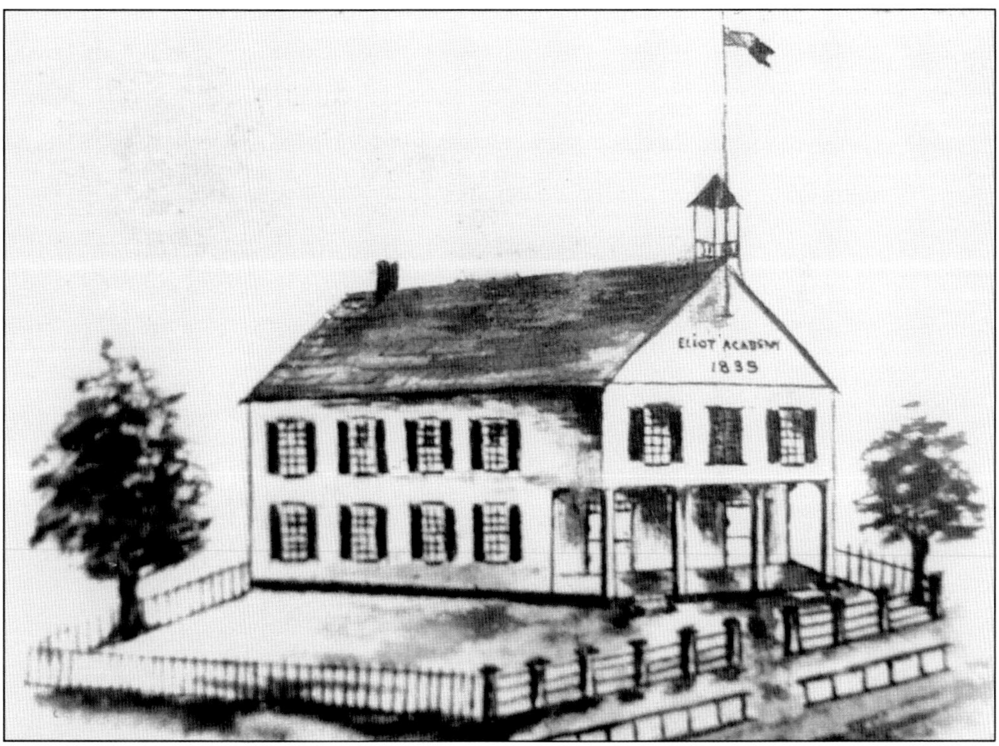

Eliot Academy stood at the corner of State and Old Roads. Built in 1839, it was destroyed by fire on December 21, 1875, and was never rebuilt. Today a marker stands at the site. (Courtesy of Edward H. Vetter.)

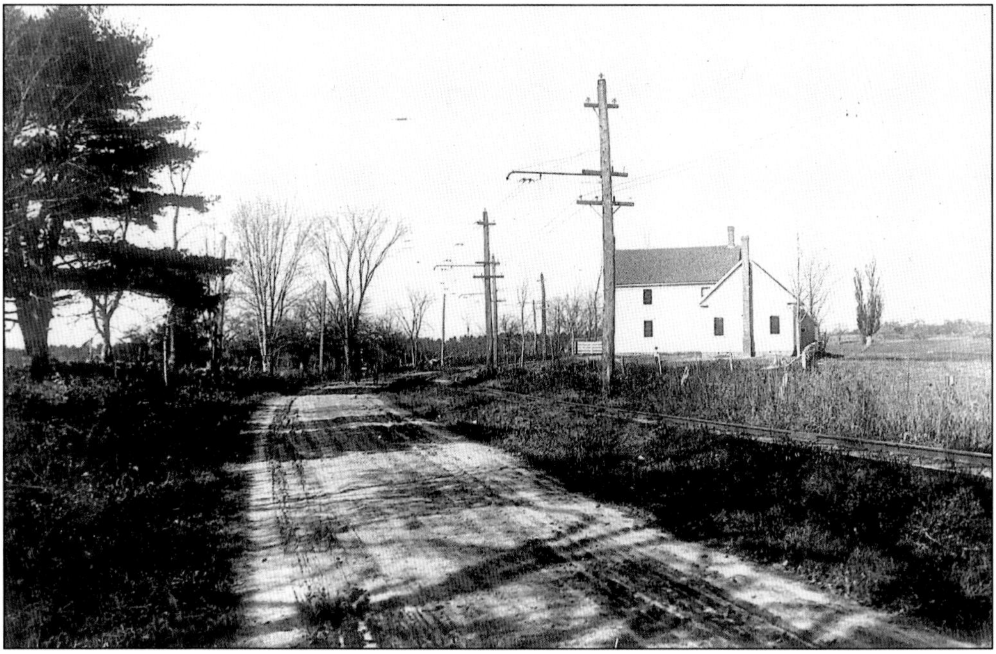

School House No. 1, also known as the Emery School, was located on Route 101 (Goodwin Road) near the Frost farm. In operation from 1810 until 1934, it was torn down in the early 1940s. Now only the foundation is left. (Courtesy of Kenneth Tuttle.)

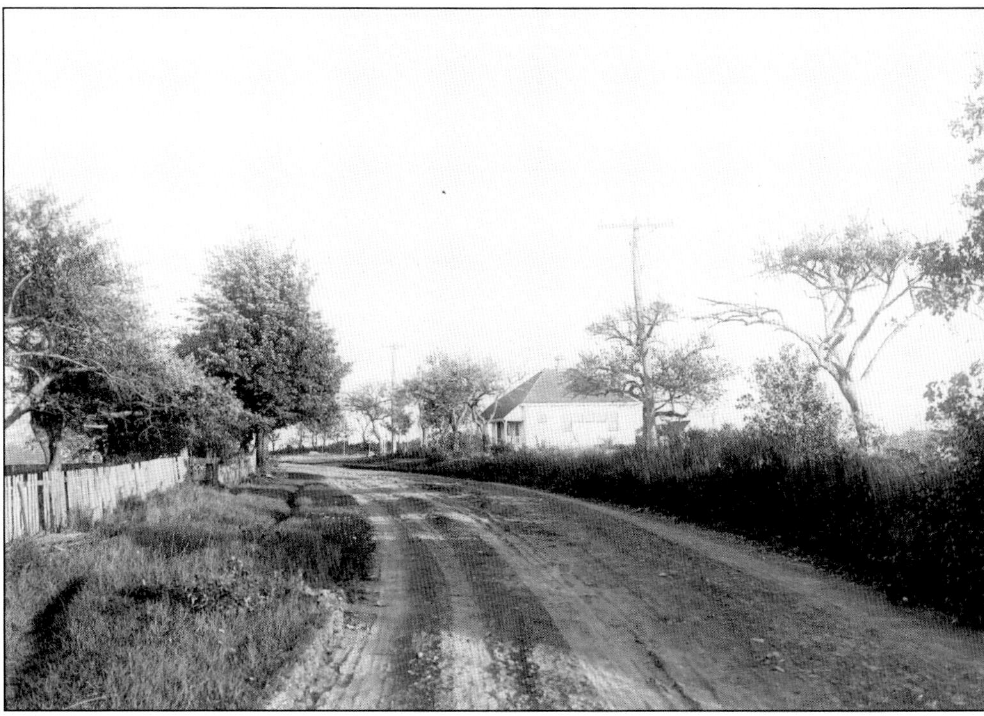

School House No. 2, at Stacy's Hill on State Road, was also known as the Lincoln School. Built in 1896, it burned down in 1940. (Courtesy of the Gov. John F. Hill Collection at the William Fogg Library.)

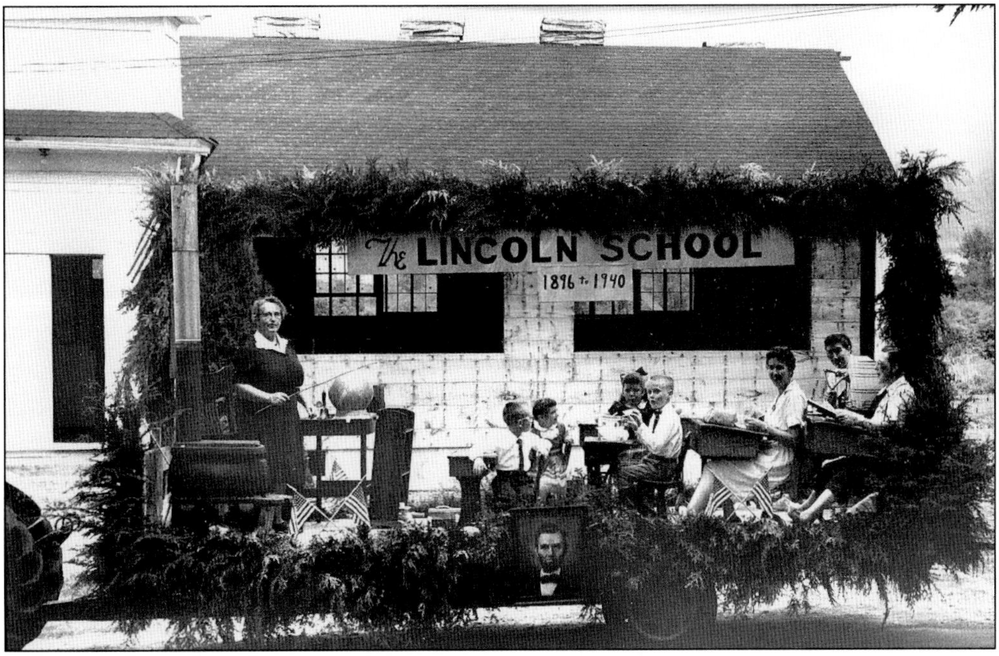

This Lincoln School float appeared in a parade in 1960 during the 150th anniversary of the incorporation of the town of Eliot. Florence Raitt Trefethen, a teacher for 20 years, portrayed a teacher on the float. (Courtesy of the Everson Collection.)

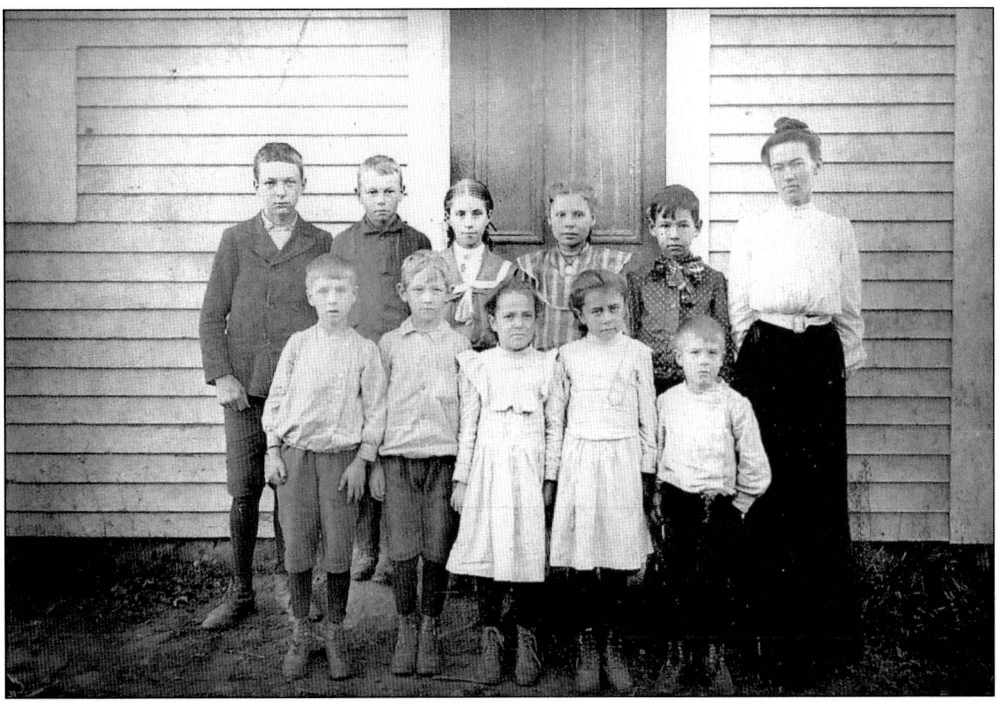

Teacher Edna Paul Fogg and her students stand in front of School House No. 3 on Brixham Road. The school, also known as the Major Charles Frost School, closed in 1940. Later, it was used as a shop and garage. (Courtesy of the Paul Family Association.)

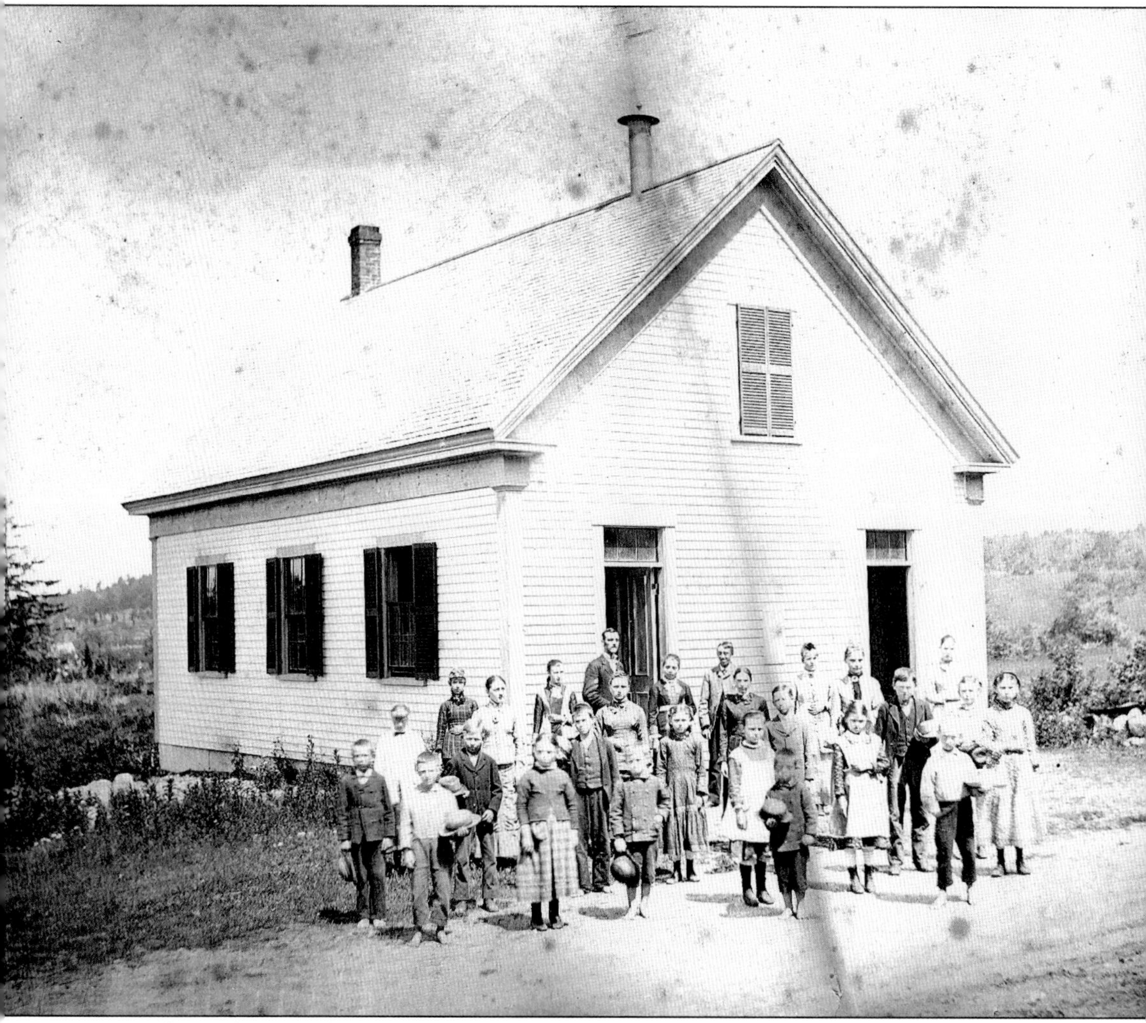

Mr. Millett's class stands in front of School House No. 3 in 1889. Pictured are Frank Peckham, Mary Peckham, George Lapham, Edith (Bartlett) Stone, Rolla Bartlett, Etta Briggs, Nellie Payne, Alma (Goodwin) Frost, Will Amee, Mr. Millett, Edith Raitt, Fred Shapleigh, Carrie Hanscom, Everett Hanscom, Mabel Raitt, Florence Emery, Oscar Shapleigh, Ralph Bartlett, Mary Frost, Alta Paul, Fannie (Briggs) Goodwin, Joe Irving, John Goodwin, Annie Raitt, Sophia Lapham, and Alice Briggs. (Courtesy of the Estate of C. Edward Bartlett Jr.)

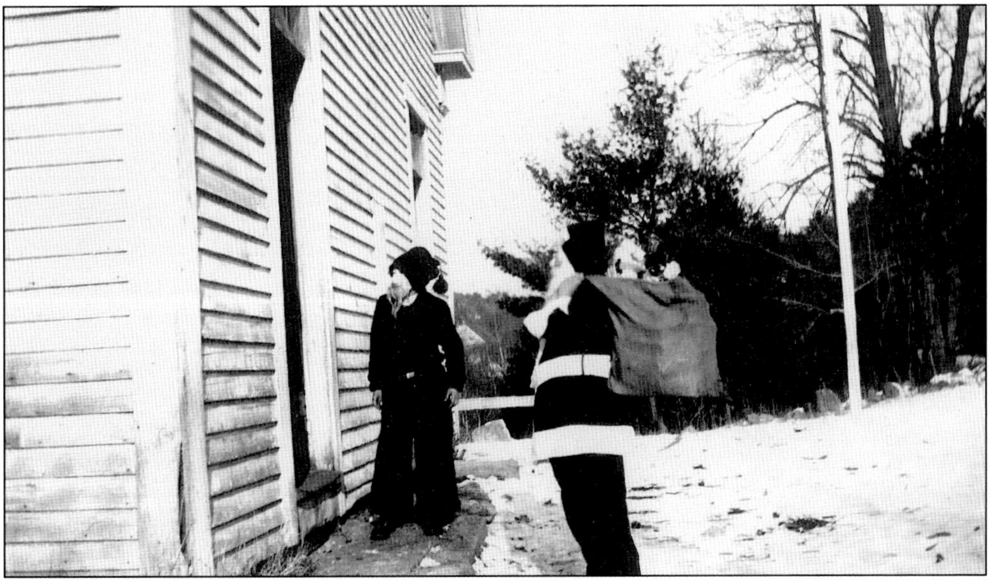

One winter's day, Santa and a helper paid a visit to School House No. 3 on Brixham Road. (Courtesy of the Estate of C. Edward Bartlett Jr.)

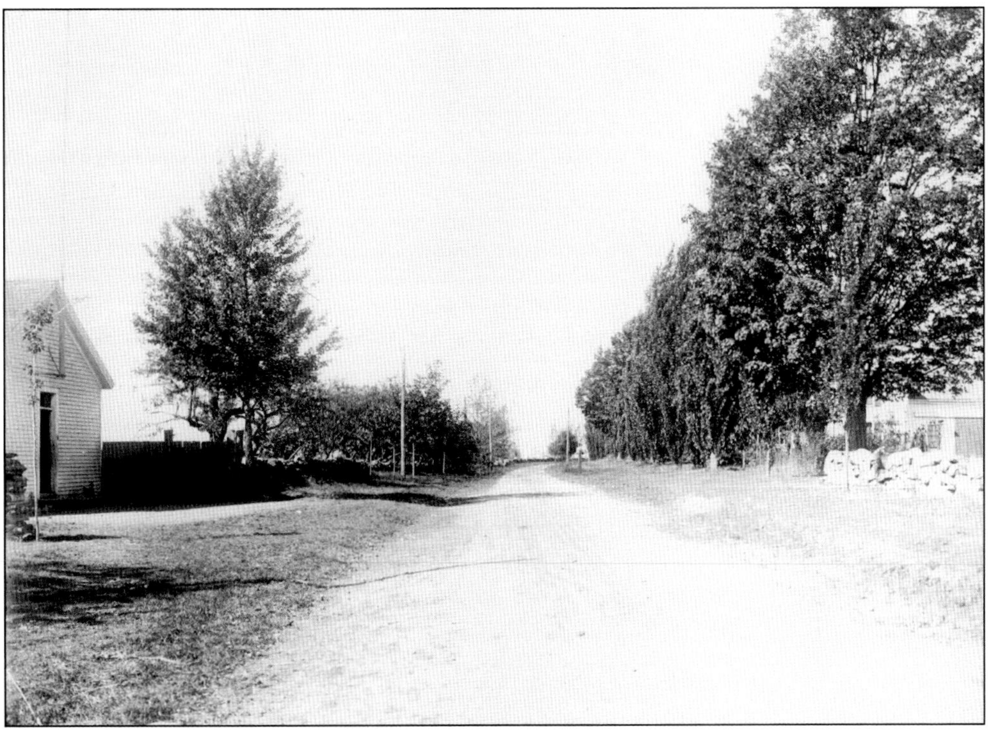

School House No. 4, built in 1810 on Goodwin Road near the Beech Road intersection, was moved to another Goodwin Road location when it became a private home. It is the oldest standing schoolhouse in Eliot. (Courtesy of the Gov. John F. Hill Collection at the William Fogg Library.)

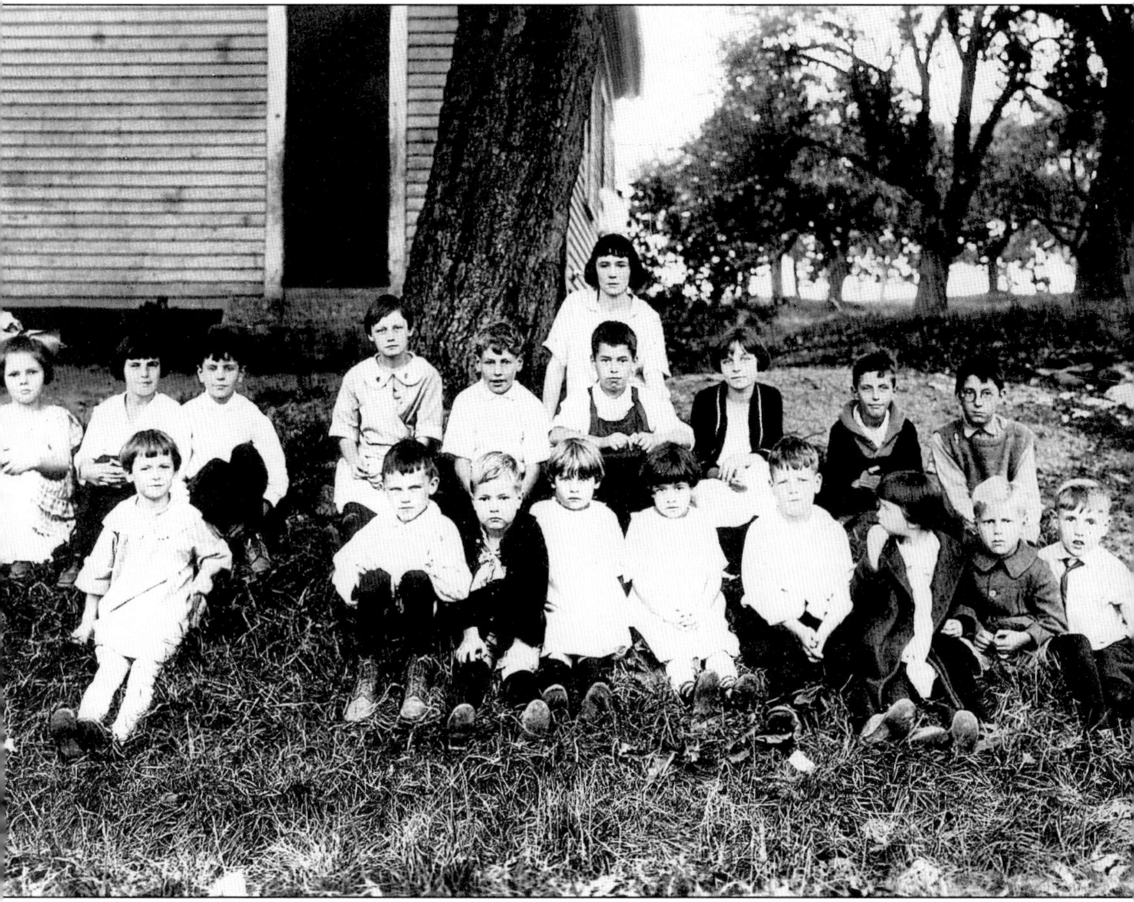

Teacher Annie Bryant's class poses outside School House No. 5. From left to right are the following: (front row) Althea Spinney, Frances Dixon, Roger Main, Helen Place, Phyllis Rogers, Lloyd Shapleigh, Estella Plaisted, Norman Main, and Martin Shapleigh; (back row) Alice Liebman, Helen Spinney, Newell Ordway, Eunice Junkins, Wilbur Place, Bernard Rogers, Evelyn Place, Raymond Mullen, and Harlon Plaisted. The very young Miss Bryant kneels behind her class. (Courtesy of the Estate of C. Edward Bartlett Jr.)

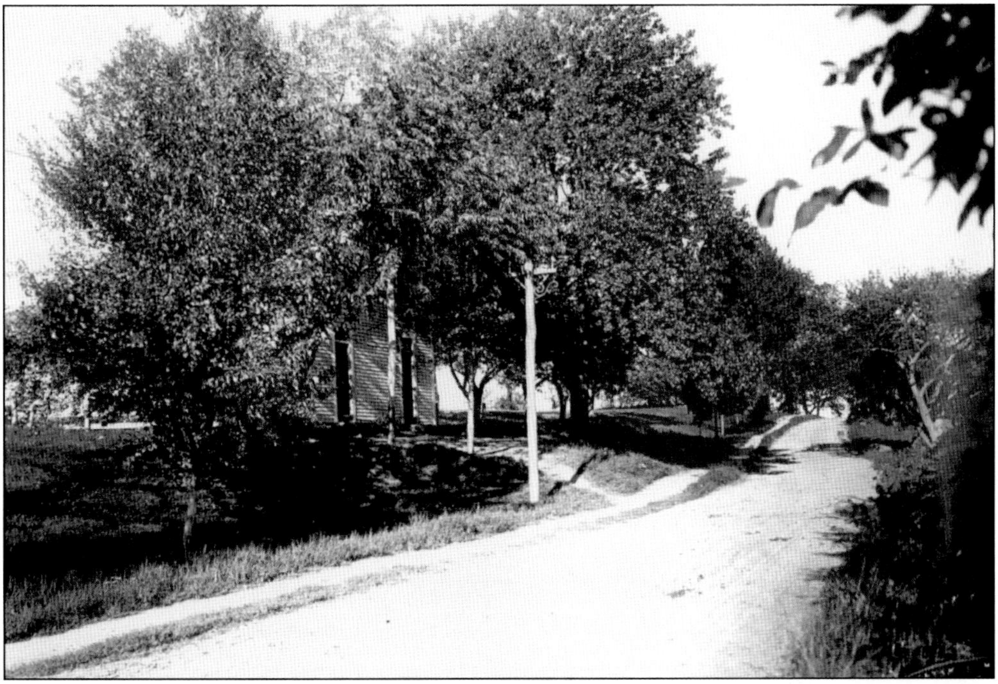

School House No. 5, on the corner of Pine Avenue and Old Road, was torn down around 1938. (Courtesy of the Gov. John F. Hill Collection at the William Fogg Library.)

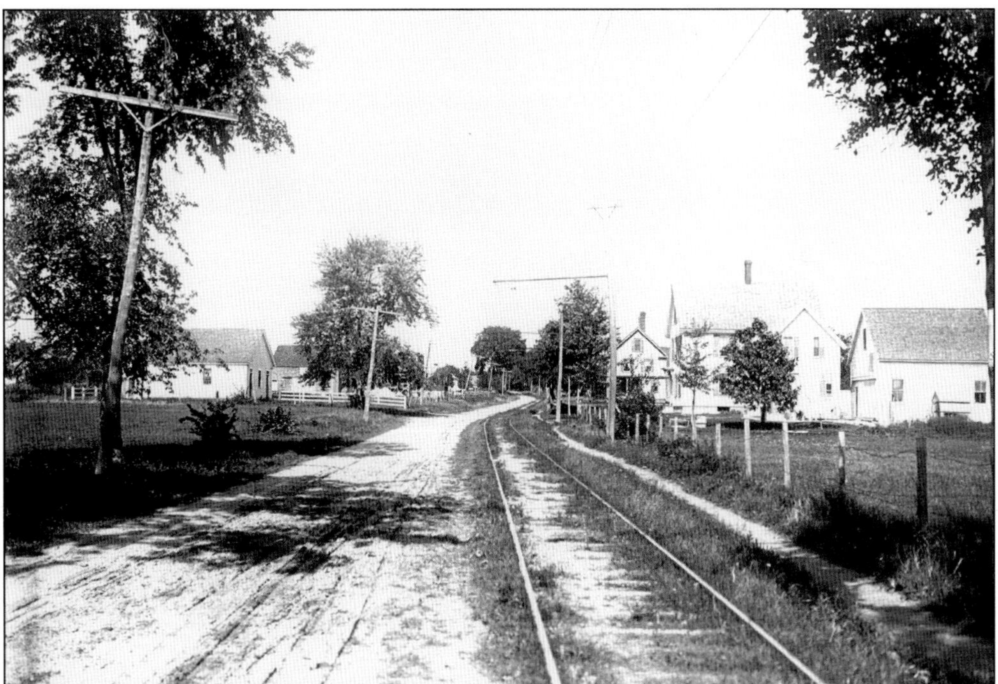

School House No. 6 (left), at the corner of Varney Lane and Main Street, closed around 1925 and was converted into a private home. (Courtesy of the Gov. John F. Hill Collection at the William Fogg Library.)

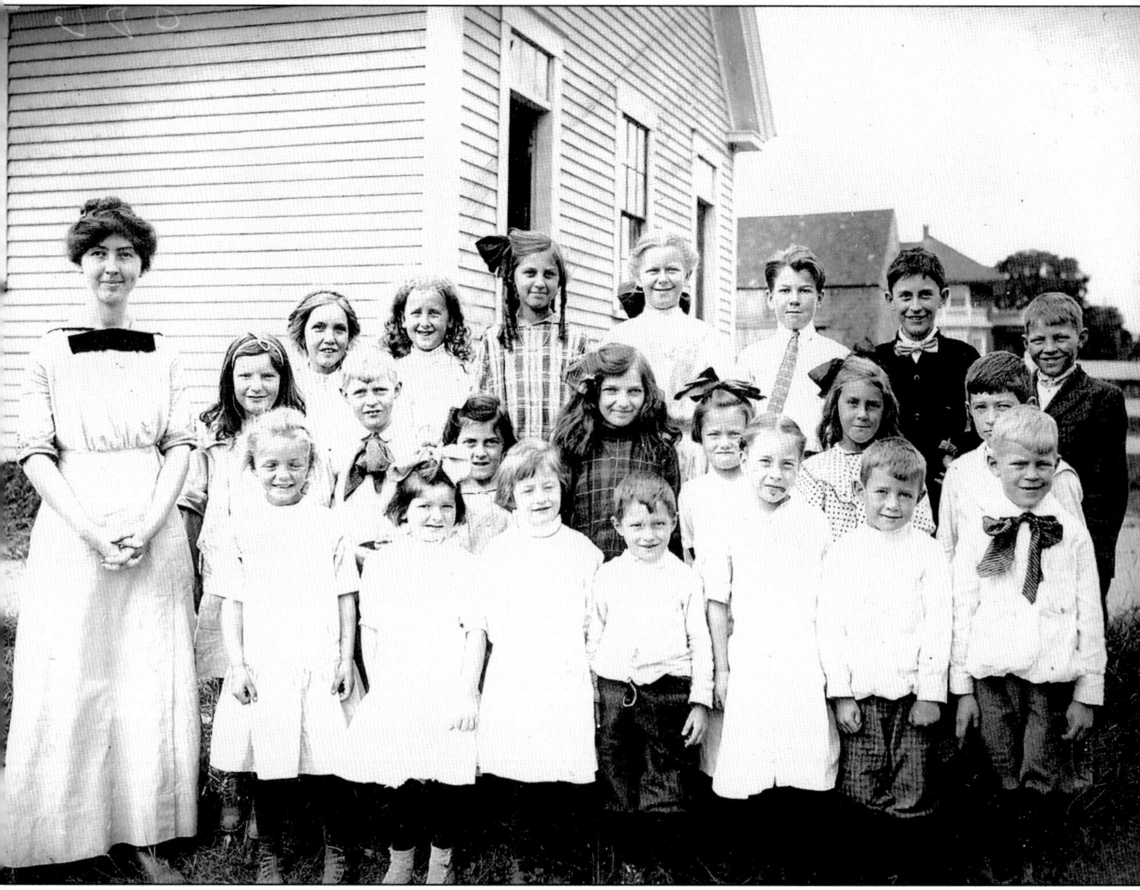

In this *c*. 1914 photograph, Miss Gove stands with her class at School House No. 6. From left to right are the following: (front row) Dagny Everson, Clara Menard, Evelyn Staples, Frank Staples, Vivian McKenny, Winfield Remick, and unidentified; (middle row) Eleanor Menard, Franklin Cole, Myra Paul, Phyllis Spinney, Isabell Remick, Alice Remick, and Linville Davis; (back row) Hilda Cole, Ada Levenseller, Phyllis York (Rowe), Dora Grover, Harvey Hill, Carl Fernald, and unidentified. (Courtesy of Jeanette Paul.)

School House No. 7, on Pleasant Street, was built in 1866. It is now a private home. (Courtesy of the Gov. John F. Hill Collection at the William Fogg Library.)

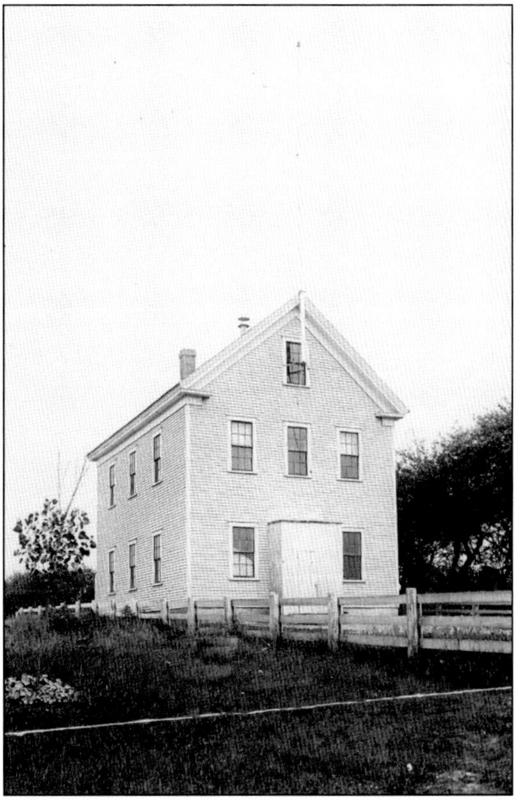

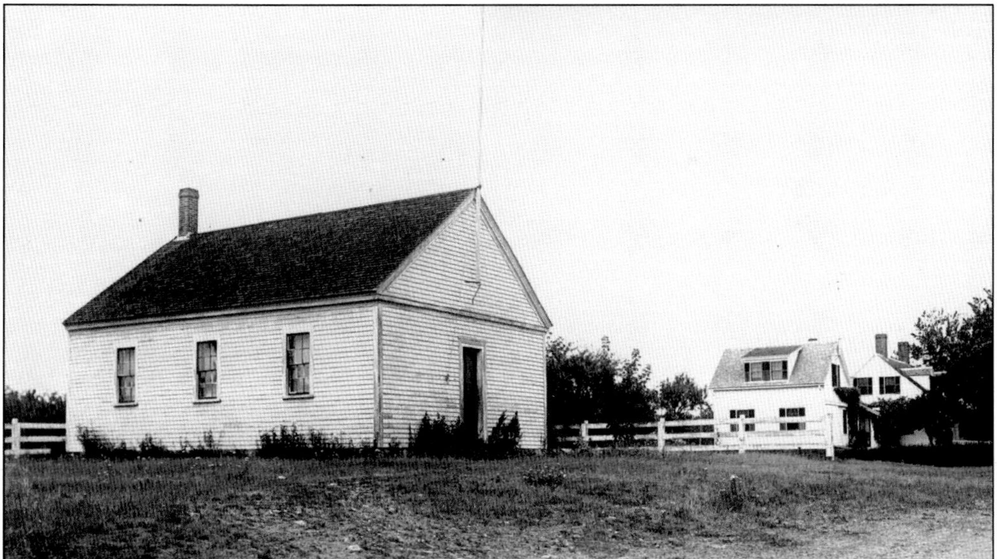

School District No. 8 was created in 1841 from parts of District Nos. 5 and 6. The Eliot Country Club, the fire department, and the Mount Pleasant Cemetery Association used the building at various times after School House No. 8, on Greenwood Street, closed. Today the Eliot Historical Society is in the process of restoring the building. (Courtesy of the Gov. John F. Hill Collection at the William Fogg Library.)

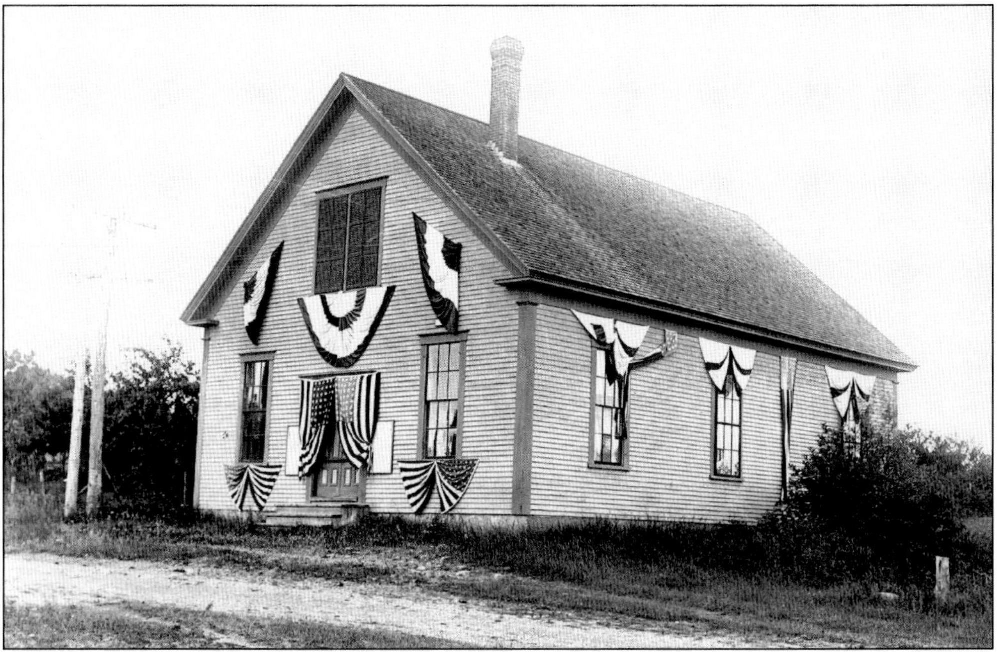

Built in 1880, the grammar school on State Road stood across from the present Eliot Elementary School. The grammar school eventually served as a town hall, before it was torn down in 1970. (Courtesy of the Carlton and Doris Grover Collection at the William Fogg Library.)

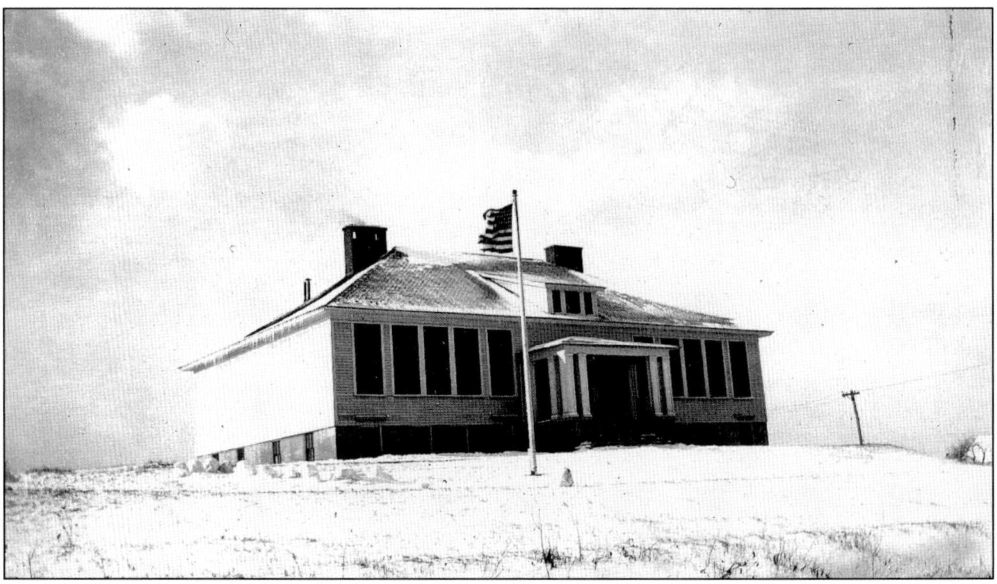

The Laura V. Dame School, on Main Street, was built in 1925 to replace several smaller schools in South Eliot. Laura V. Dame taught in Eliot for many years. The school closed around 1966 and was converted to apartments. This photograph was taken in 1927. (Courtesy of Jeanette Paul.)

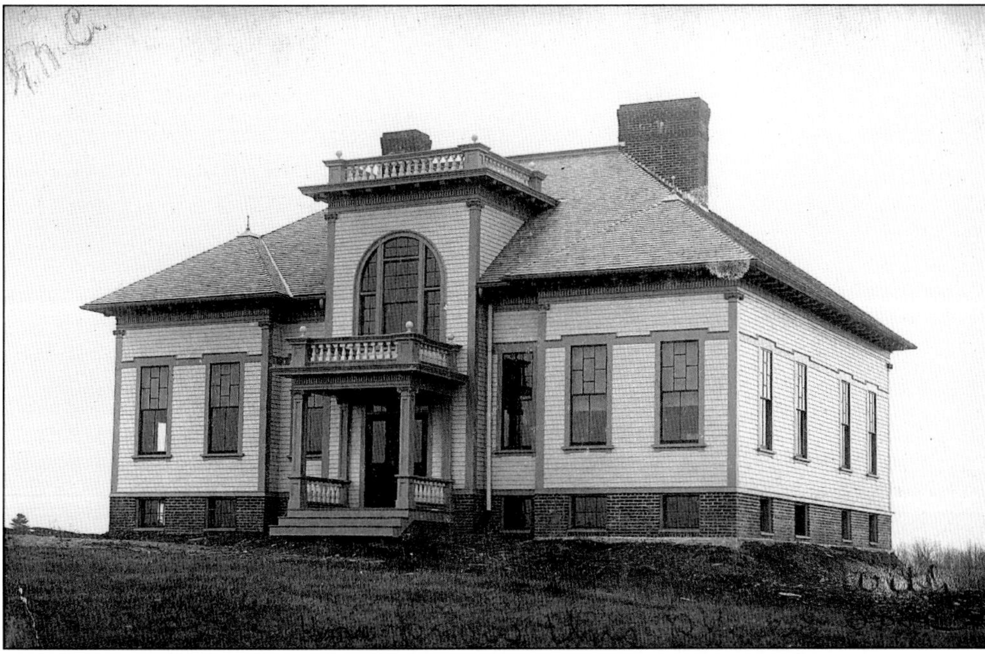

Eliot High School, also known as the Central School, operated from 1906 until 1940, when a new junior-senior high school was built across the street. The building stood in the vicinity of the present town hall. It remained in use by the school department until July 1963, when the fire marshal closed it. Later, it reopened as a town office and police station until it was torn down in August 1987. (Courtesy of Jeanette Paul.)

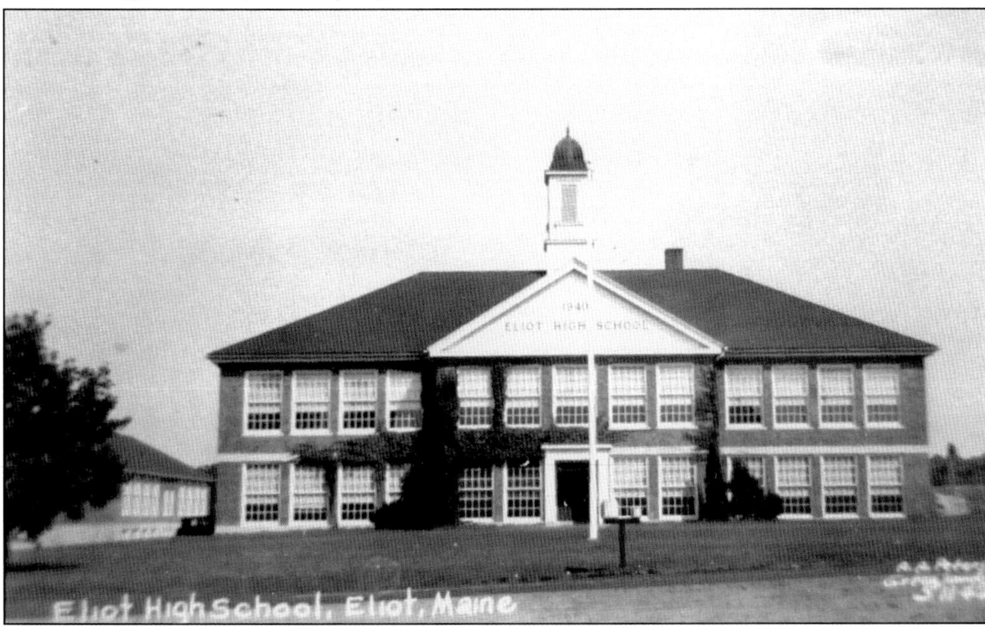

Built in 1940, the new Eliot High School housed both junior and senior high schools. In the 1950s, a primary school was built on the west side of the high school. In 1956, a gymnasium, which joined the two buildings, was built. The entire complex became Eliot Elementary School in 1966. (Courtesy of the Eliot Historical Society.)

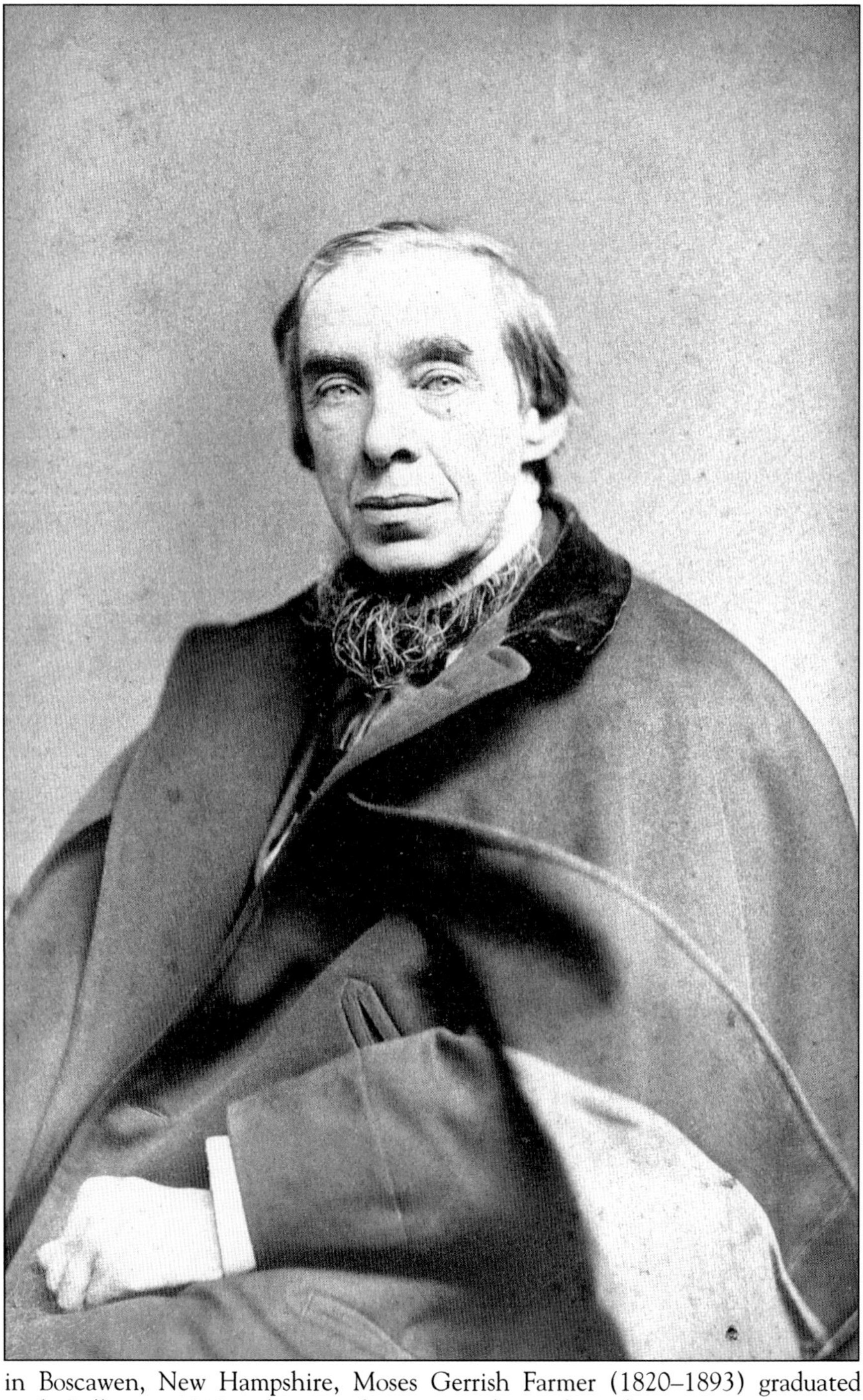

Born in Boscawen, New Hampshire, Moses Gerrish Farmer (1820–1893) graduated from Dartmouth College in 1840 and received a master's degree from the same institution in 1853. Inventor of the Boston Fire Alarm, electric streetcar, and many other innovations, he was at one time the principal of Eliot Academy. He taught electrical science at the United States Torpedo Station at Newport, Rhode Island. In 1882, he retired and returned to Eliot. (Courtesy of the Estate of C. Edward Bartlett Jr.)

Seven

NOTABLE CITIZENS

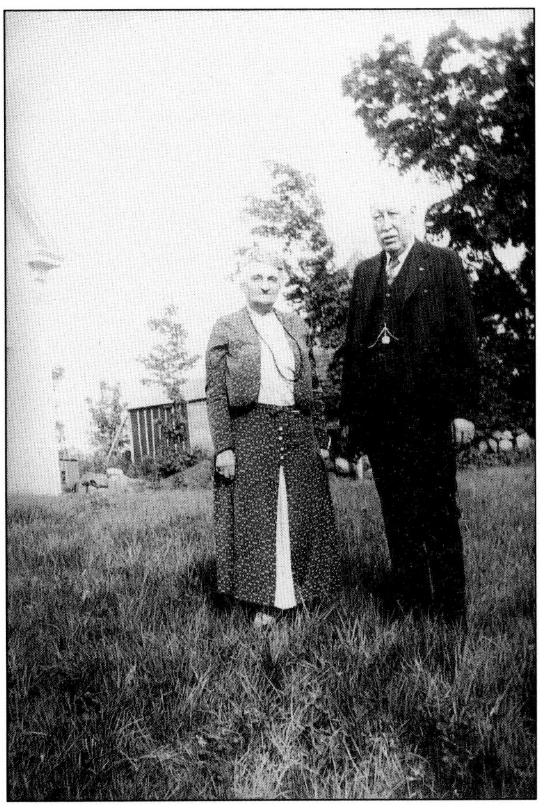

Dr. Henry I. Durgin began practicing medicine in Eliot soon after graduating from the University of New York City medical department in 1889. Born in Freedom, New Hampshire, in 1864, he attended the New Hampshire Literary Institute. He married Alta Moulton on December 3, 1890. Dr. Durgin served on many town committees. At one time, he was also the superintendent of schools. (Courtesy of the Estate of C. Edward Bartlett Jr.)

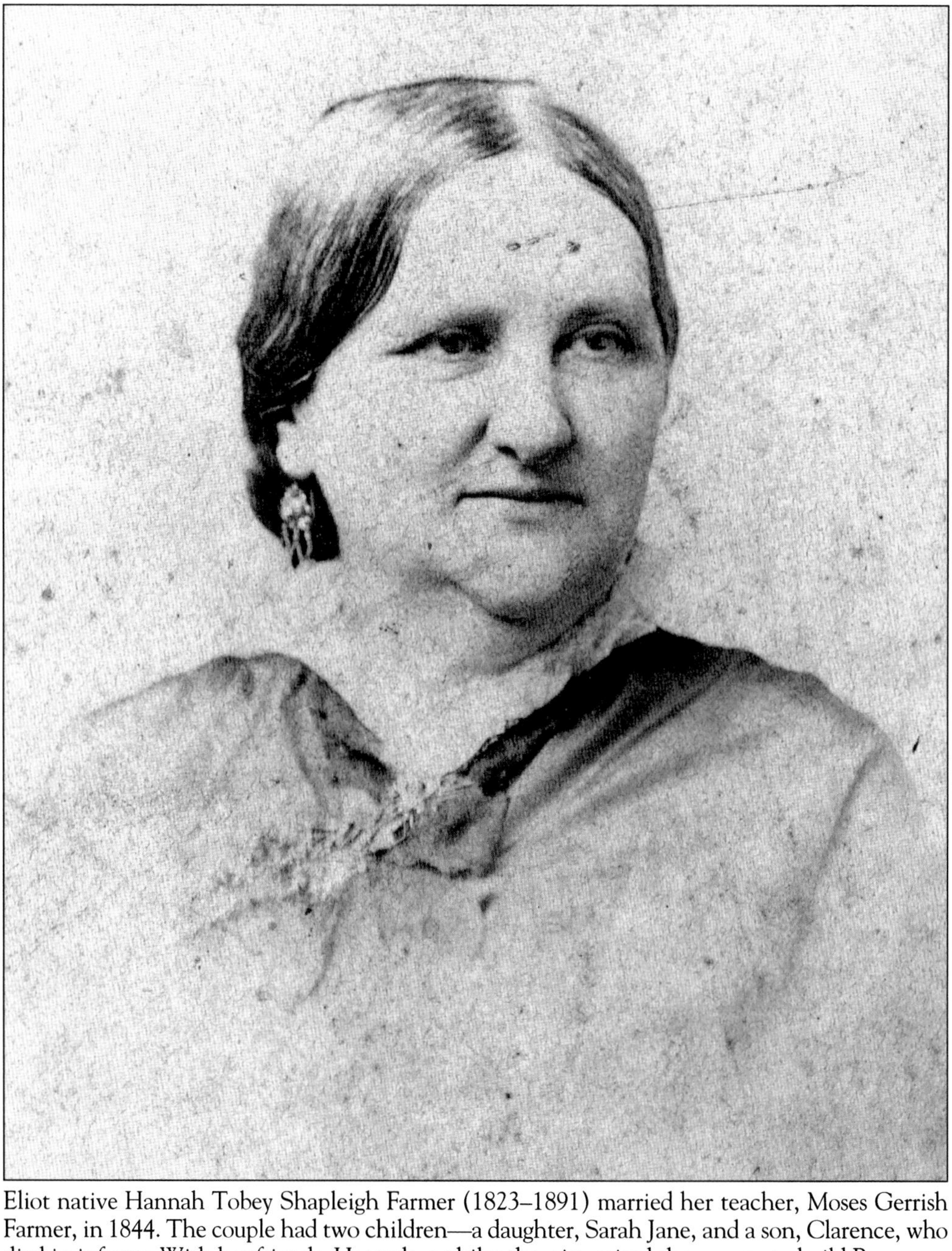

Eliot native Hannah Tobey Shapleigh Farmer (1823–1891) married her teacher, Moses Gerrish Farmer, in 1844. The couple had two children—a daughter, Sarah Jane, and a son, Clarence, who died in infancy. With her friends, Hannah, a philanthropist, raised the money to build Rosemary Cottage (1888), a respite for underprivileged mothers and their children. Hannah dedicated this endeavor to the memory of her son. (Courtesy of the Estate of C. Edward Bartlett Jr.)

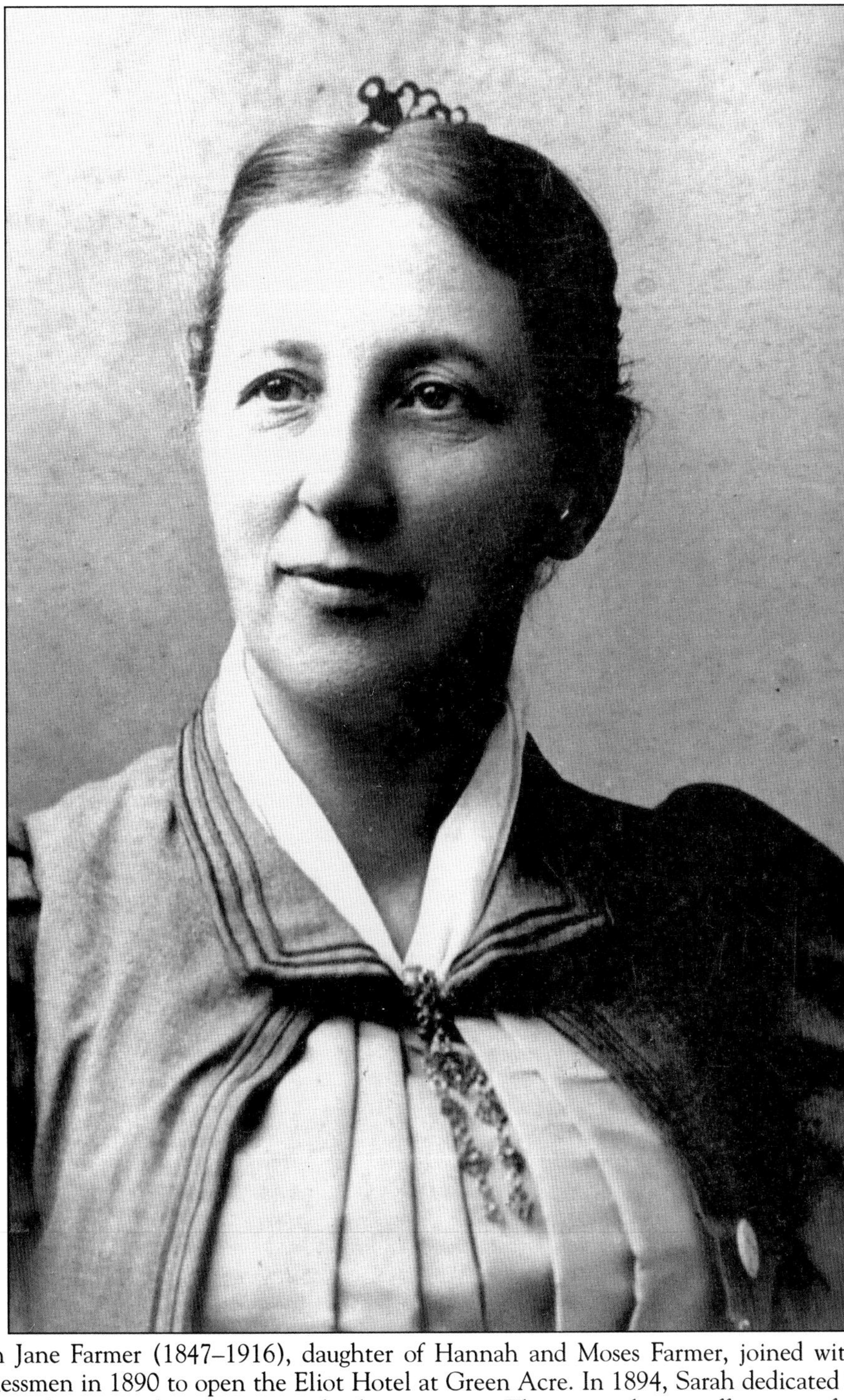

Sarah Jane Farmer (1847–1916), daughter of Hannah and Moses Farmer, joined with four businessmen in 1890 to open the Eliot Hotel at Green Acre. In 1894, Sarah dedicated Green Acre to the principles of peace and religious unity. The center began offering conferences on the sciences, arts, and religion. Farmer was the lone woman to witness the signing of the Russo-Japanese Peace Treaty at the Portsmouth Naval Shipyard in 1905. (Courtesy of the Eliot Baha'i Archives.)

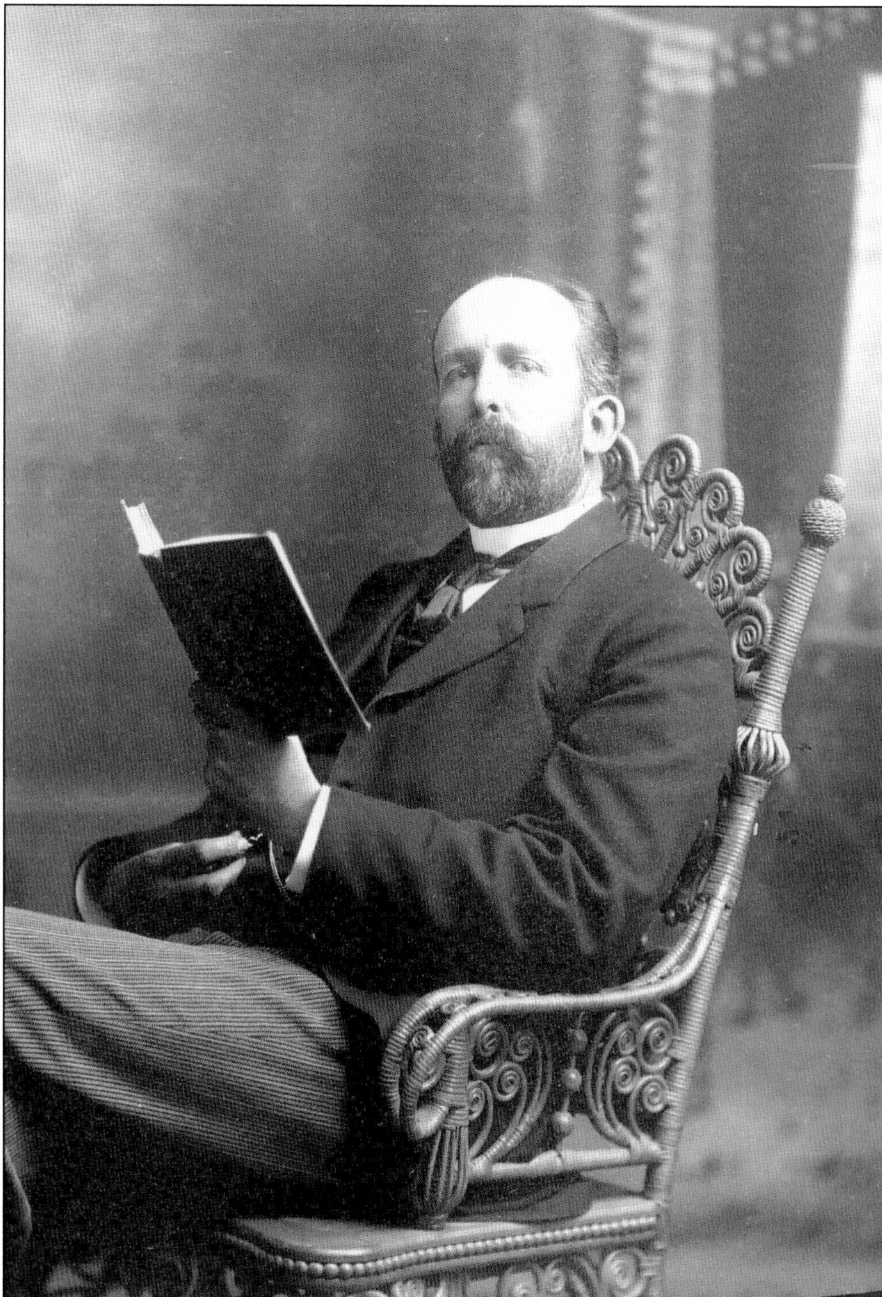

Dr. John L. M. Willis (1856–1924) practiced medicine for 50 years. He was the founder (February 8, 1897) and first president of the Eliot Historical Society. Educated at Eliot and Berwick Academies, he had a medical degree from Bowdoin. Willis also studied at New York University, becoming a doctor in 1877. His belief that the preservation of historical records was important for future generations led him to produce nine volumes of the magazine *Old Eliot*. Instrumental in planning the Eliot centennial celebration in 1910, Willis edited the event's resulting book, *History of the Centennial of the Incorporation of the Town of Eliot, Maine. August 7th–13th, 1910*. (Courtesy of the Paul Family Association.)

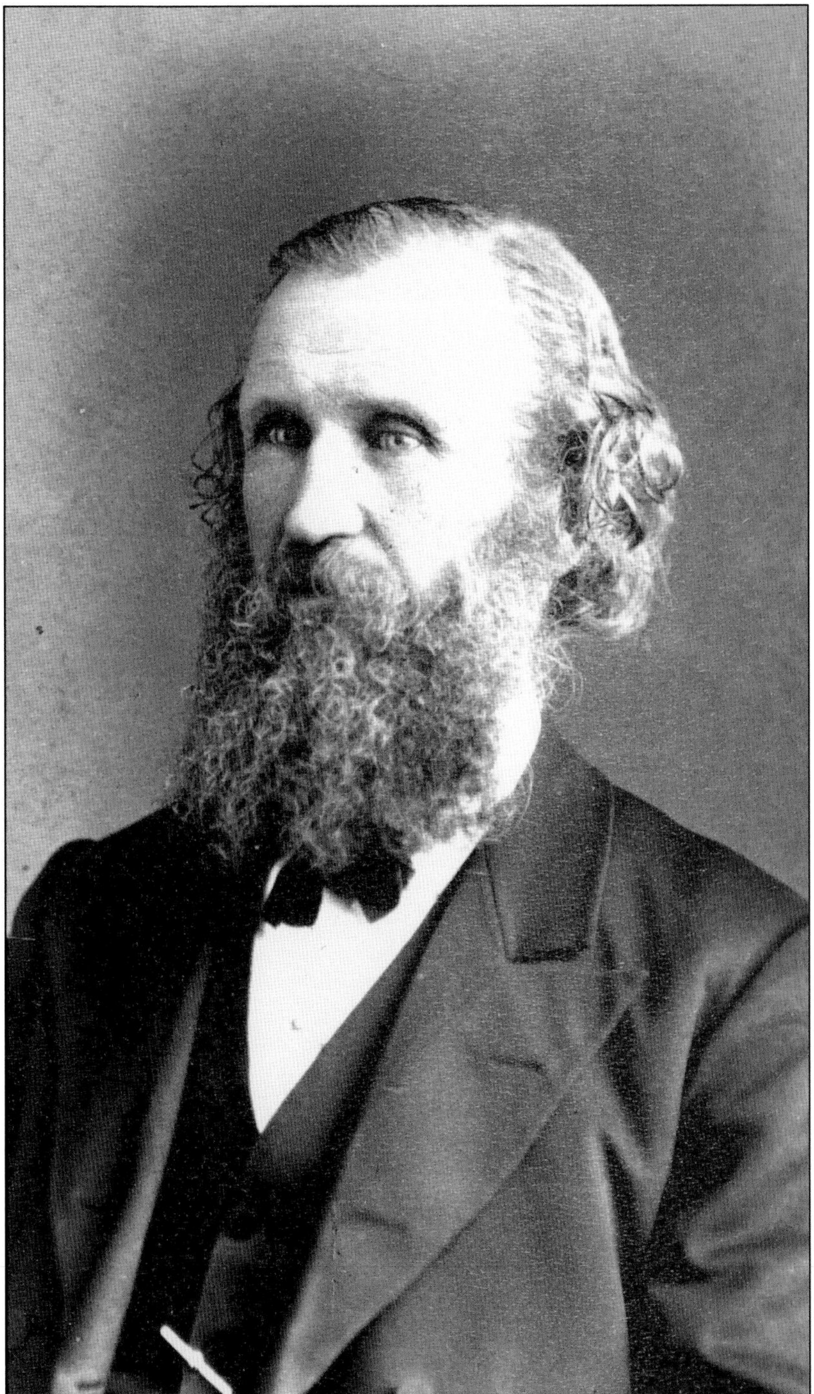

Farmer Sylvester Bartlett (1822–1901) proved to be a man of many talents. He sang, played a clarinet in his church choir, and wrote poetry for his church newspaper (the *Eliot Epworthian*) and for New York newspapers. From 1895 to 1896, he represented Eliot in the Maine legislature. (Courtesy of the Estate of C. Edward Bartlett Jr.)

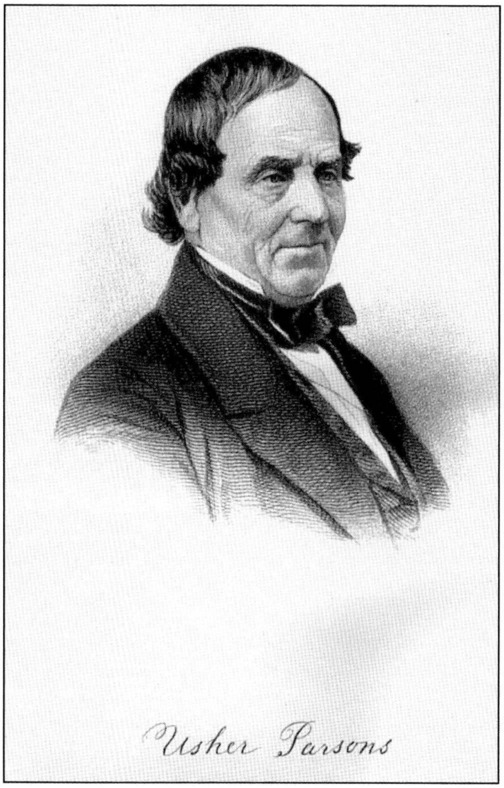

At one time, Usher Parsons (1788–1868) taught at Eliot School House No. 4. Because he had such a burning desire to become a physician, he walked from Alfred to Portland, and then to Boston, in search of a medical doctor who would mentor him. Parsons was the brother-in-law of Dr. Oliver Wendell Holmes and a surgeon at the Battle of Lake Erie in 1812. (*Memoir of Usher Parsons, M.D.*, courtesy of Joseph W. P. Frost.)

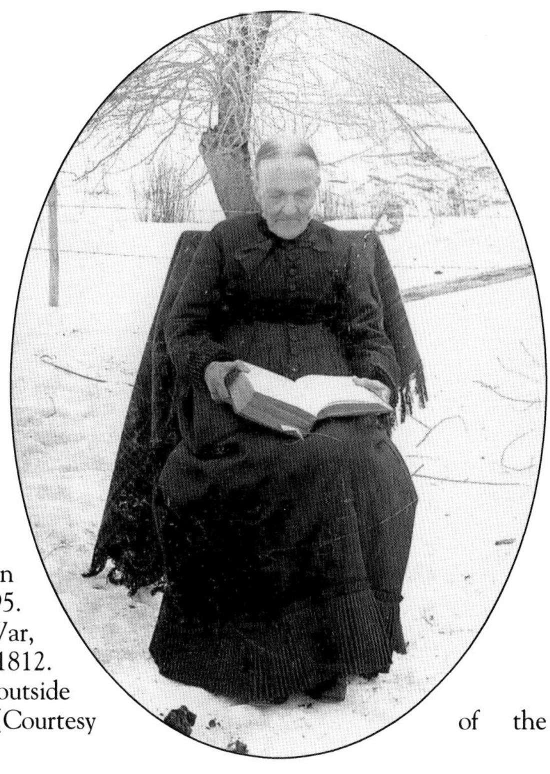

This photograph of Thirsa Emery was taken on her 100th birthday on March 12, 1895. Her father fought in the Revolutionary War, and her two brothers fought in the War of 1812. She must have been a hardy soul, sitting outside in the March snow. She lived to be 103. (Courtesy of the Paul Family Association.)

No one would ever call this lovely lady an old maid, but indeed, she never married. Annie E. Raitt was the daughter from the third marriage of Jefferson Raitt. A very self-sufficient woman, she maintained the old homestead. She lived her entire life in the home where she was born until she entered a nursing home. (Courtesy of the Estate of C. Edward Bartlett Jr.)

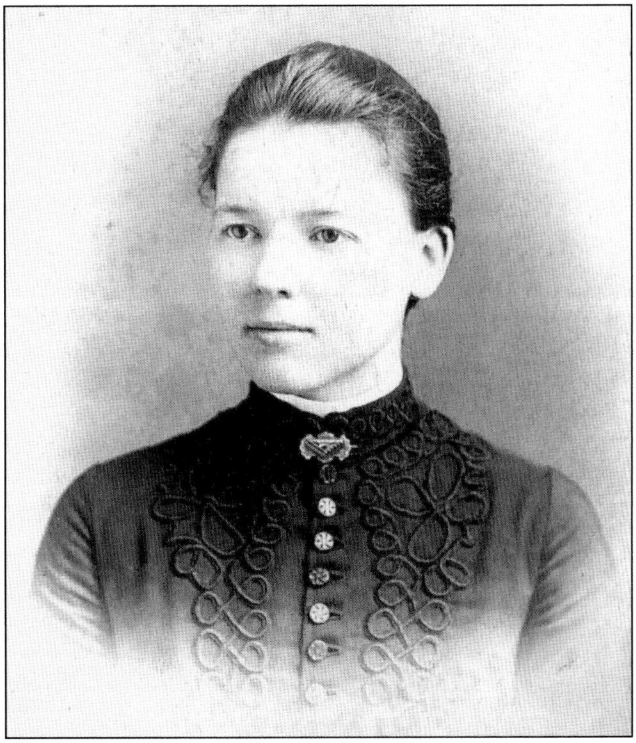

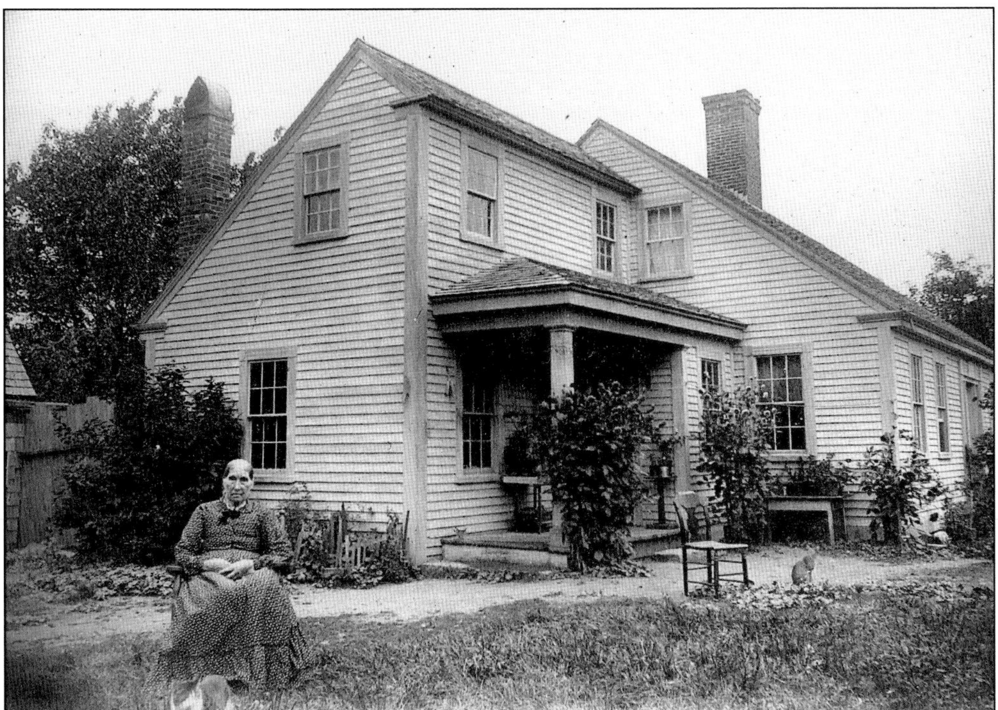

Eliot Frost, the father of Rachel Frost Fernald (pictured here), fought in the American Revolution. (Courtesy of the Paul Family Association.)

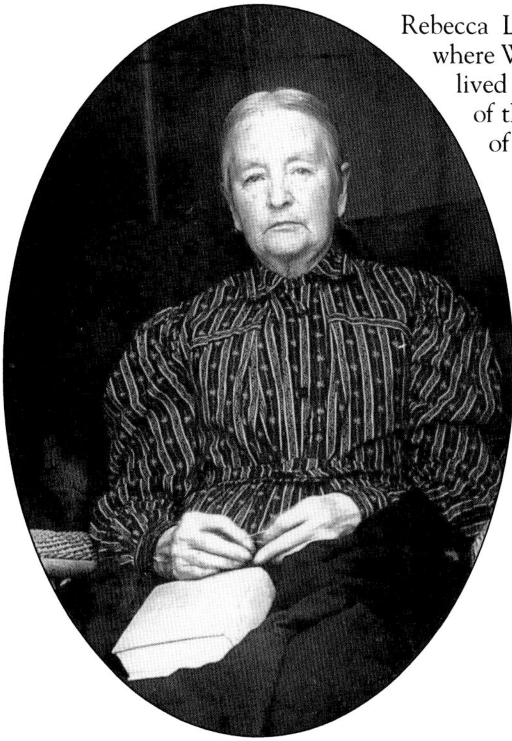

Rebecca Leighton Hammond resided on River Road where William Everett's tavern once stood. When she lived on the property, one could still see the marks of the tavern's cellar in her front yard. (Courtesy of the Paul Family Association.)

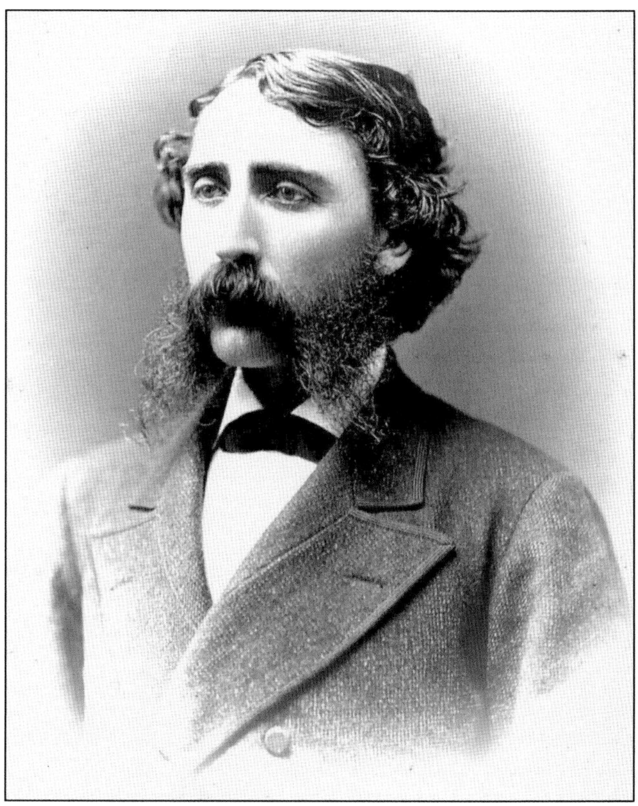

Eliot native Dr. George Melville Frost (1843–1898) traveled far from Eliot in his lifetime. Son of Joshua and Catherine Frost, he received his degree from the Medical School of Maine in 1869. He moved to Peabody, Massachusetts, gaining celebrity for his work during a smallpox epidemic there. Later, he worked in London hospitals. (Courtesy of the Paul Family Association.)

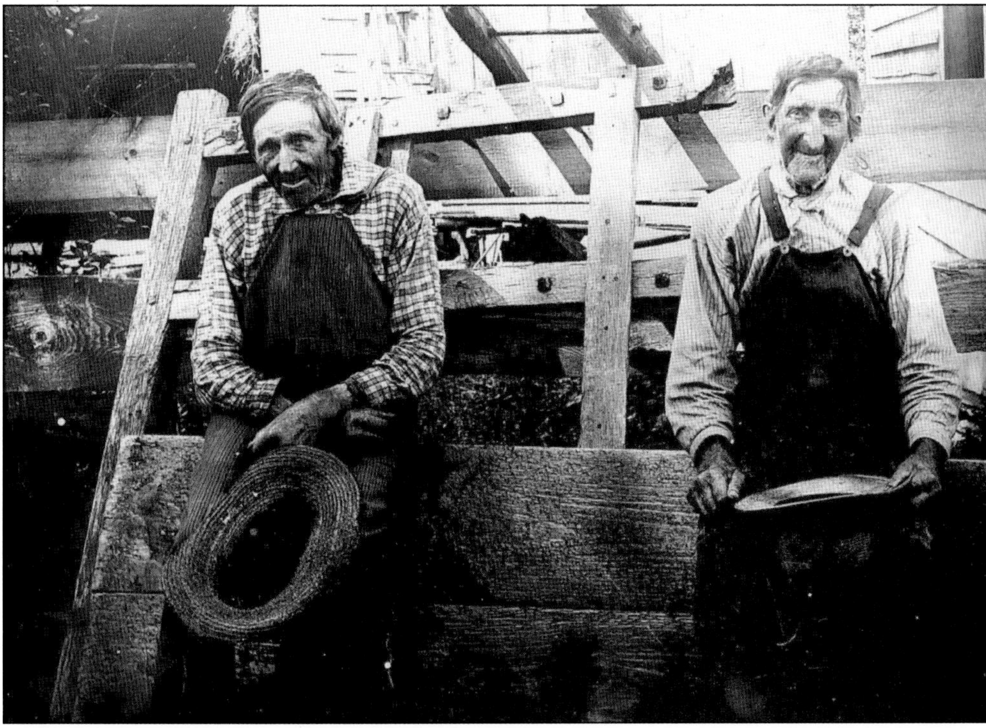

Brothers Ivory and James Gould were the youngest sons of Alexander Gould. The brothers remained bachelors and lived together at Gould's Corner. Ivory died in 1896 at the age of 87. James was still alive in 1903. (Courtesy of the Paul Family Association.)

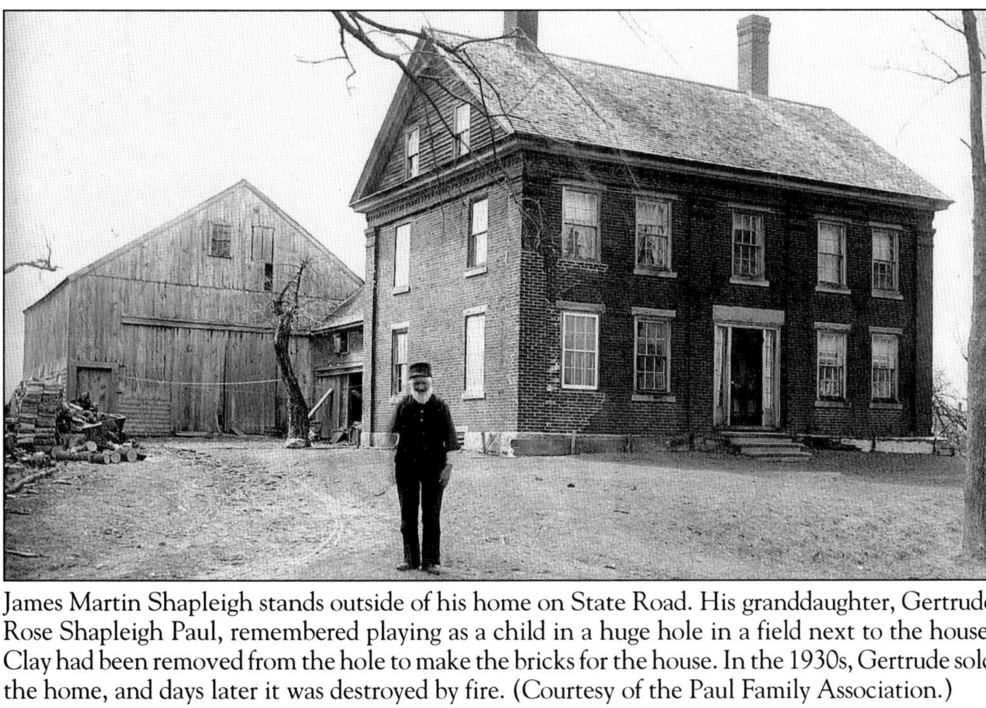

James Martin Shapleigh stands outside of his home on State Road. His granddaughter, Gertrude Rose Shapleigh Paul, remembered playing as a child in a huge hole in a field next to the house. Clay had been removed from the hole to make the bricks for the house. In the 1930s, Gertrude sold the home, and days later it was destroyed by fire. (Courtesy of the Paul Family Association.)

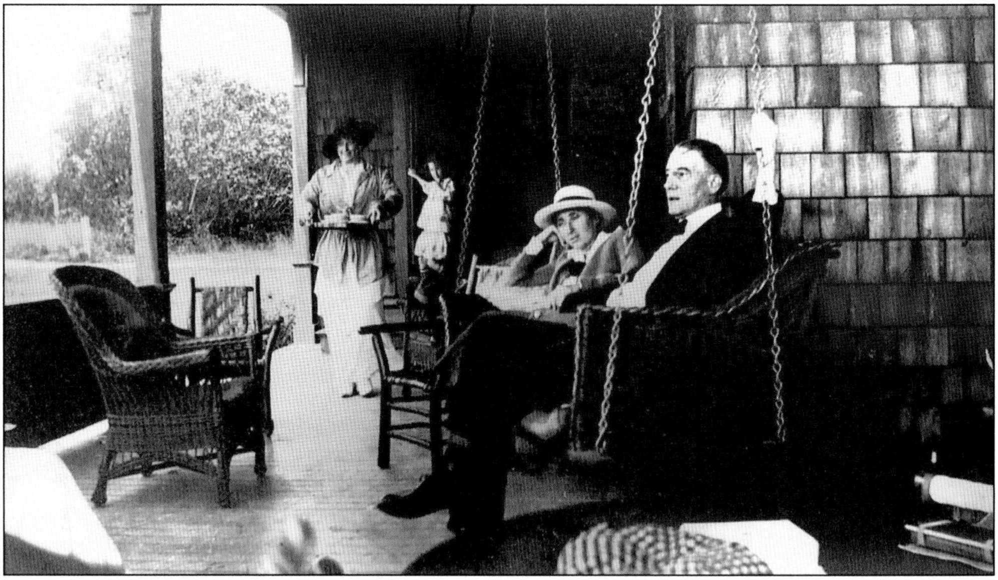

Ruth and William H. Randall were early supporters of Eliot's Baha'i community. William owned a steamer line and was involved in the shipping business. Ruth was the hostess of the Golden Cock Tea House and Gift Shop at Rogers Cottage near Green Acre. (Courtesy of the Eliot Baha'i Archives.)

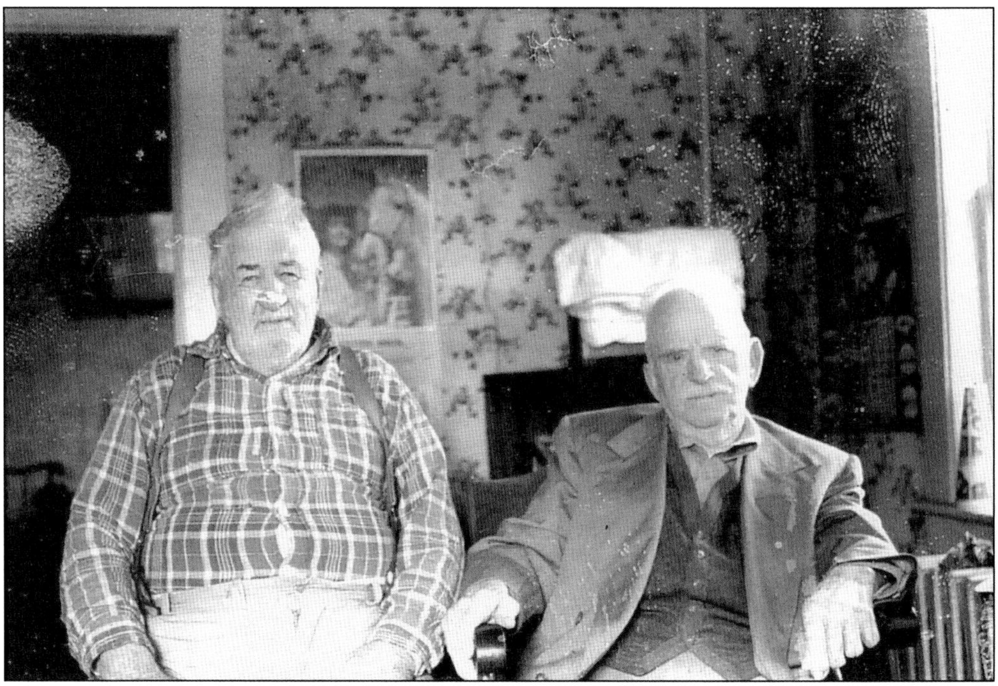

Bertram Tuttle (left) sits with his good friend, Mr. Emery. Tuttle was the founder of Tuttle's Cider Mill. (Courtesy of Kenneth Tuttle.)

Maurice Foss was a longtime principal of Eliot High School. This photograph was taken in 1932. (Courtesy of Jeanette Paul.)

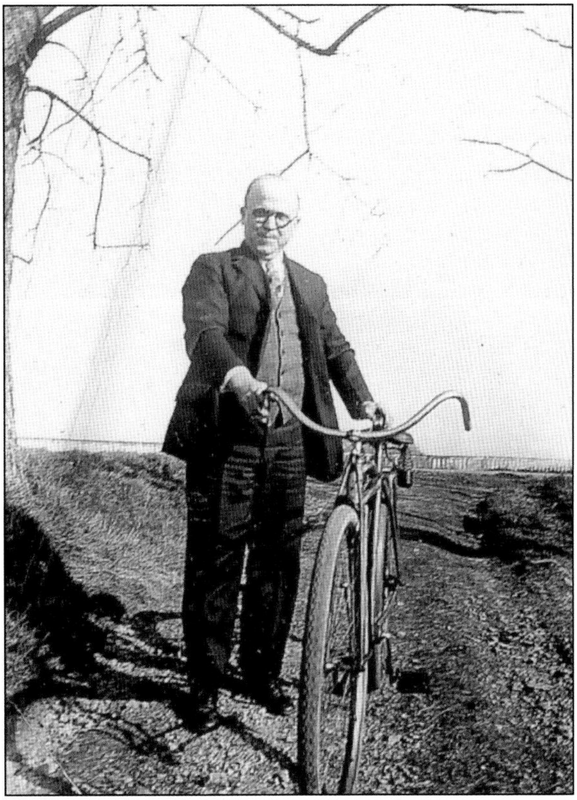

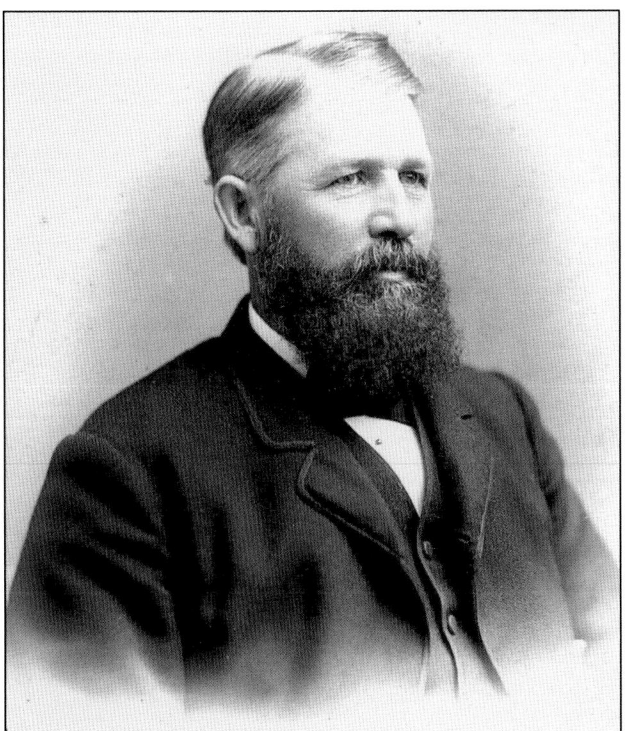

In 1887, Samuel Clark of the Clark Brickyard sold over a half-million bricks for the construction of a new factory in Dover, New Hampshire. (Courtesy of the Estate of C. Edward Bartlett Jr.)

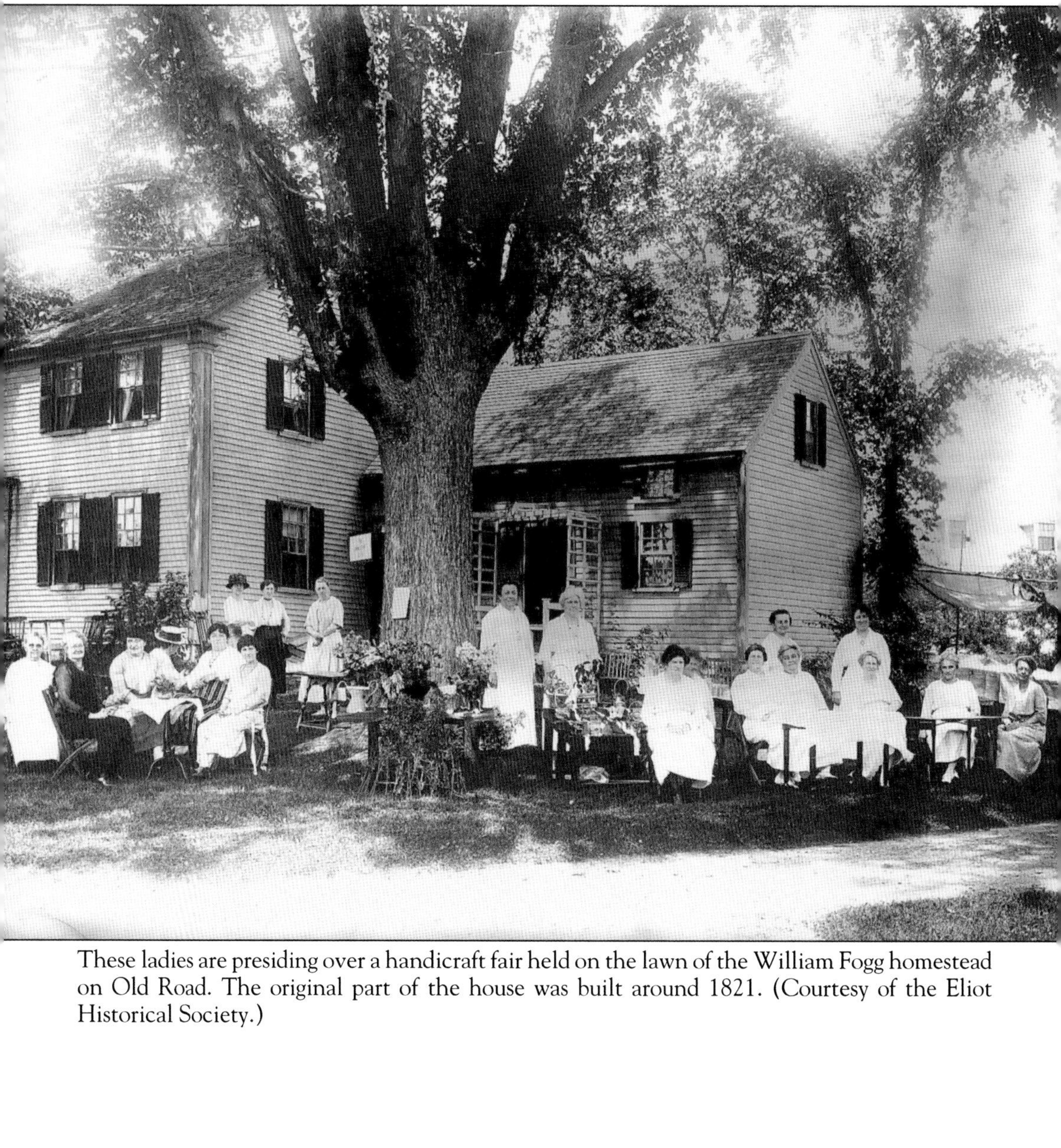

These ladies are presiding over a handicraft fair held on the lawn of the William Fogg homestead on Old Road. The original part of the house was built around 1821. (Courtesy of the Eliot Historical Society.)

Eight

Leisure Activities

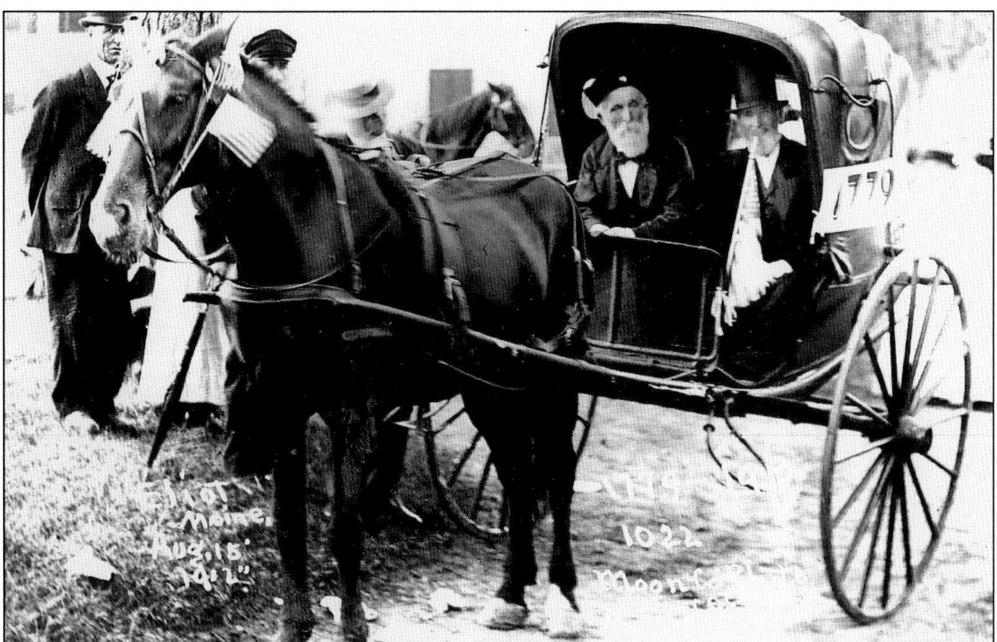

In August 1912, Eliot celebrated Old Home Week. Charles Hanscom (left) and John Shapleigh rode in the parade. (Courtesy of Kenneth Tuttle.)

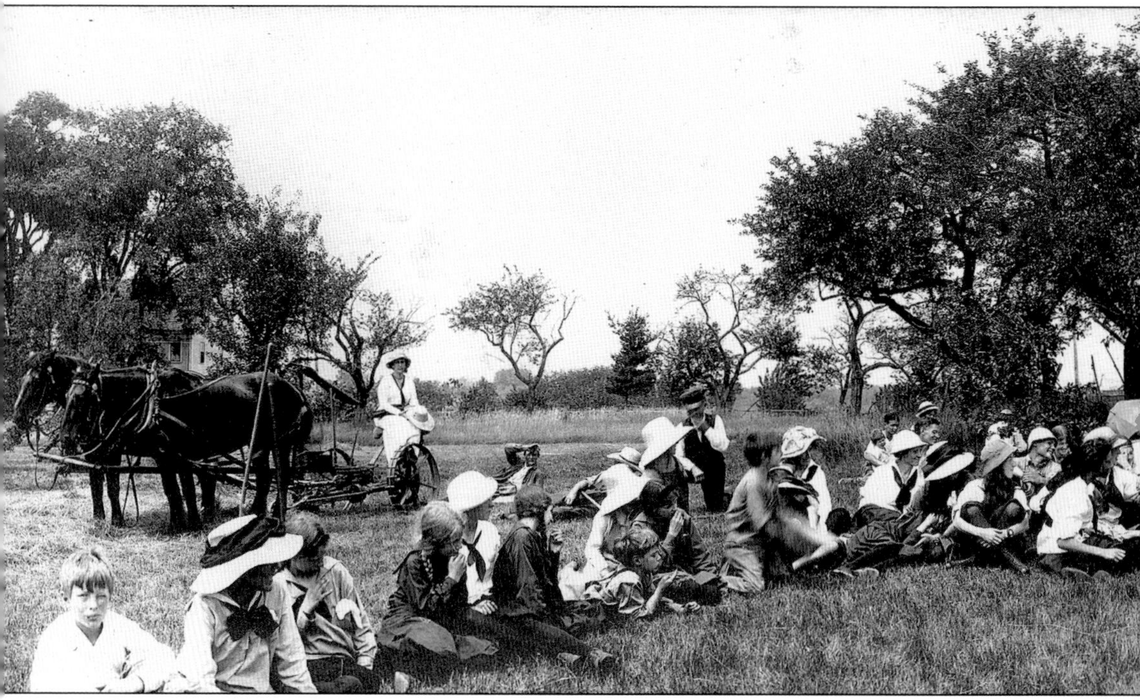

Sidney Lanier Jr. and his wife, Elizabeth, founded one of the first coeducational children's camps in the country. Mr. Lanier was the son of Southern poet Sidney Lanier. The camp ran from 1908 until 1939. In this rare photograph, Elizabeth sits behind the horses on the left. Sidney

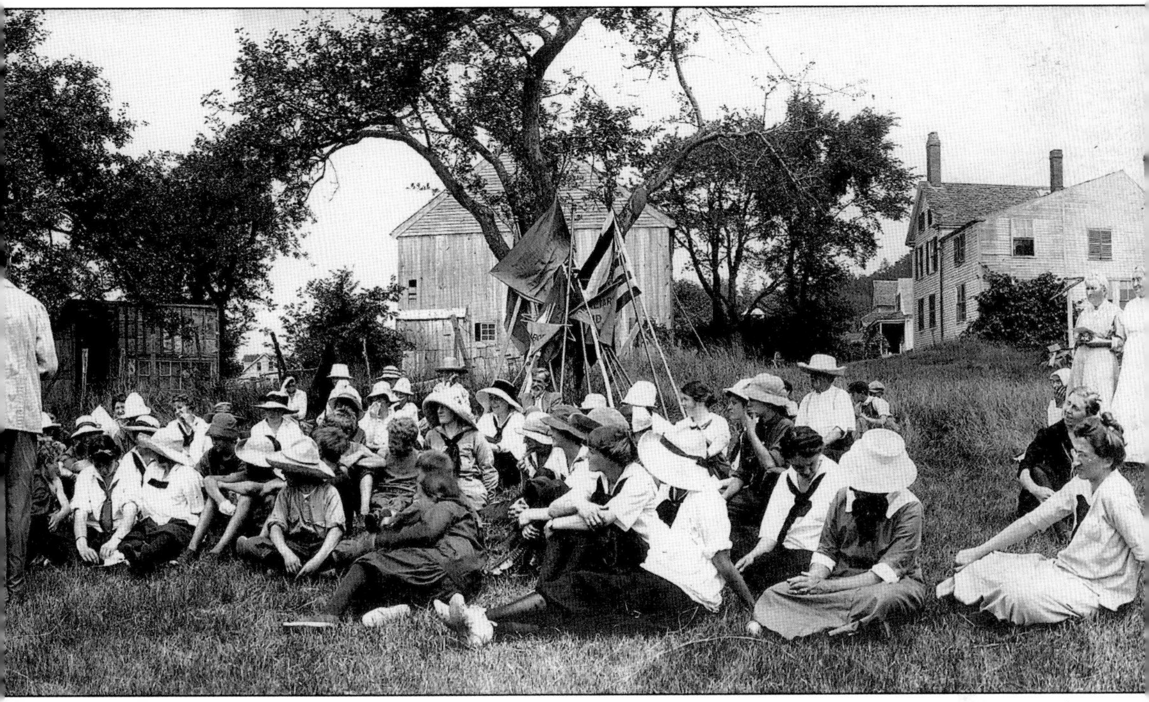

Lanier Jr. is the man in the center with his back to the camera. The hired hands, nannies, and other staff resided in the large house on the right, the Plasterboard House. The house no longer exists. (Courtesy of Dr. and Mrs. William Gilbert.)

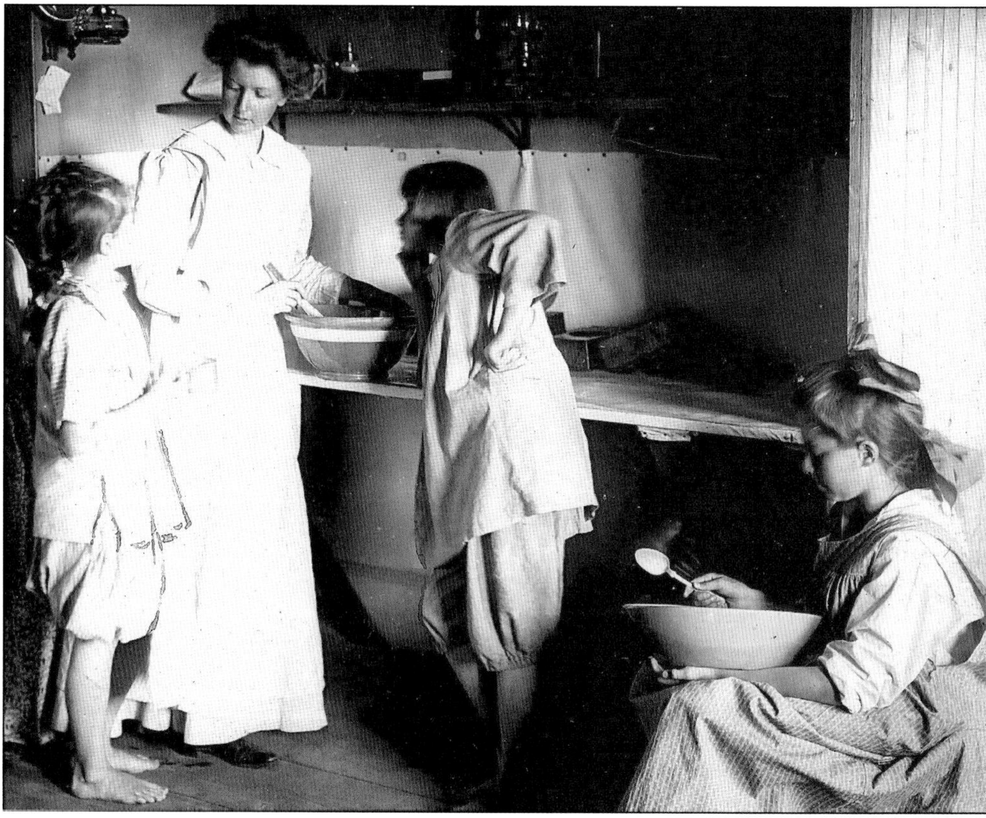

In the Lanier Camps' practice kitchen, girls learn how to prepare meals. A large portion of the camp's bread supply was made here. Female campers ranged in age from 8 to 20 years. This photograph was taken before 1910. (Courtesy of Dr. and Mrs. William Gilbert.)

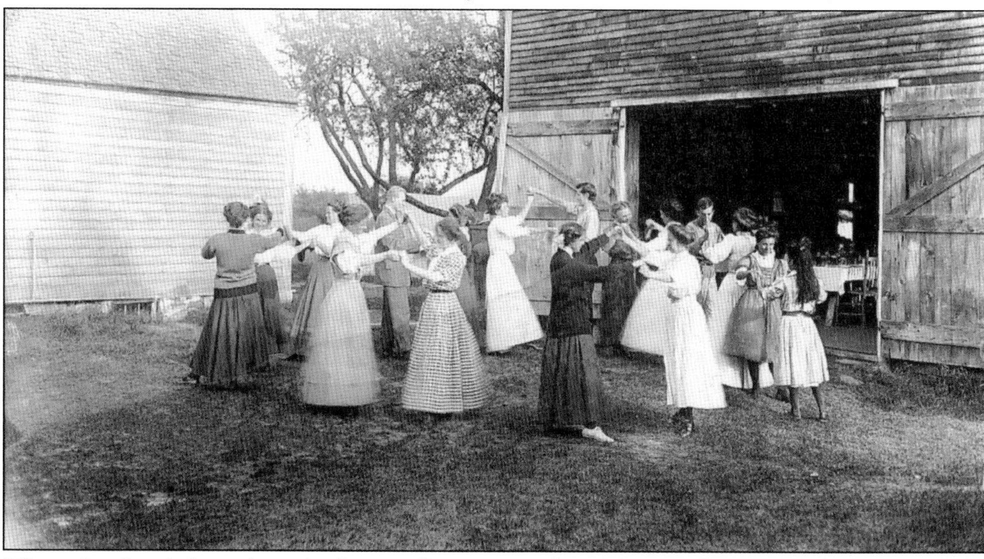

When the Swedish cook at the Lanier Camps introduced Morris dancing to the campers, she was one of the first to do so in the United States before 1909. The folk dancers pictured here are outside the camp's dining room. (Courtesy of Dr. and Mrs. William Gilbert.)

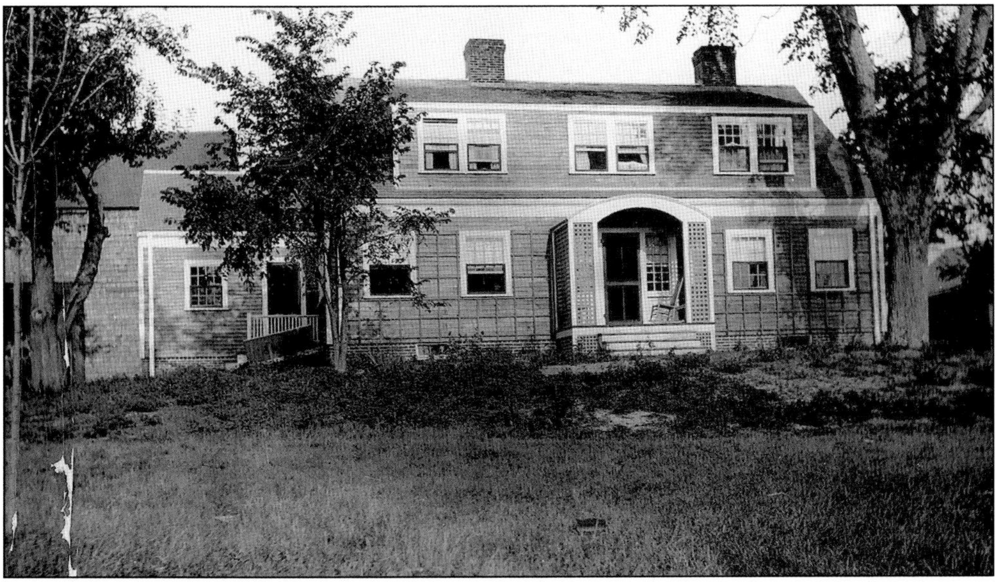

In 1913, Elizabeth and Sidney Lanier Jr. built the Lanier Inn on River Road. The location was once the site of William Everett's tavern. Visiting parents of children at the Lanier Camps stayed in this building. The camp was one of the first coeducational camps for children in the country and was in operation from 1908 to 1939. The property remained in the Lanier family until 1978. (Courtesy of Dr. and Mrs. William Gilbert.)

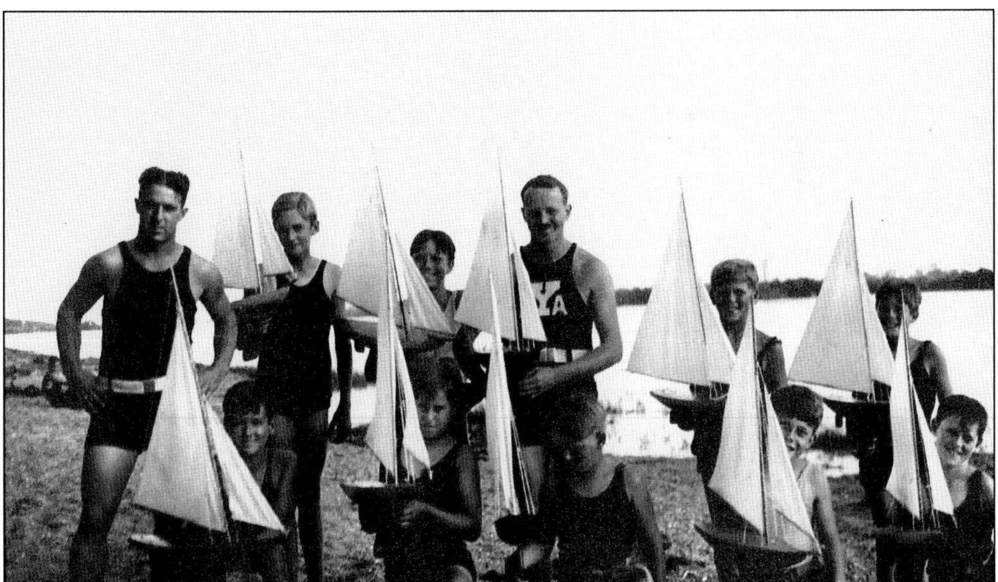

These young men are about to launch their sailboats in the Piscataqua River. They made the boats at the Lanier Camps. Male campers ranged in age from 8 to 14 years. (Courtesy of Dr. and Mrs. William Gilbert.)

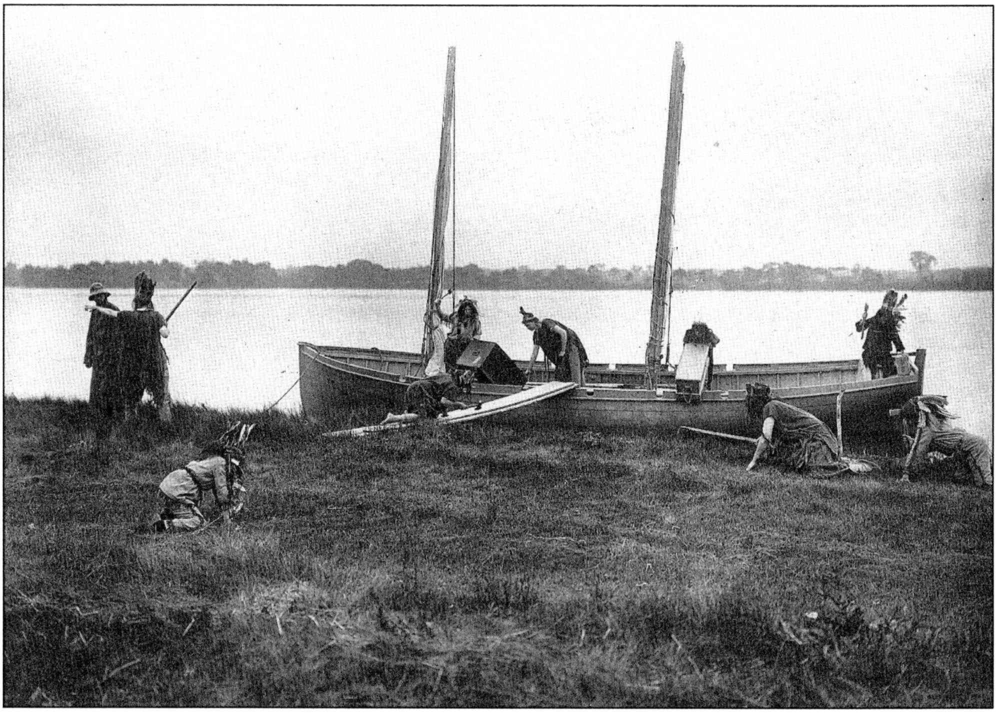

Pageants became part of the Lanier Camps experience. Here are two scenes from a typical dramatic presentation performed by the campers. (Courtesy of the Paul Family Association.)

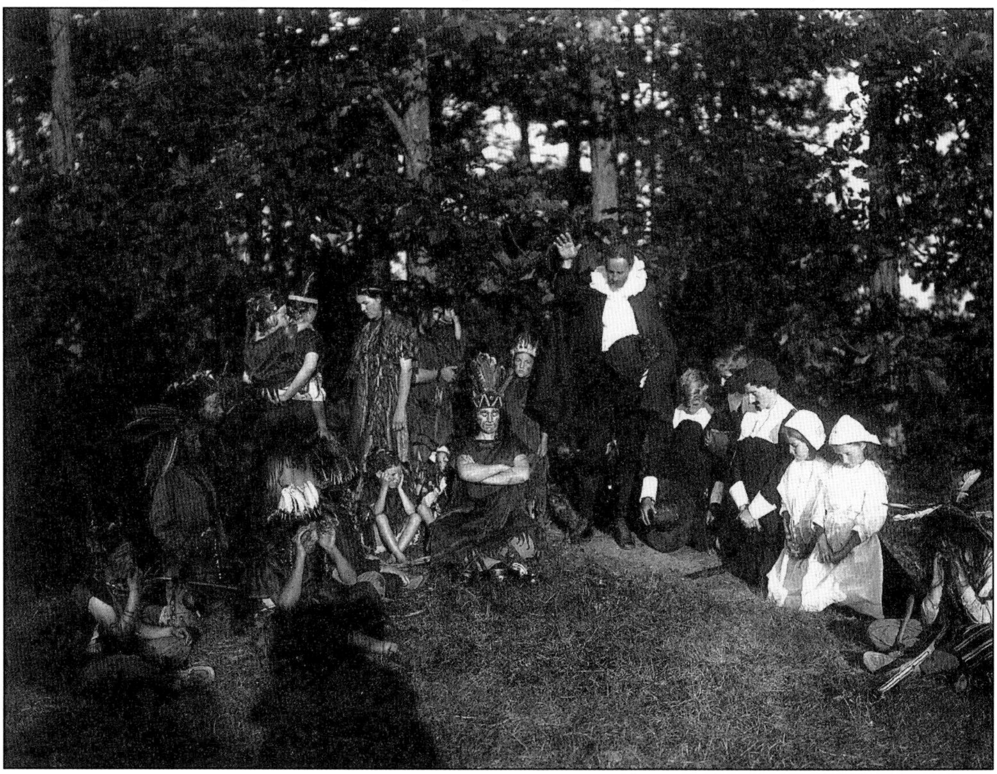

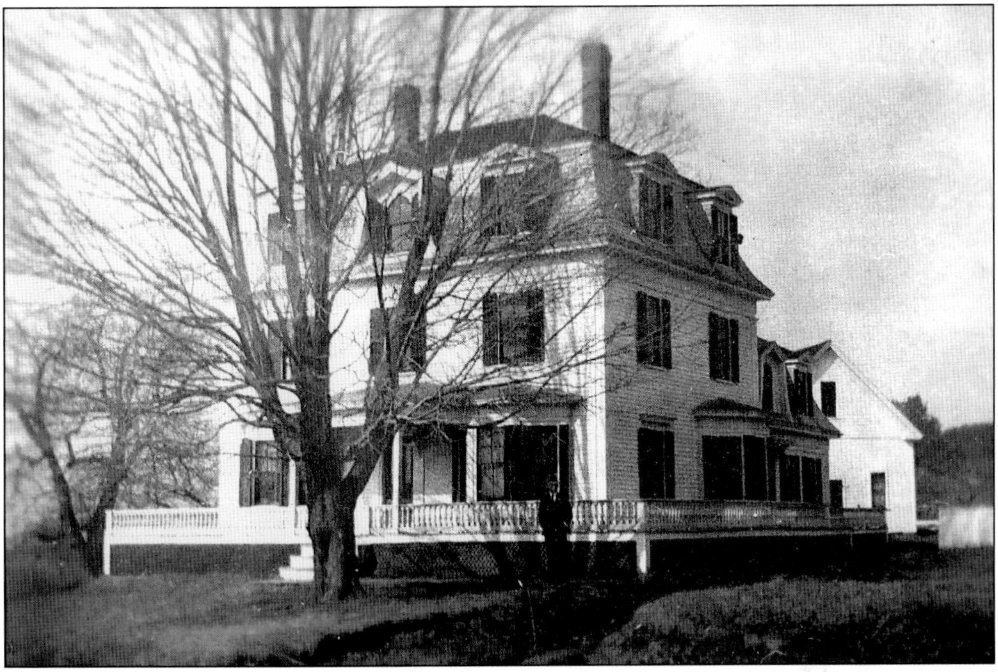

Hannah Farmer built Rosemary Cottage in the Second Empire style in 1888 with the support of her friends. It was a memorial to her son, Clarence, who died as an infant. The building was a summer respite for underprivileged woman of Boston and their children. (Courtesy of the Paul Family Association.)

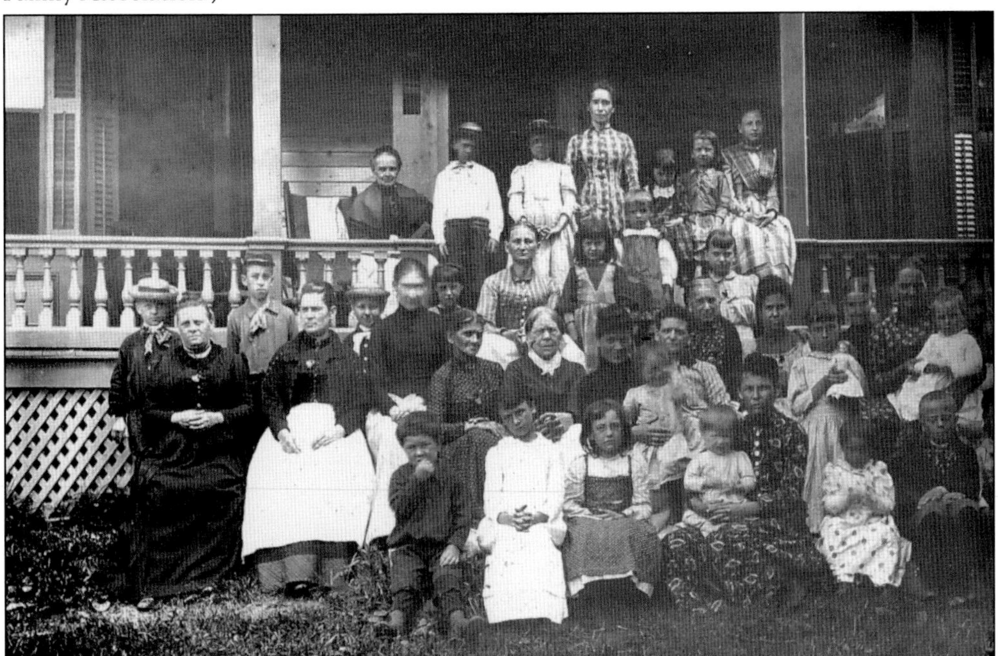

These women and children are enjoying a stay at Rosemary Cottage in July 1891. Hannah Tobey Shapleigh Farmer was instrumental in creating this respite for Boston's underprivileged mothers, their children, and shop girls. (Courtesy of the Estate of C. Edward Bartlett Jr.)

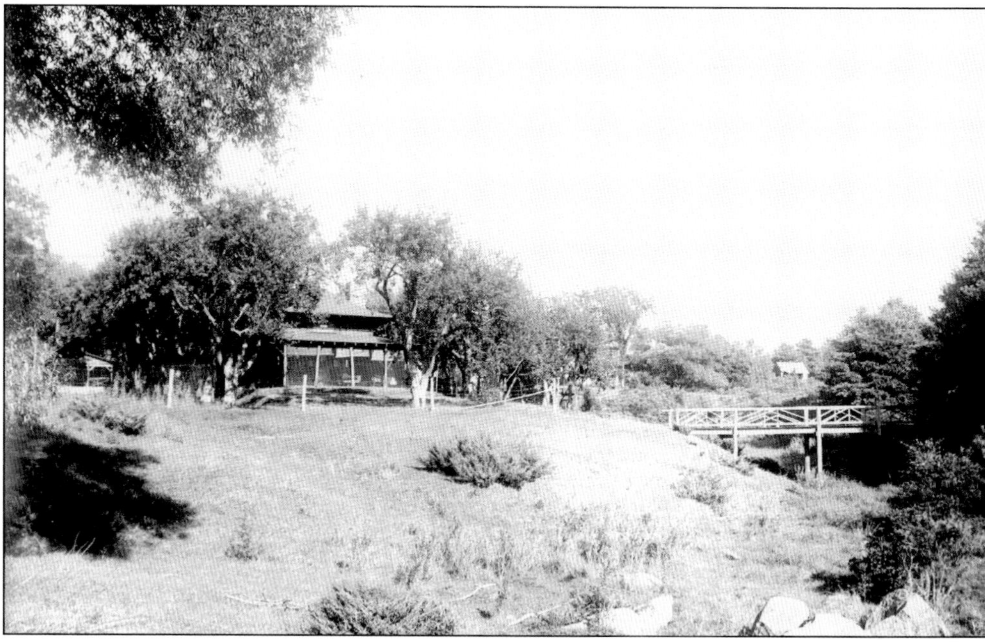

Mrs. Ida Aline Devin's cottage stands at the end of Mast Cove Road. Built around 1909 as a summer home, the structure is thought to be the work of architect Frank Lloyd Wright or one of his associates. A member of the Baha'i faith, Devin wintered in Chicago. (Courtesy of the Gov. John F. Hill Collection at the William Fogg Library.)

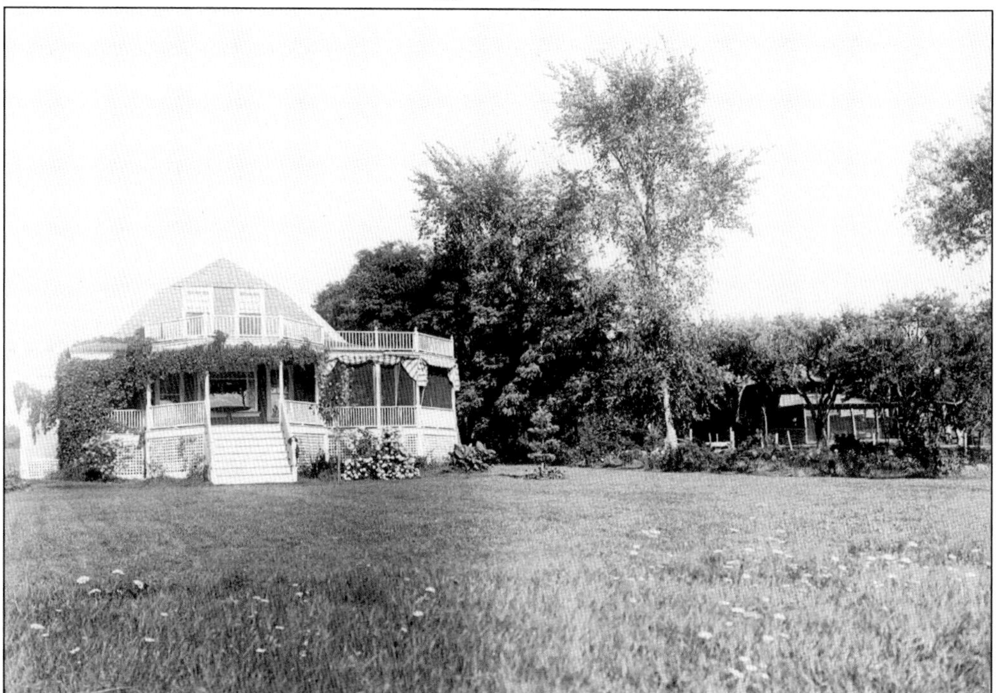

The Morrill Cottage was off Mast Cove Road on Tobey's Lane. (Courtesy of the Gov. John F. Hill Collection at the William Fogg Library.)

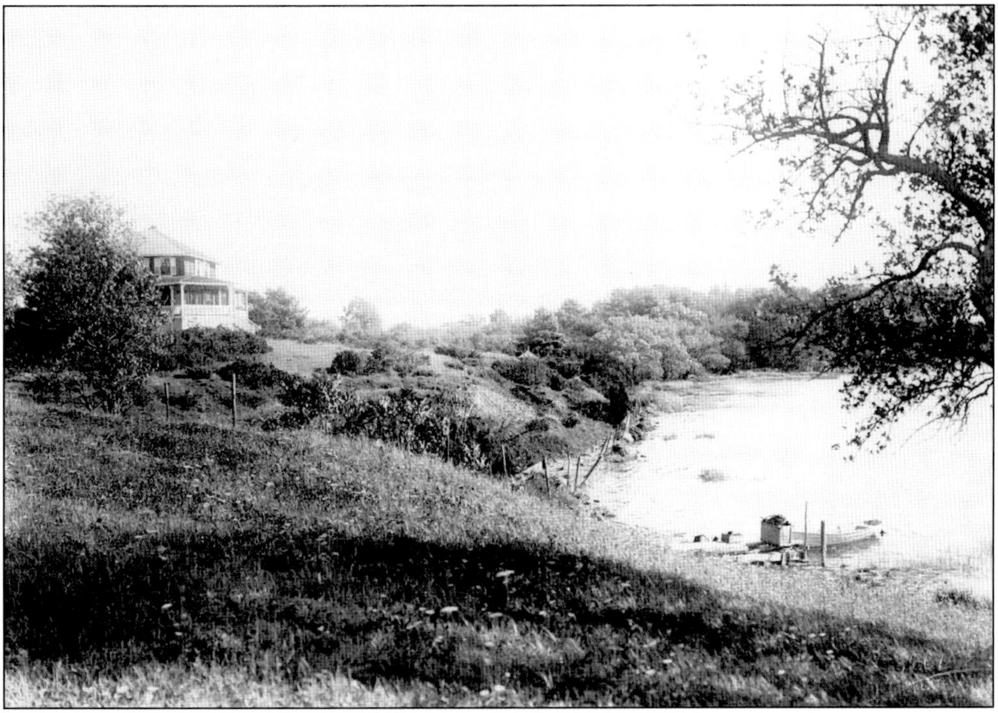

What a wonderful vacation spot! Arthur Hall's cottage stood at Tobey's Landing off Mast Cove Road. (Courtesy of the Gov. John F. Hill Collection at the William Fogg Library.)

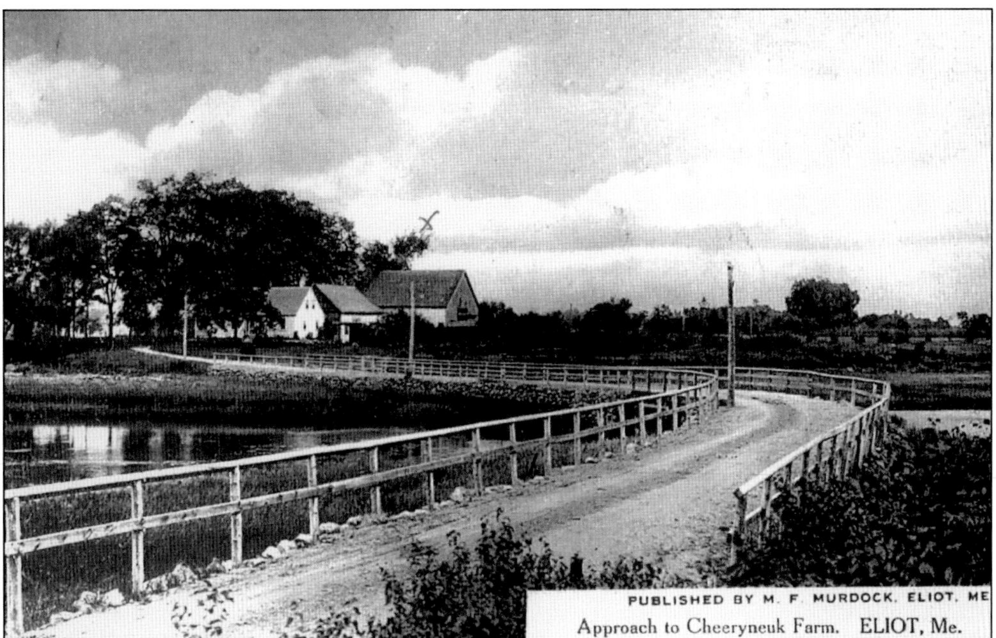

In the 1930s, the Cheeryneuk Tea Room did business at the Cheeryneuk Farm on River Road. The sender of this postcard reported that she enjoyed tea at the tearoom and found the atmosphere very fashionable. (Courtesy of the Eliot Historical Society.)

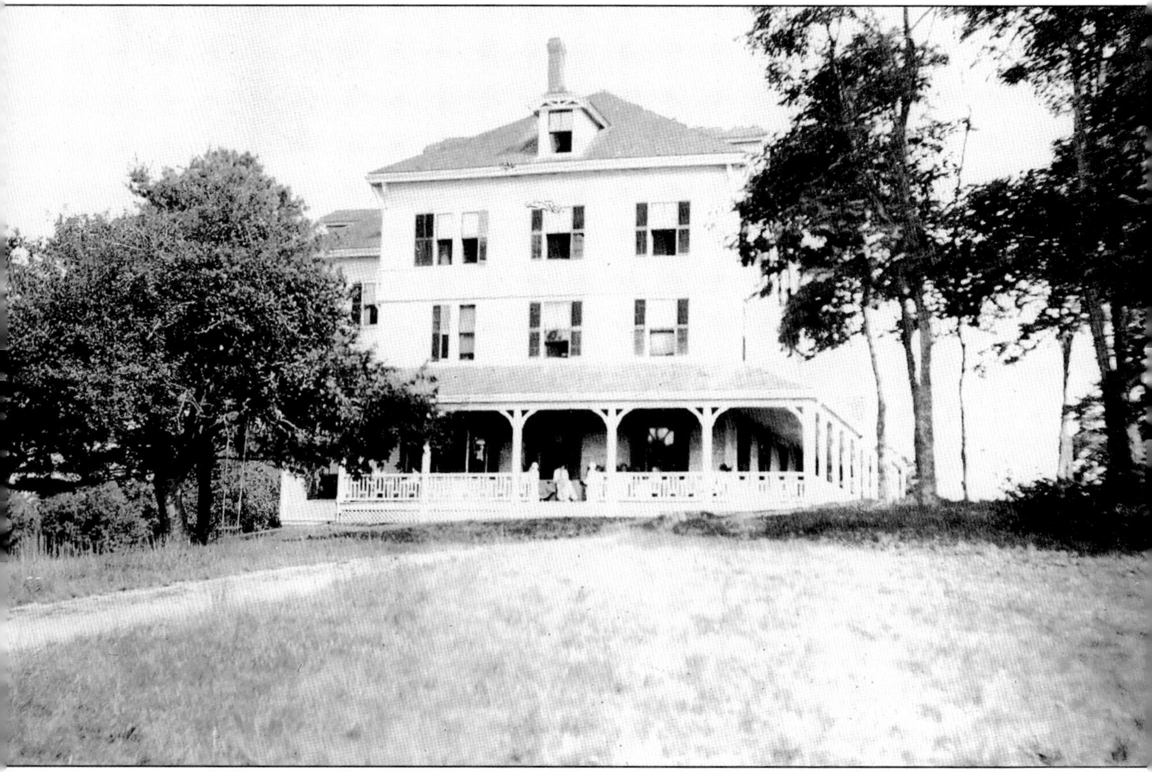

Sarah Farmer, Francis Keefe, Dr. John L. M. Willis, G. Everett Hammond, and Martin Parry Tobey opened the Eliot Hotel in 1890. Two years later, Sarah envisioned the property as a conference center, and in 1894, she dedicated the spot to the ideals of peace and religious unity. Guests included John Greenleaf Whittier and Edward Everett Hale. The Eliot Hotel became the Sarah Farmer Inn at Green Acre. (Courtesy of the Eliot Baha'i Archives.)

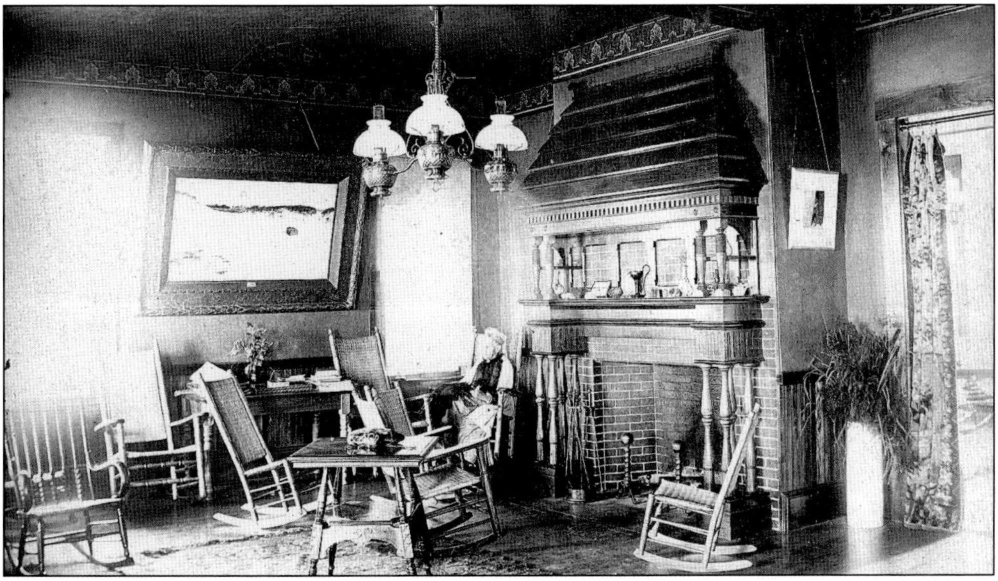

This interior photograph shows the lobby of the Green Acre Inn. John Greenleaf Whittier visited during the hotel's first summer and gave it the name Green Acre. (Courtesy of the Estate of C. Edward Bartlett Jr.)

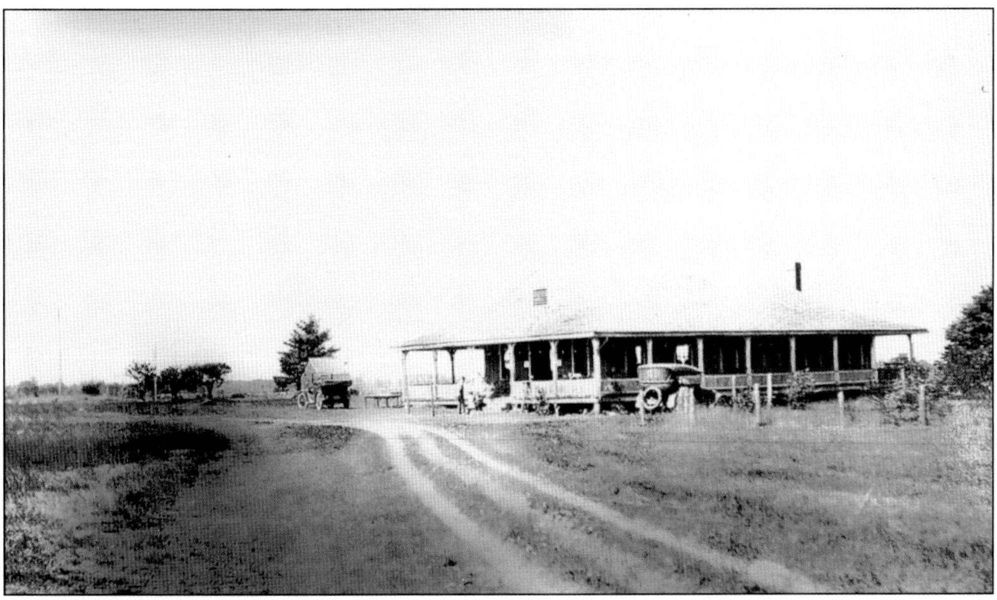

Abdu'l-Baha, son of the founder of the Baha'i faith, presented his first talk at Green Acre in this building in 1912. Constructed in 1897, Eirenion was a lecture hall. In the background, the small shack on the left was Green Acre's first library. Eirenion burned in 1924. (Courtesy of the Eliot Baha'i Archives.)

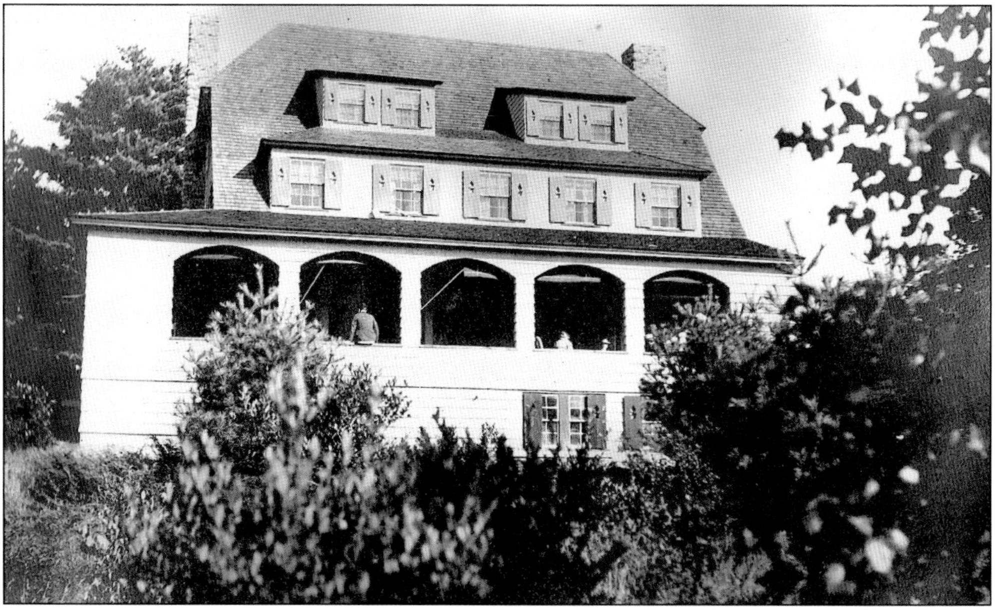
This view of the back of Fellowship House at Green Acre looks toward the Piscataqua River. Fellowship House was built in 1916 with funds bequeathed by Helen Ellis Cole, a member of the Baha'i faith. (Courtesy of the Eliot Baha'i Archives.)

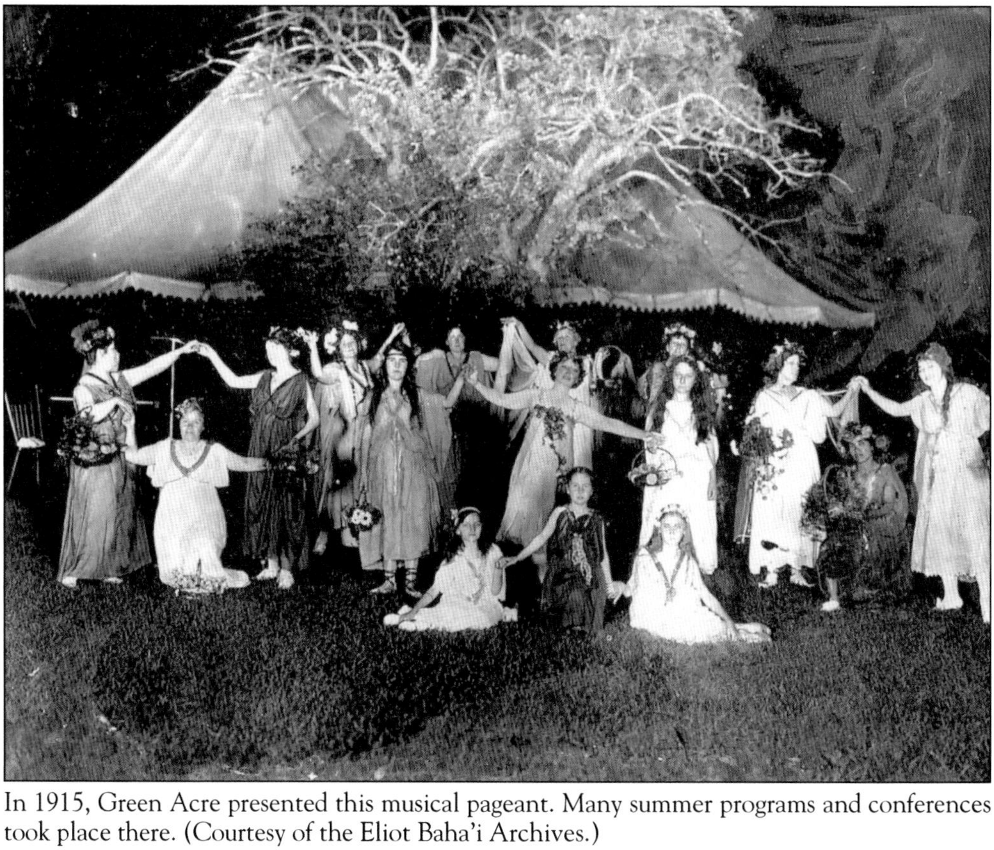
In 1915, Green Acre presented this musical pageant. Many summer programs and conferences took place there. (Courtesy of the Eliot Baha'i Archives.)

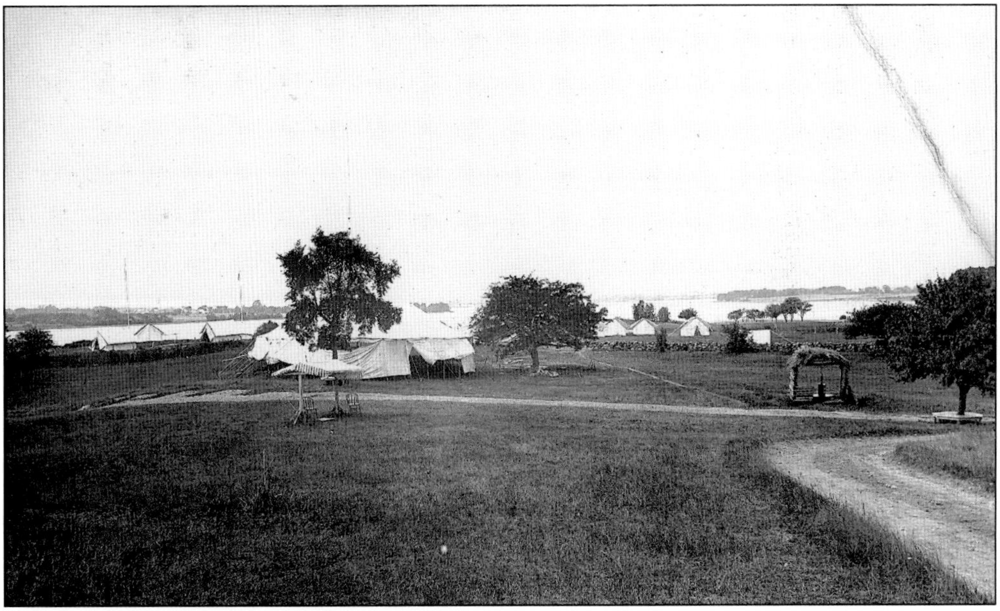

Tents covered the Green Acre grounds during summer months. Campers attended educational lectures at the school. These summer programs flourished during the years from 1894 through 1916. (Courtesy of the Estate of C. Edward Bartlett Jr.)

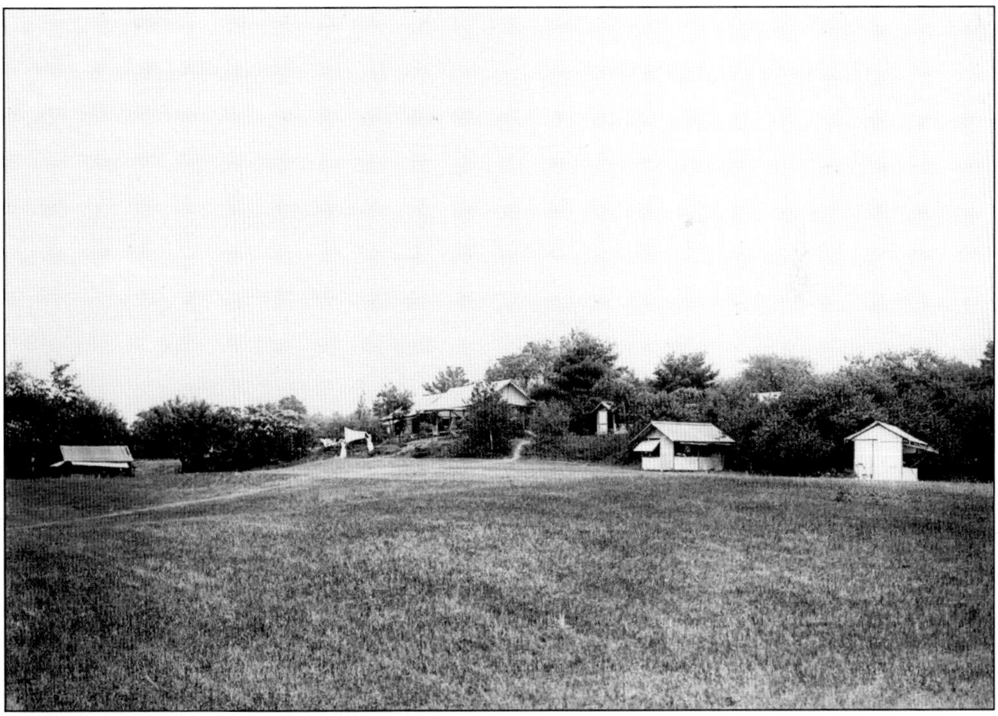

Dr. Fillmore Moore ran the Bungalow Camp in the early 1900s. The health camp was located off Farmer Road. Moore was very involved with the Baha'i community. (Courtesy of the Gov. John F. Hill Collection at the William Fogg Library.)

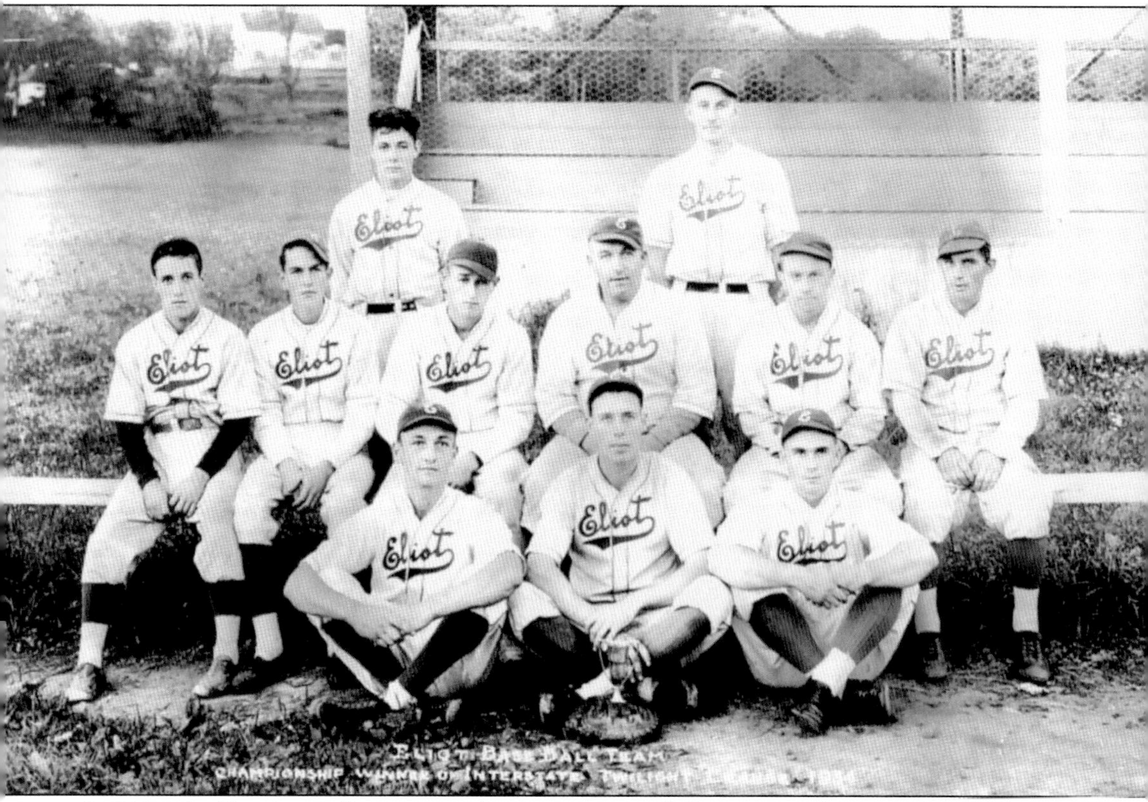

In 1934, the Eliot baseball team won the Interstate Twilight League Championship. (Courtesy of the Everson Collection.)

Nine

Centennial Celebration

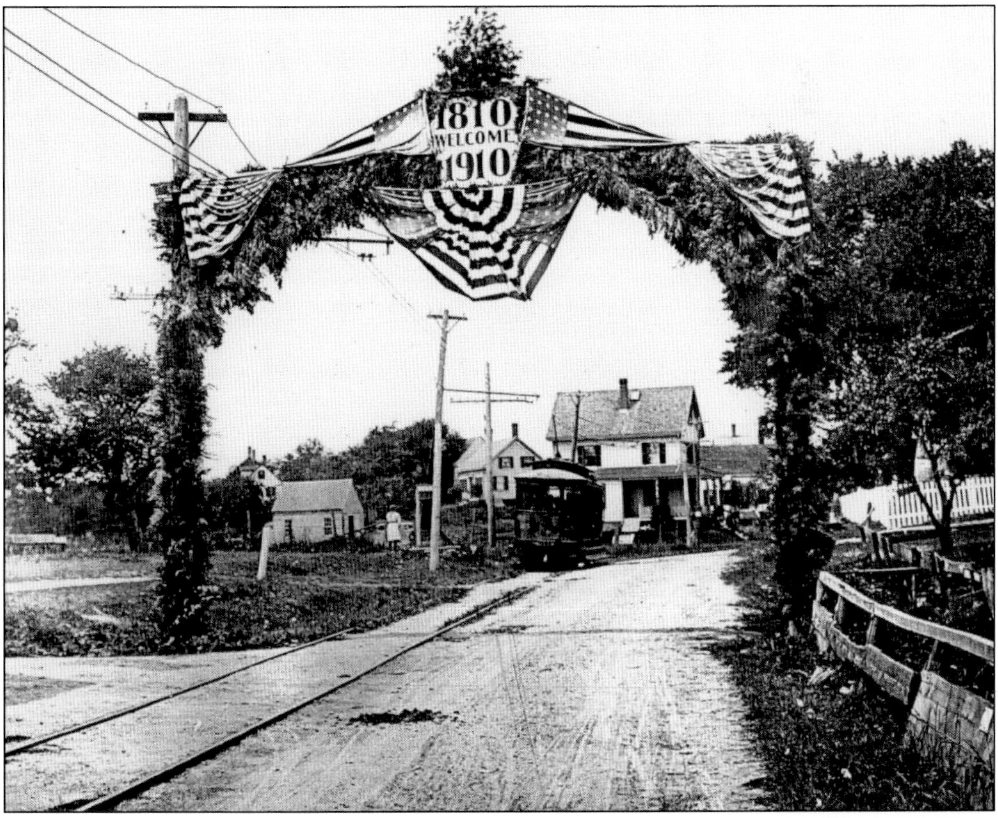

Eliot marked the 100th anniversary of its incorporation as a town with a weeklong celebration from August 7 through August 13, 1910. Residents decorated their houses with flags and bunting. The festivities included a parade, speeches, tableaus, musical programs, fireworks, a tour, and field events. Evergreen branches and flags decorated this archway in South Eliot. (Courtesy of the Everson Collection.)

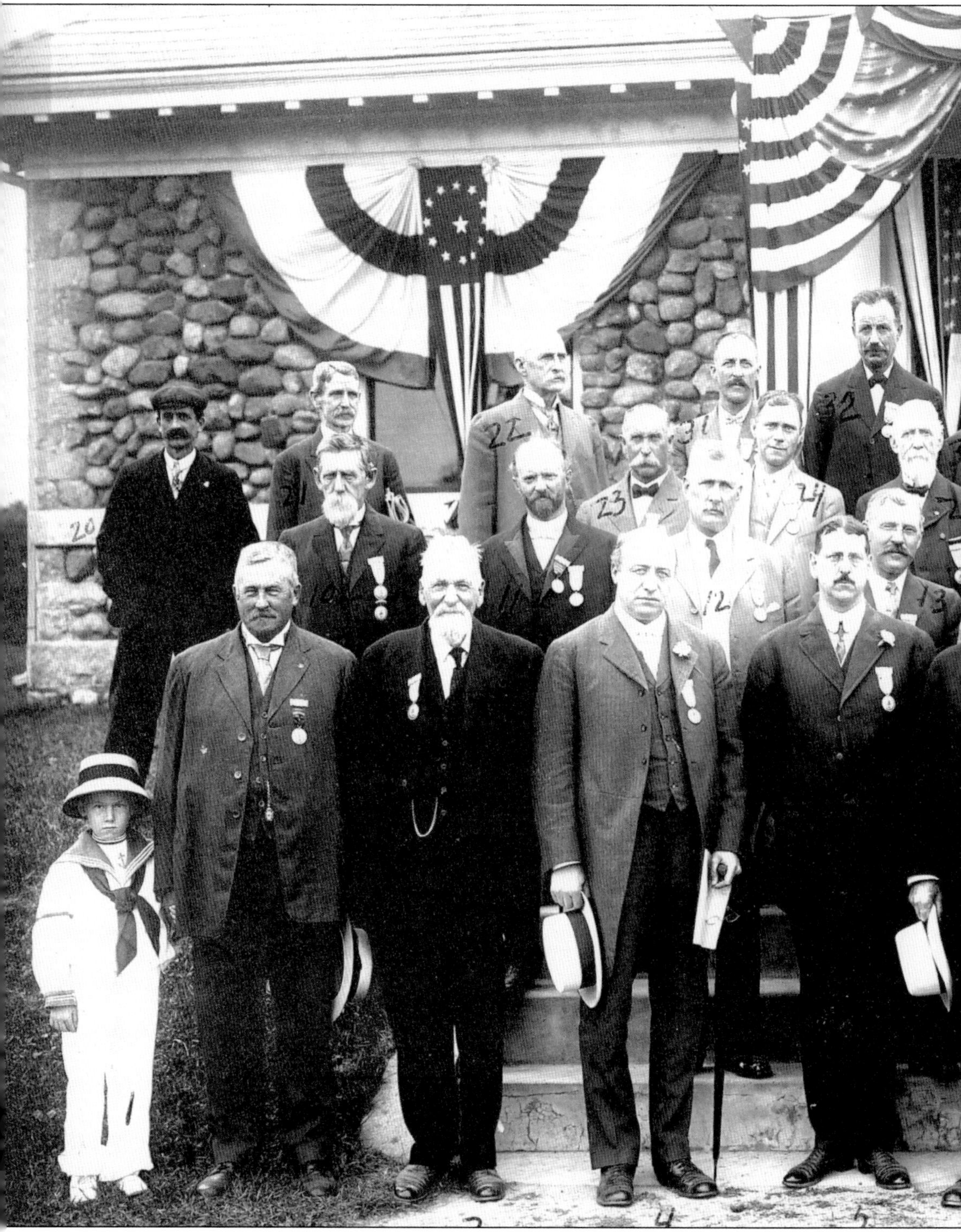

The executive committee for the 1910 centennial celebration and invited guests include, in the front row, Gov. Bert M. Fernald (third from right), Dr. John L. M. Willis (second from right, committee chairman), and C. E. Bartlett (far right, committee treasurer). In the second row are

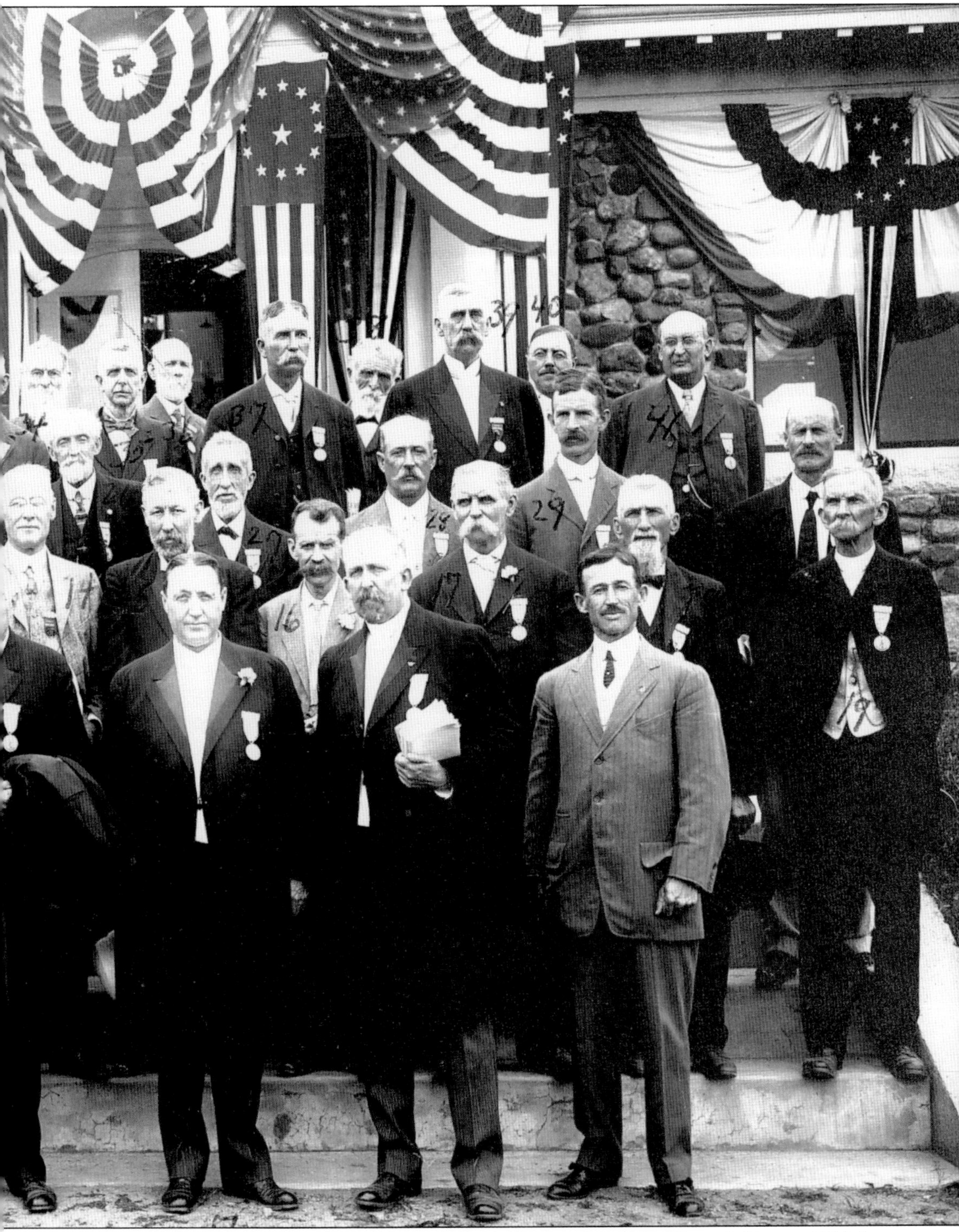

former governor John F. Hill (standing sixth from the right) and Dr. Henry I. Durgin (fifth from the right). (Courtesy of the Eliot Historical Society.)

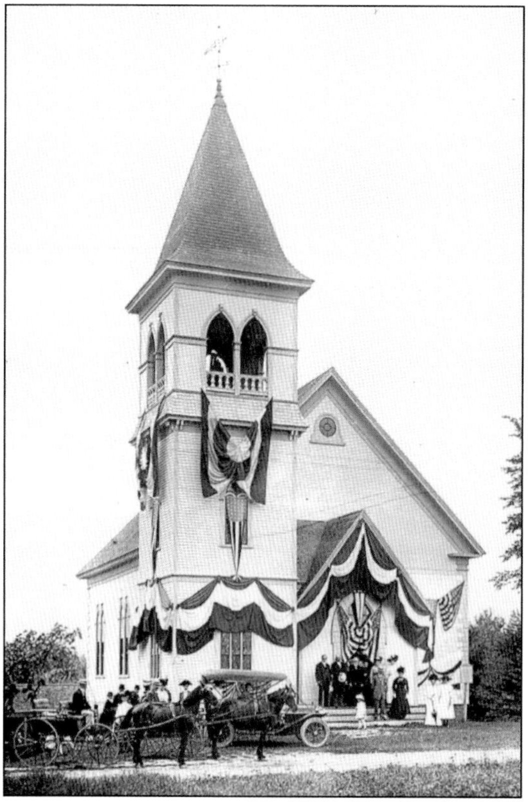

The First Parish Congregational Church is decked out for Eliot's centennial. Dedicated on March 9, 1881, the church replaced an earlier building, which burned in 1880. (Courtesy of the Everson Collection.)

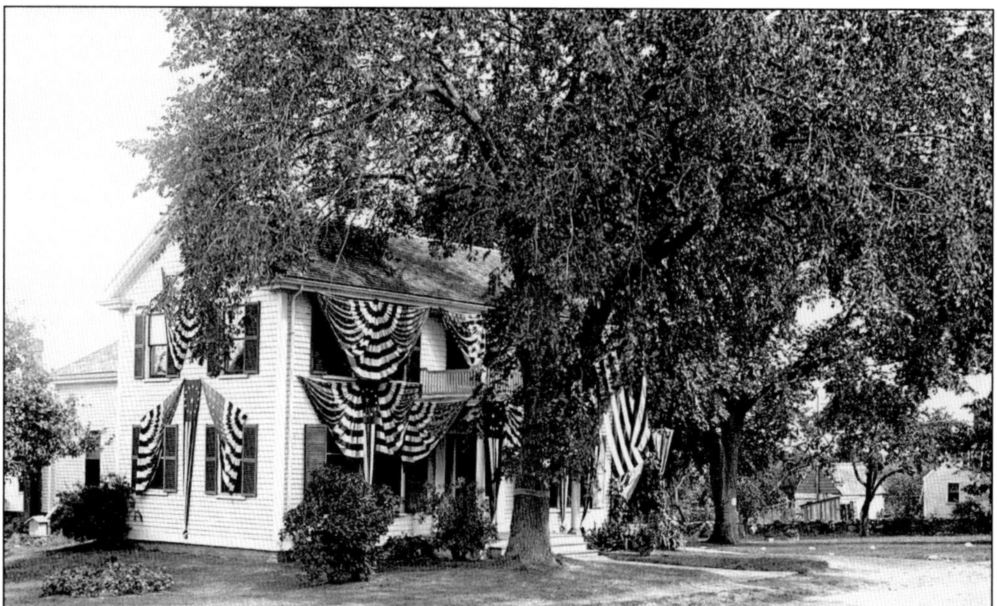

Centennial committee member Dr. Henry I. Durgin decorated his State Road home with plenty of bunting. The residence formerly belonged to Gen. Mark Wentworth, Medal of Honor recipient who commanded the 26th Regiment from Maine during the Civil War. (Courtesy of the Carlton and Doris Grover Collection at the William Fogg Library.)

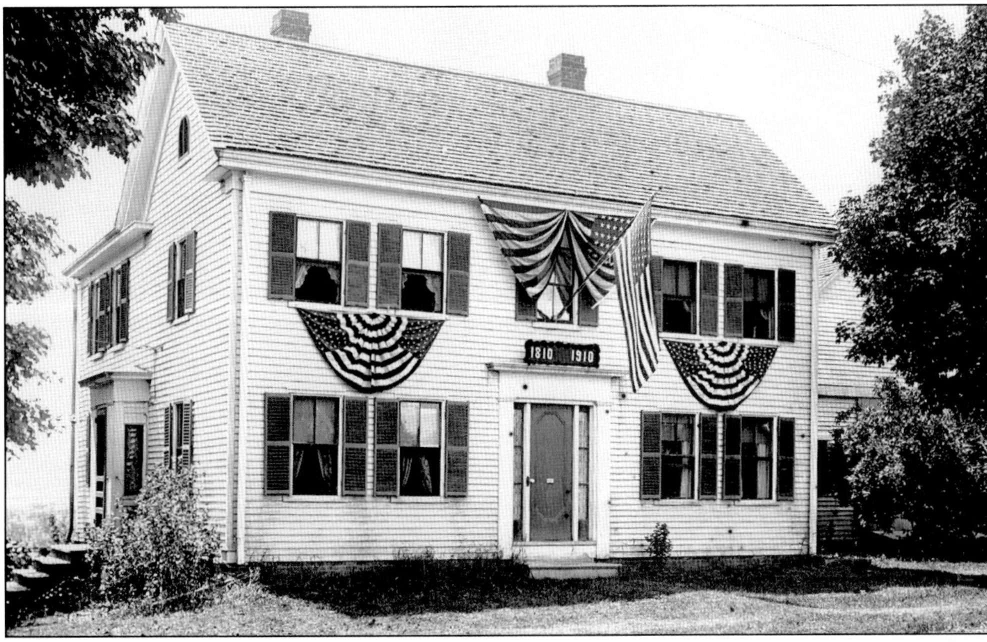

Charles Drake, a centennial committee member, placed a sign over his front door marking the 100 years of Eliot's incorporation as a town. This State Road home was built around 1835. (Courtesy of the Carlton and Doris Grover Collection at the William Fogg Library.)

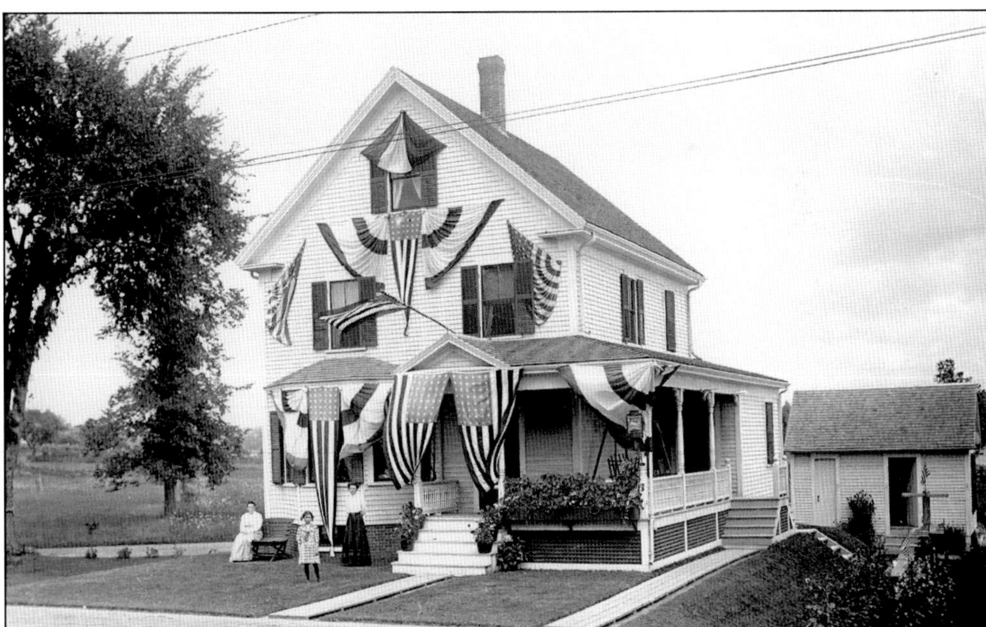

Charles Cole and his wife, Alma, decorated their house on Main Street for the celebration. Their daughter, Ethel, married Malcolm Davis, the oilman. (Courtesy of the Carlton and Doris Grover Collection at the William Fogg Library.)

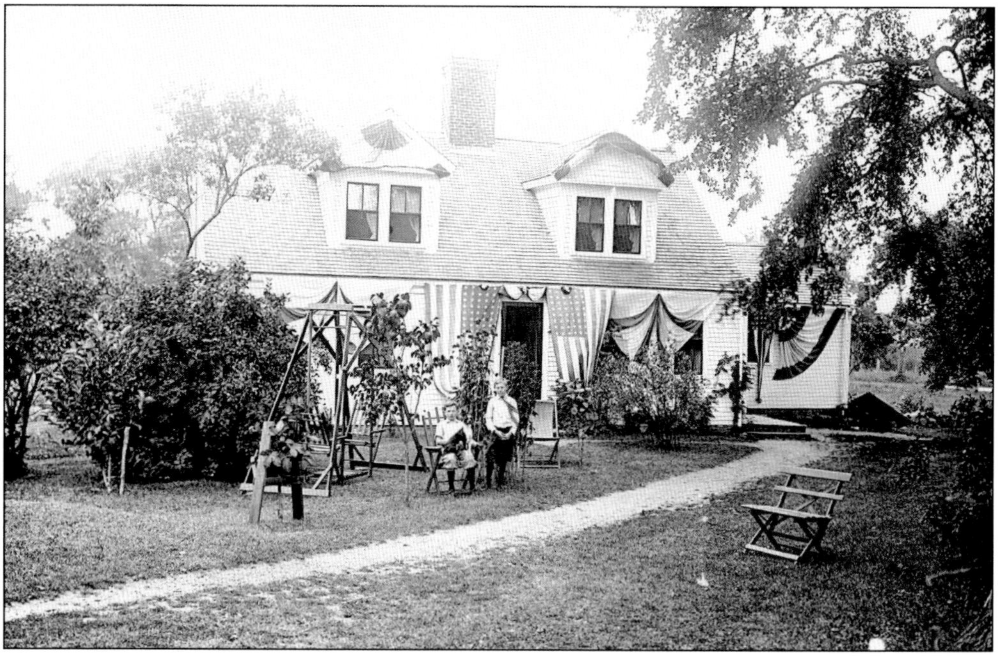

The Stanley Parmley House, on Main Street, was built around 1800. Behind the house, Tobey's Pasture ran to the river's edge. (Courtesy of the William Fogg Library.)

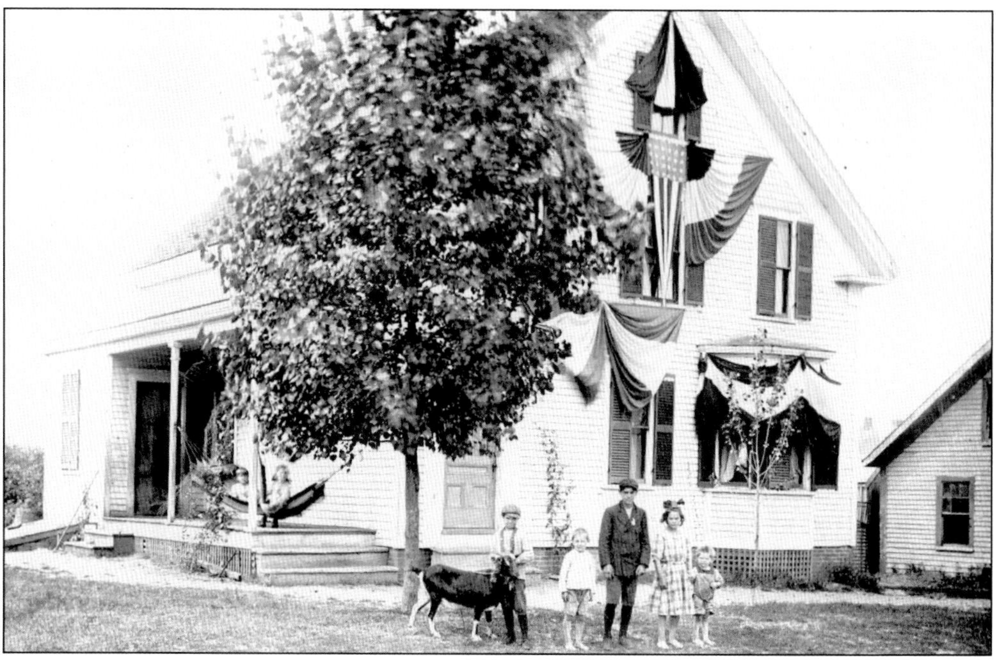

Mel Dixon lived in this house on Pleasant Street, but he owned a shop on Dixon Road. (Courtesy of the William Fogg Library.)

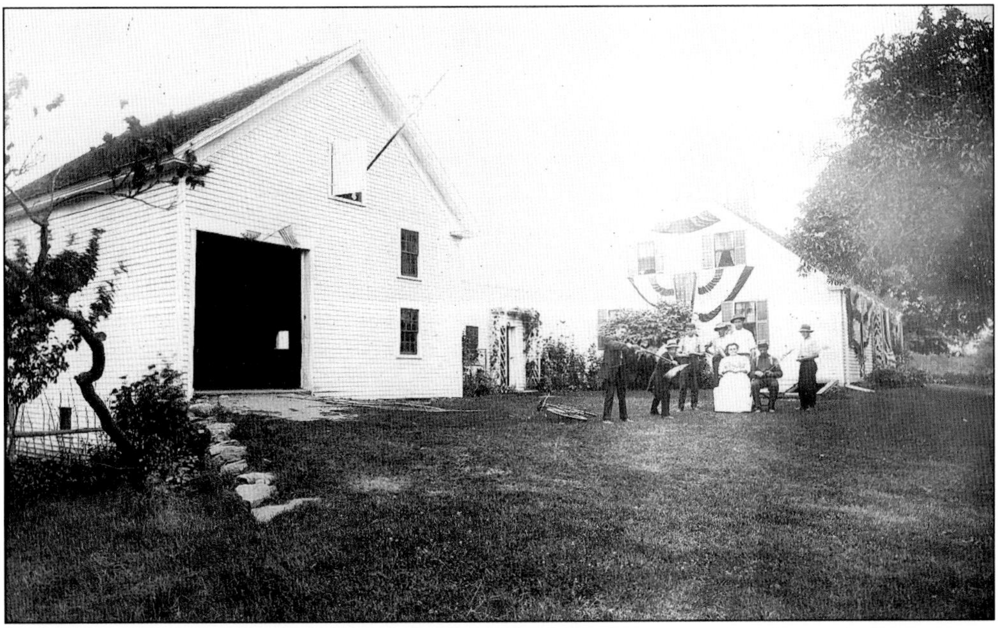

Frank E. Liebman and his family posed for these photographs next to their home. Liebman was a carpenter. In the photograph below, the men dressed in suits on each end of the group decorated the exterior of the Liebman home on Farmer Road for the centennial celebration. Others are, standing from left to right, Frank Dixon, Ernest Liebman, Harry Dixon, and Austin Liebman. Seated are Lillie and Frank Liebman. (Courtesy of the Estate of C. Edward Bartlett Jr.)

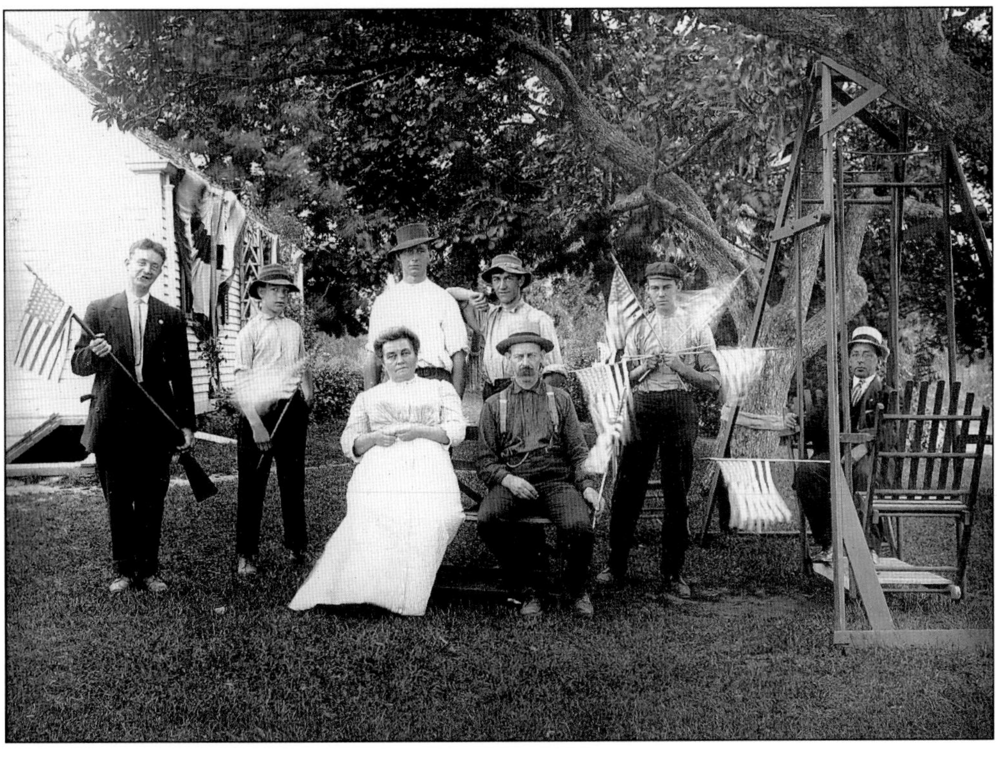

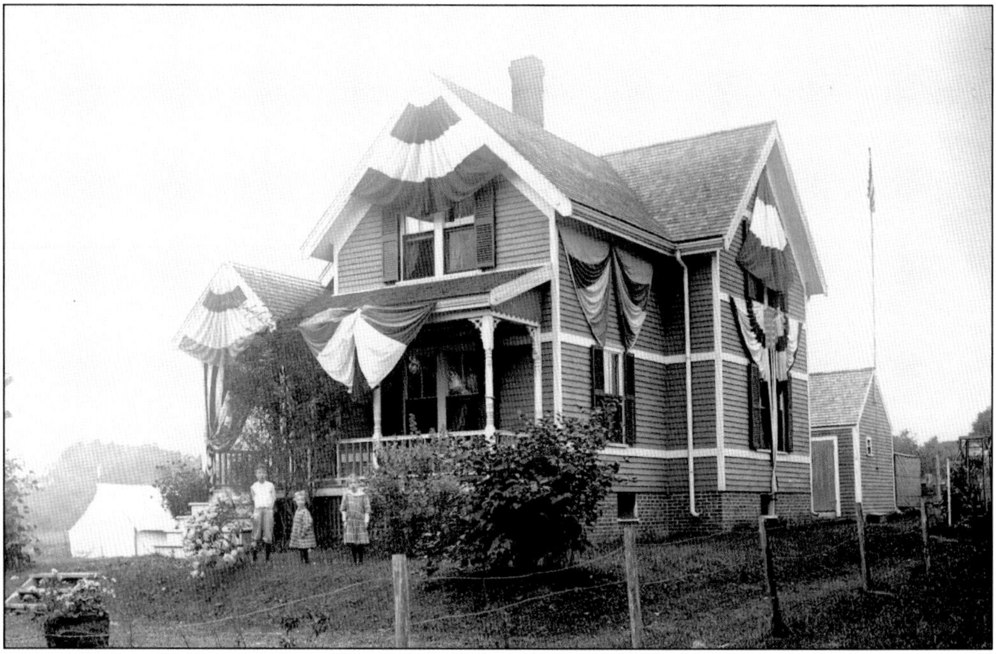

Only 10 years old at centennial time, the Cecil Babkirk home, on Main Street, was built by Milo Spinney. Cecil's father-in-law, Irving Mitchell, first lived in the house. (Courtesy of the William Fogg Library.)

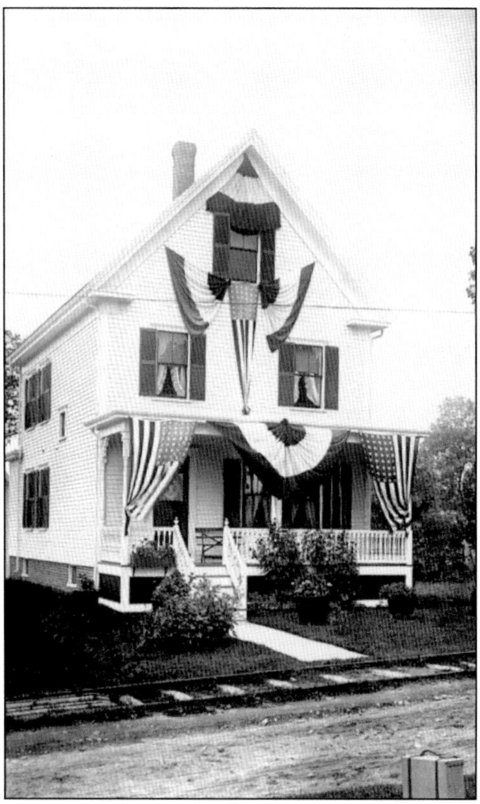

The Bowden house, on Pleasant Street, was built around 1900 in the Queen Anne style. (Courtesy of the William Fogg Library.)

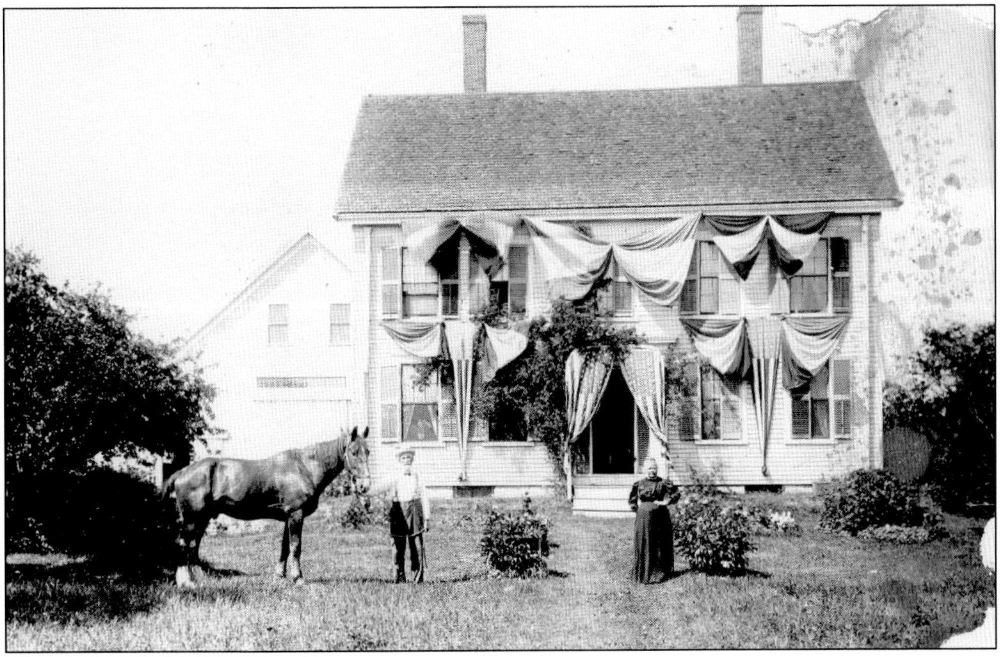

Omer Clement's home on Pleasant Street was built by Samuel Dixon in the early 1800s. (Courtesy of the William Fogg Library.)

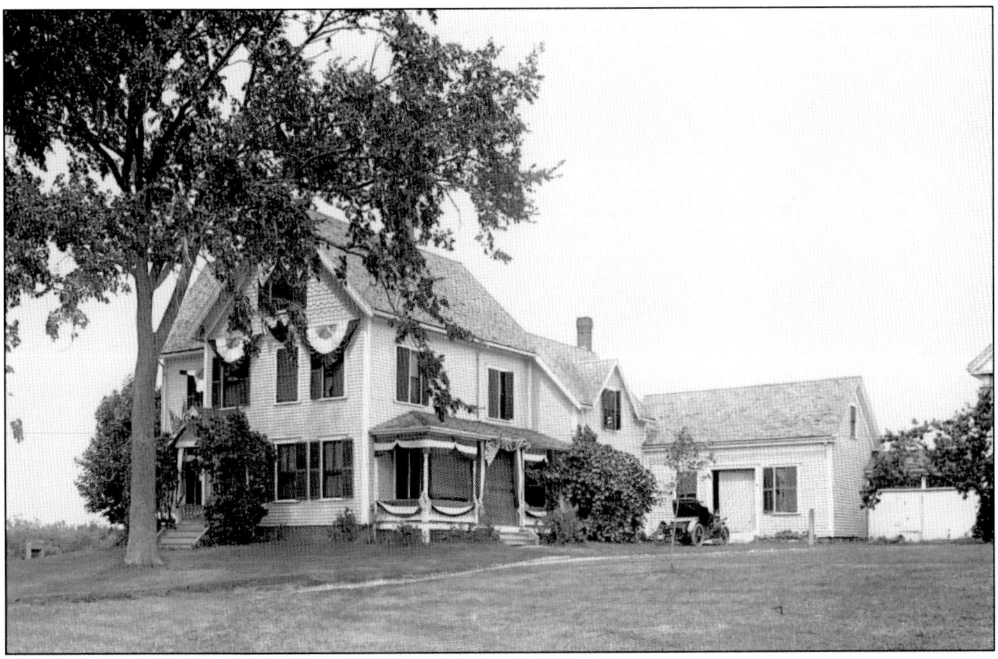

Built around 1860 across from the Congregational church, the Libbey home on State Road displays characteristics of the Queen Anne style. (Courtesy of the William Fogg Library.)

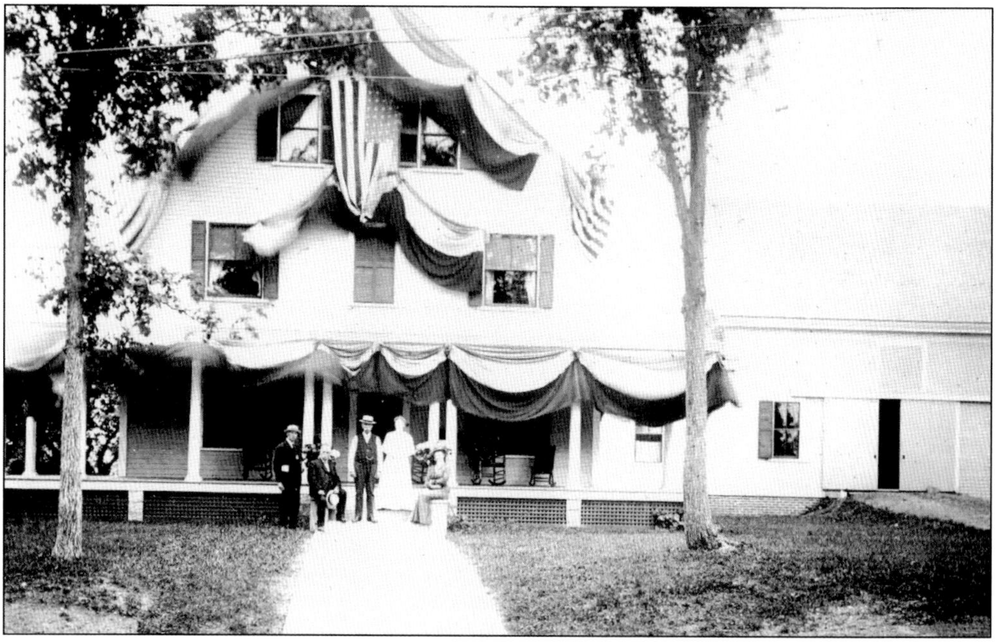

Adorned with flags and bunting, the old Kennard home on State Road is ready for the celebration. The residence, built around 1900, stands on the same land where Eliot Academy once stood. (Courtesy of the Carlton and Doris Grover Collection.)

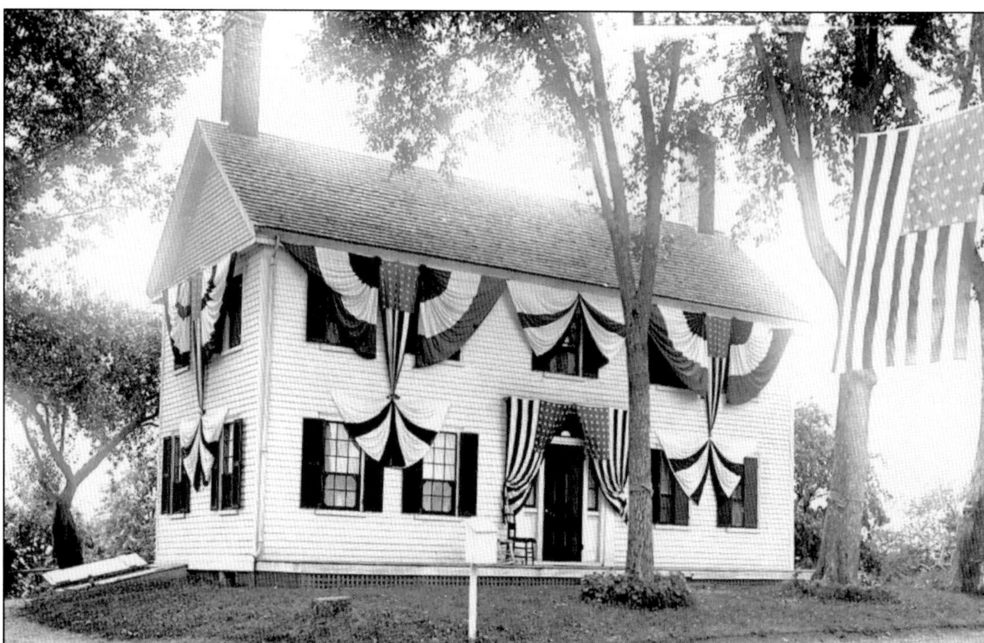

The Kennard House on Old Road stands in the Kennard's Corner area, a location that was the center of town activity in the early 19th century. (Courtesy of the Carlton and Doris Grover Collection at the William Fogg Library.)

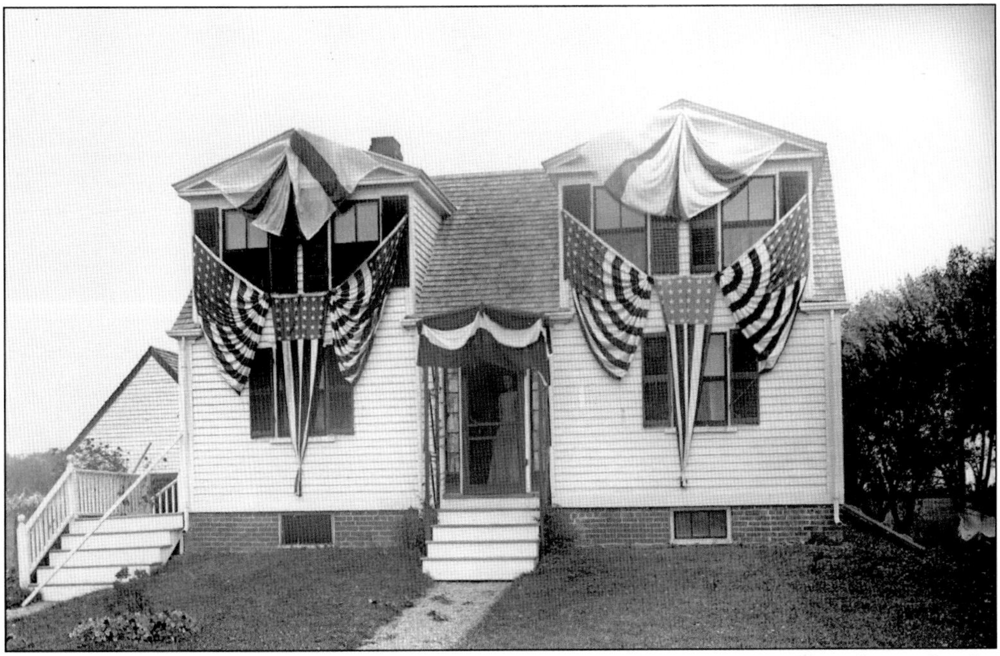

Everett "Pop" Cole and his wife, Ethel, lavishly decorated their Pleasant Street home for the celebration. The couple had four children. (Courtesy of the William Fogg Library.)

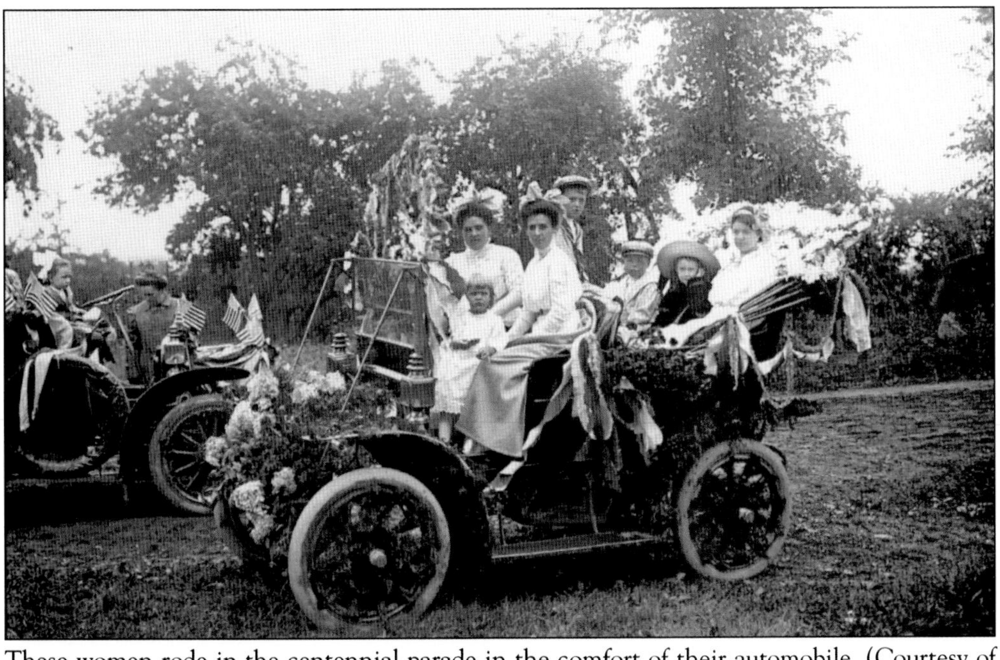

These women rode in the centennial parade in the comfort of their automobile. (Courtesy of the Gov. John F. Hill Collection at the William Fogg Library.)

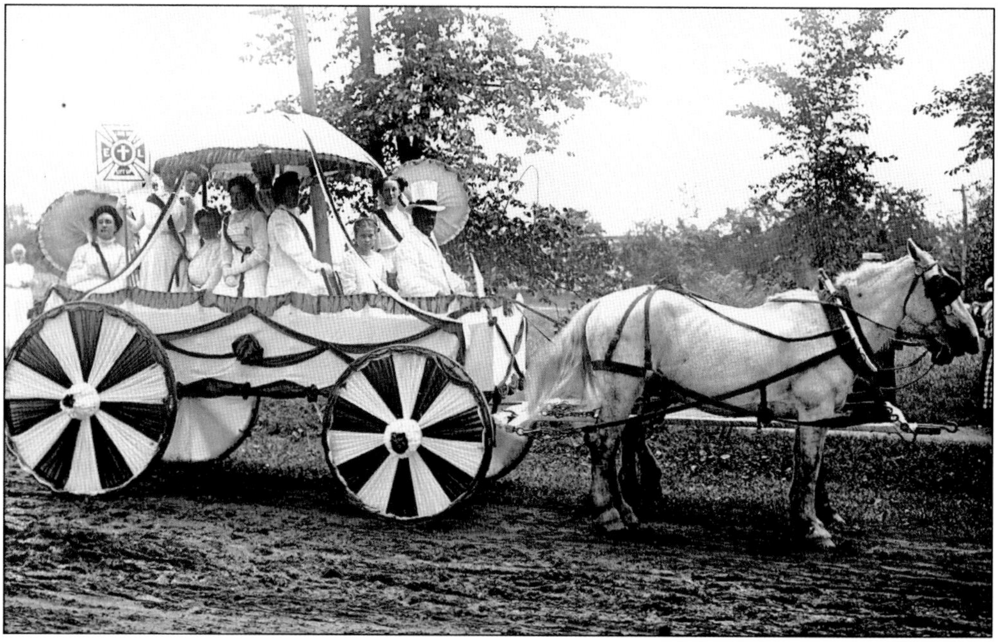

The Epworth League of the Methodist Church rode in a horse-drawn carriage in the centennial parade. (Courtesy of the William Fogg Library.)

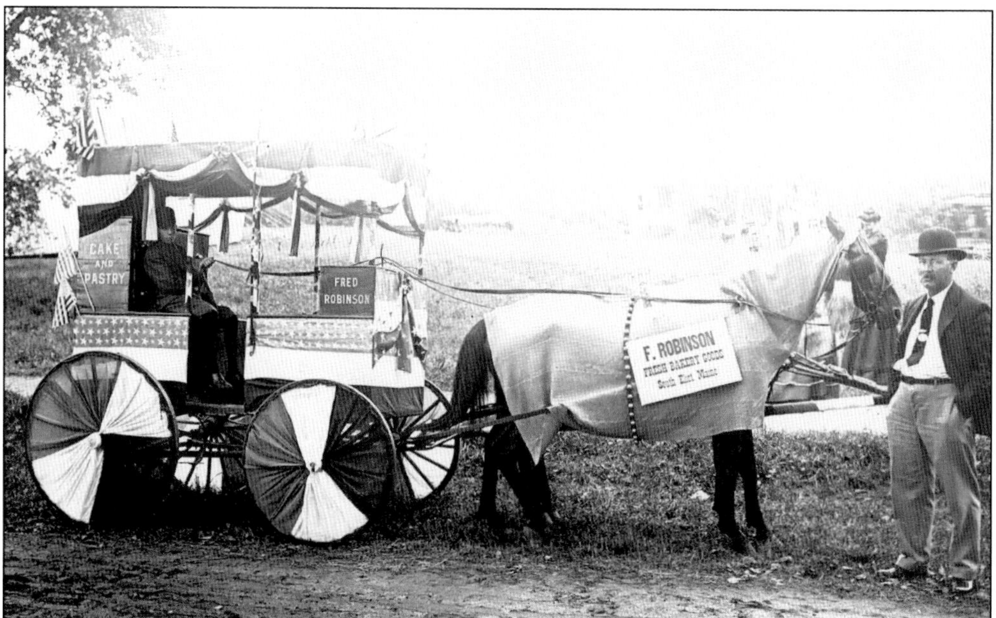

Fred Robinson's bakery had a float in the 1910 centennial parade. (Courtesy of the William Fogg Library.)

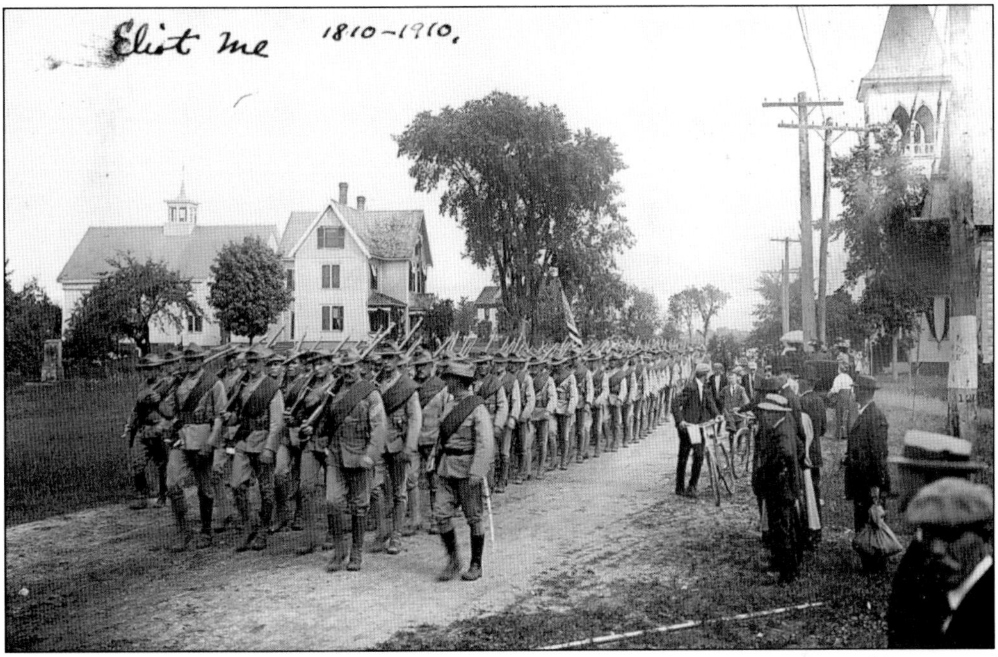

A contingent of U.S. Marines marched in the centennial parade in August 1910. (Courtesy of the Estate of C. Edward Bartlett Jr.)

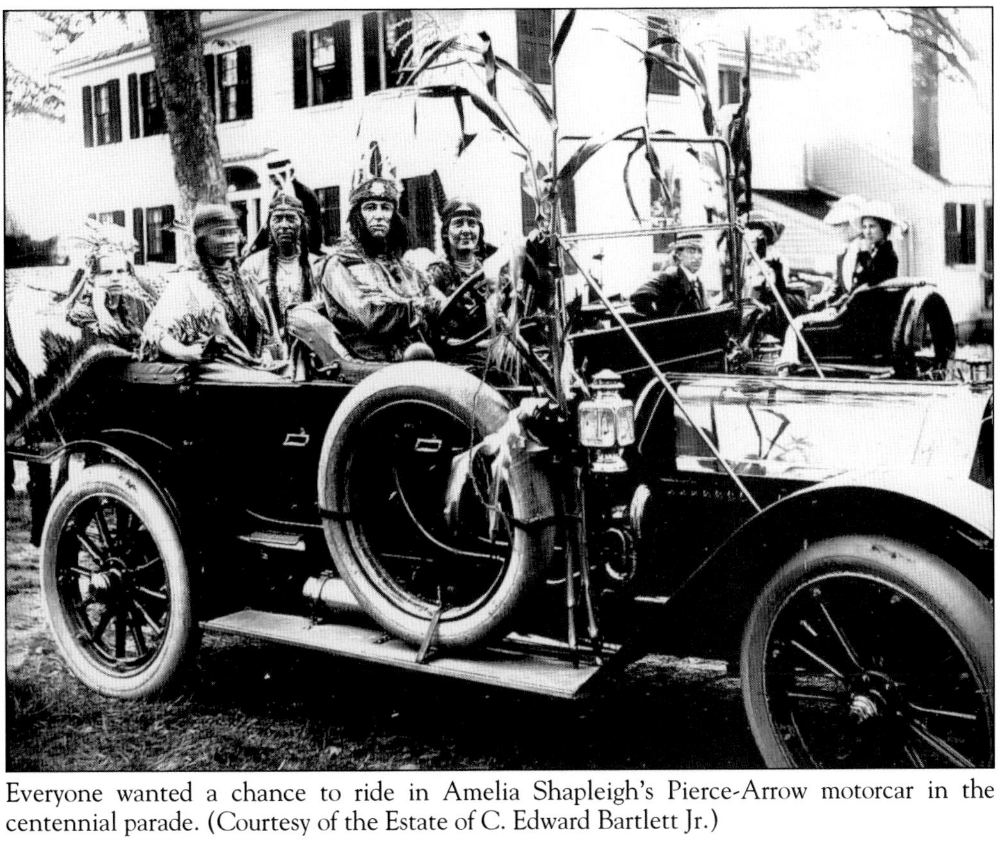

Everyone wanted a chance to ride in Amelia Shapleigh's Pierce-Arrow motorcar in the centennial parade. (Courtesy of the Estate of C. Edward Bartlett Jr.)

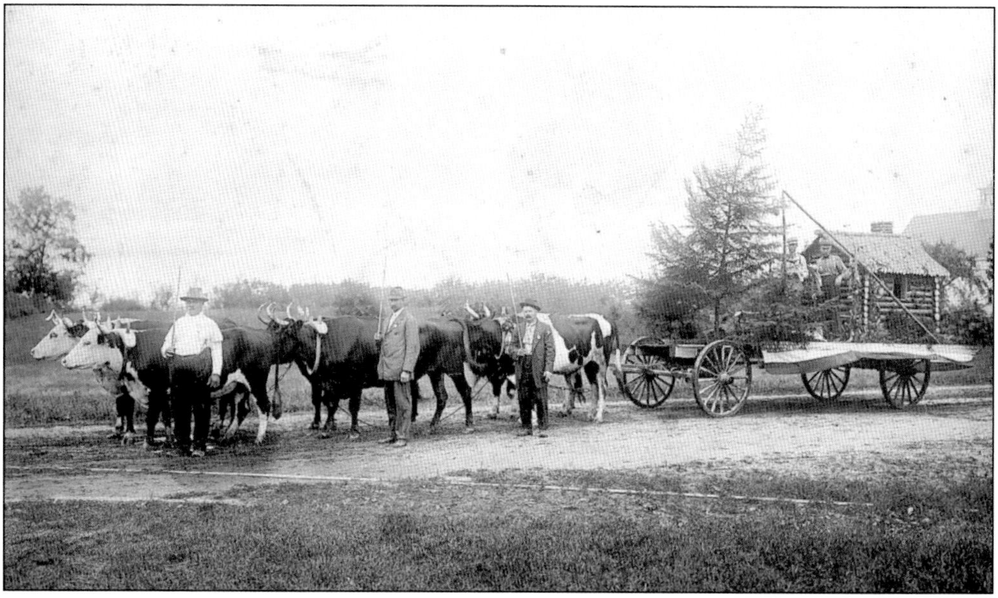

The Old Log Cabin float, drawn by oxen, won second prize in the centennial parade of 1910. The men standing beside their oxen are Moses Morrell, J. Albert Stacy, and Walter Rowe. (Courtesy of the Libby Collection.)

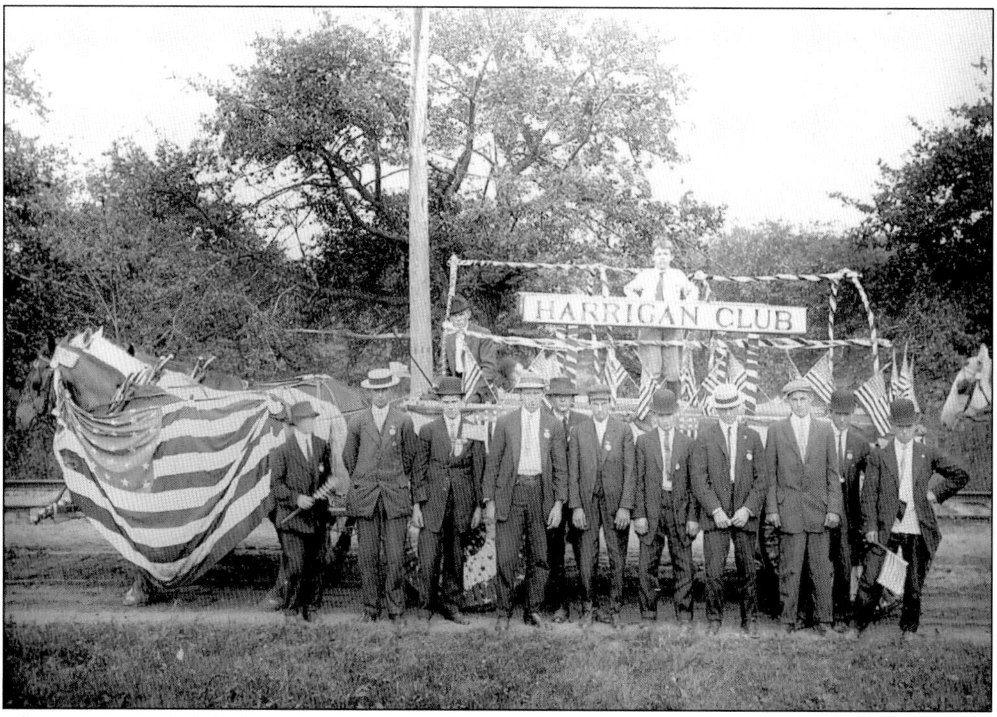

The Harrigan Club had a float in the centennial parade. (Courtesy of the Estate of C. Edward Bartlett Jr.)